Hope Springs Eternal

Hope Springs Eternal

French Bondholders and the
Repudiation of
Russian Sovereign Debt

KIM OOSTERLINCK

Translated by

ANTHONY BULGER

Yale UNIVERSITY PRESS/NEW HAVEN & LONDON

Published with assistance from the foundation established in
memory of Amasa Stone Mather of the Class of 1907,
Yale College.

Publié avec le concours de la
Fondation Universitaire de Belgique
Published with assistance from the
University Foundation of Belgium

Yale University Press books may be purchased in quantity for
educational, business, or promotional use. For information,
please e-mail sales.press@yale.edu (U.S. office) or
sales@yaleup.co.uk (U.K. office).

Set in Minion type by Integrated Publishing Solutions.
Printed in the United States of America.

Library of Congress Control Number: 2015952078
ISBN 978-0-300-19091-5 (cloth: alk. paper)

A catalogue record for this book is available
from the British Library.

This paper meets the requirements of ANSI/NISO Z39.48-1992
(Permanence of Paper).

10 9 8 7 6 5 4 3 2 1

Contents

About This Book

The repudiation of Russia's debt by the Bolsheviks affected French investors for several generations. The reason for this was the sheer volume of money lent by institutional investors and private citizens alike. Although estimates of the precise amounts lent to the Russian empire vary, there is general agreement about their size relative to the French economy—approximately 4.5 percent of national wealth at the time.

Despite the huge amounts involved, few economists have attempted to analyze this extreme example of debt repudiation. René Girault's seminal book (1973) offers a fascinating and meticulous account of the appearance of Russian bonds in French investors' portfolios. But the scope of that study is limited to the period from 1887 to 1914 and therefore does not address the repudiation and its consequences. Several more recent books appeared when negotiations with Russia were reopened. However, these seek to express a position on repayment, analyze the legal aspects of the repudiation, or denounce the "scandalous spoliation."

This book analyzes the repudiation from the angle of modern financial theories. It concentrates on sovereign debt issued by the former tsarist empire and therefore excludes bonds issued by private companies. The first section describes the development of sovereign default and repudiation theory, before examining the case of Russian debt repudiation. The analysis rests largely on a phenomenon of some significance: counterintuitively, market prices for Russian debt remained remarkably high, both in absolute and relative terms, for several years after the repudiation. Far from being a sign of irrational behavior, this trend can be attributed to expectations that one or more extreme events could occur. The subsequent sections of this book analyze these expectations. Each chapter considers the historical and financial factors that encouraged French investors to hope their bonds would be redeemed. The final chapter presents the econometric and financial analyses performed on the Russian data to determine the relative importance, in quantitative terms, of each of these reasons for hope.

Preface

This book follows several of my articles on Russian debt. Having worked for several years on this topic, I felt there were still many elements to be discussed. Additional sources kept being added to the already long list I had been working on. Each new article raised new questions and generated new ideas. One obvious limit of the articles I had written was the period I had considered. My articles cover only the period up to 1919 and therefore leave out the negotiations of the 1920s. All these elements gradually convinced me to write a book about Russian debt between 1918 and 1921. As well as including the negotiations, this time frame coincides roughly with the period of the Russian civil war, which plays a central role in the analysis.

Historians have focused mostly on the political aspects related to the Russian bonds and the negotiations held after 1918. Specialists in international law have analyzed the legal aspects of the repudiation. Eventually, journalists as well as members of bondholders' associations condemned the repudiation and asked for a higher reimbursement from Russia.[1] The analysis presented here focuses instead on market prices for Russian bonds. Indeed, contrary to common sense, Russian debt continued to be listed and traded long after it was repudiated. Aside from some periods of inactivity, when prices may not have been representative, the price series can be analyzed using quantitative techniques. Although the emphasis here is on investor perceptions at that time, the book also contributes to the broader debate on sovereign debt, one of the most singular financial instruments in existence.

In efficient markets, prices respond to information, the nature of which varies according to the type of market efficiency. Analyzing the information available to French investors at the time is therefore of critical importance. Contemporary archives were a key source for this book. Commenting on the Russian position during the Second World War in a radio broadcast in 1939, Winston Churchill described Russia as "a riddle wrapped in a mystery inside an enigma." That description was probably apt thirty years earlier. Information from Russia, particularly news about the Russian civil war, could take a long time to reach Paris. Furthermore, the number and complexity of revolutionary and counterrevolutionary movements and governments active across the vast expanse of Russia could only add to the confusion about what was happening on the ground. The combination of incomplete and incorrect information and high financial stakes kept the rumor mill turning.[2]

Market prices are as responsive to rumor as they are to accurate information. The archives of the Paris Prefecture (which oversees law enforcement) provided valuable insights into the nature of the rumors. In late 1917 the Prefect of Paris, whose mandate included surveillance of the stock exchange, sent large numbers of inspectors into the city to ascertain citizens' attitudes toward the war.[3] The reports they submitted were collated under the title *Physionomie de Paris* (A physiognomy of Paris). They include a description of rumors and activity on the stock exchange from December 1917 to May 1919. For the period 1920–21 the letters from the special commissioner for the stock exchange to the prefect were similarly enlightening.

A second key source for the analysis was the archives of the National Association of French Securities Holders (Association Nationale des Porteurs Français de Valeurs Mobilières),[4] particularly the archives of the committees that dealt with Russian debt, such as the General Commission for the Protection of French Interests in Russia (Commission générale pour la protection des intérêts français en Russie), the Committee of Holders of Russian Government Bonds, Securities Guaranteed by the Russian State and Municipal Debt (Comité de Porteurs de Fonds d'Etat Russes, de Valeurs Garanties par l'Etat Russe et d'Emprunts Municipaux), and the Defense Committee of French Holders of Russian Industrial and Banking Stocks (Comité de Défense des porteurs français de valeurs industrielles et bancaires russes). These extremely comprehensive records probably contain most of the information that a French investor could have known at the time. They include translations of Russian documents such as newspaper articles and decrees as well as an enormous volume of correspondence. References to the archives in this book use the numbering system devised by Laurence Lesueur, which was operational when I consulted them. The documents have since been transferred to another location and may now be classified by a different system.

Last, the French press had a preponderant influence on the Paris financial market for many years. The Russian debt market was exemplary in this regard since the very issuance of Russian securities on the Paris market was hugely facilitated by favorable articles, often written by journalists in the pay of Russia. I therefore paid attention to contemporary articles on Russian debt in the general and financial press, in particular those in *Le Rentier, L'Economiste Français,* and *The Economist.* My choice of these titles may be questioned, but there were several reasons for it. *Le Rentier* is an interesting source because its journalists did not simply report market price movements, as many other newspapers did, but also attempted to analyze the reasons for market trends. The longer, denser articles of *L'Economiste Français* provide a more detailed picture of contemporary perceptions of the repudiation. The two newspapers did not take a neutral stance on Russian bonds, however, since Arthur Raffalovitch, an agent of the tsar, was a regular contributor to them. Given the number of journalists bribed by the Russian government, one may justifiably wonder whether there was a neutral newspaper in France at the time. Emile Zola said that the French financial press could be divided into two categories: "The venal, and the so-called 'incorruptible' that sells itself only in exceptional cases and at a very high price."[5] Finally, in order to step outside the French framework, I chose *The Economist* for its foreign perspective on the situation.

Acknowledgments

It is with pleasure that I follow the tradition of thanking the very many people whose invaluable support helped me to write this book.

First of all, I would like to thank Professor Ariane Szafarz, who introduced me to academic research by agreeing to supervise, first, my master's dissertation and then my doctoral thesis. Her discerning eye, her insightful, always constructive comments, and her encouragement have always been of enormous help to me. I have also benefited from the sound advice and support of other colleagues from Université Libre de Bruxelles. My thanks therefore also go to Professors Kenneth Bertrams, Ariane Chapelle, Jean-Luc De Meulemeester, André Farber, Jean-Jacques Heirwegh, Marie-Paule Laurent, Pierre-Guillaume Méon, Hugues Pirotte, Véronique Pouillard, and Mathias Schmit.

Outside ULB, the opportunity of a postdoctoral position at Rutgers, the State University of New Jersey, was a major turning point in my career as a researcher. I would especially like to thank Professors Michael Bordo, Hugh Rockoff, and Eugene White for the welcome they extended to me. My time in New Brunswick was an unforgettable experience, both academically and personally.

A researcher's career is not confined to the walls of his or her original institution. Over the years, my work on the issue of Russian debt has brought me into contact with academics from other institutions, all of whom have helped me in various ways to progress in my work. The following deserve special mention: Olivier Accominotti, Martha Bailey, Vincent Bignon, Frans Buelens, Stéphanie Collet, Géraldine David, Claude Dieboldt, Rui Esteves, Marc Flandreau, Georges Gallais-Hamonno, Pierre-Cyrille Hautcoeur, John Landon-Lane, David Le Bris, Chris Meissner, Kris Mitchener, Larry Neal, Anders Ögren, Sébastien Pouget, Philippe Raimbourg, Christian Rietsch, Angelo Riva, Michaël Schiltz, Max-Stephan Schulze, Richard Sylla, Loredana Ureche-Rangau, Karine van der Beek, Jacques-Marie Vaslin, Daniel Waldenström, and Marc Weidenmier.

I have been assisted by the comments of various participants at conferences where I have presented my research on Russian debt. I would like to thank all the people who offered helpful feedback on my work at the following conferences: AFFI (2004), the Annual International Conference on Macroeconomic Analysis and International Finance (2009), the Economic History Society (2004), the European Historical Economics Society Conference (2005 and 2013), the Journées d'Histoire de la comptabilité et du management (2012), the Tor Vergata Conference on Banking and Finance (2005), the International Economic History Congress (2006) as well as seminars at Rutgers University (2004 and 2012), the Laboratoire d'Economie d'Orléans (2006), the London School of Economics (2011), Tokyo University (2012), Uppsala University (2011), and the joint ULB (Solvay)-Sorbonne conference.

The subject matter of this book required collecting a large quantity of data, a task that could have become tedious were it not for the skill, availability, and kindness of the administrators of archive collections. I would particularly like to thank Ms. Bodilsen, Ms. Lesueur, and Mr. Douezi for their invaluable assistance with my research at the Association Nationale des Porteurs Français de Valeurs Mobilières and the Société de Bourse Française.

I would, of course, like to thank my family and friends, who have supported me throughout this long project. Many other people have assisted in the writing of this book, in some cases unwittingly. I would like to thank them all for their help and support.

Hope Springs Eternal

Introduction

This is a book about hope and international finance. From time immemorial investors have been eager to invest abroad in risky undertakings, attracted by the hope of huge potential gains. When hope is mentioned in a financial context, it is usually related to investments entailing substantial risk but promising high returns.

Even though international investments are often risky, some foreign assets are perceived as being risk free. This was the case with Russian sovereign bonds at the beginning of the twentieth century. They were considered so creditworthy that in some countries they were among the assets in which funds set up for the benefit of orphans and widows were allowed to invest. Since these bonds were supposed to be risk free, investors had little reason to hope for anything other than the normal coupon payments. That was the case until the Bolsheviks took the dramatic decision to repudiate.

This book focuses on the reasons which prompted French investors to hope they would eventually be repaid. In this financial context, hope was reflected in the fluctuations of Russian bond prices. Indeed, in view of the extreme nature of the repudiation, the prices of Russian sovereign debt experienced only a modest decline. As a matter of fact, they actually increased after the repudiation, and their yields were well below those observed nowadays when sovereign debts are repudiated. I will argue that these seemingly strange price movements reflected investors' hopes for reimbursement. I will further defend the idea that, far from being a sign of irrational behavior, investors based their hopes on an expectation of one or more extreme events that would lead to repayment. Even though none of these events materialized, there were numerous reasons to be hopeful. My project here is to investigate those reasons. What prompted investors to refuse to view their bonds as valueless? But first I want to describe the context of the repudiation and the data used to analyze the fate of these Russian bonds.

International investments were a common feature of financial markets in the eighteenth century. The benefits of international diversification were well understood at the time. As a result, some early investment vehicles took international diversification explicitly into account (Rouwenhorst 2004). At the end of the nineteenth century, Great Britain was not the only country exporting capital on a massive scale. The Paris stock exchange had gradually become one of the leading exchanges for sovereign debt issues, with Russian sovereign bonds representing one of its largest segments. By the turn of the twentieth century, approximately 50 percent of British savings were invested abroad (Feis 1930). By contrast Heathcote and Perri (2013) mention that on average, foreign assets represented 32 percent of holdings owned by U.S. residents for the 1990–2007 period.

The first foreign loan issued by tsarist Russia was floated in 1769 (Bovykin, 1990). At the beginning of the twentieth century, Russian bonds were listed on all major European stock exchanges (Amsterdam, Berlin, Paris, and London). France was the largest market for Russian securities. At a time when Paris was one of the major exchanges and France was exporting capital on a massive scale, Russian securities as a whole represented 25 percent of French foreign investment (Feis 1930). By contrast, in 2012 French foreign investment was much more diversified, with no single country accounting for more than 15 percent of French foreign portfolio investment holdings.[1]

Just before the outbreak of the First World War, almost half of Russian sovereign bonds were held outside Russia. Ukhov (2003) estimates that the percentage of foreign-held sovereign bonds rose from roughly

43.5 percent in 1893 to 49.7 percent in 1913. Russian sovereign bonds represented only part of the investments made in Russia. In the late nineteenth century many investors had also bought industrial securities from firms active in the country. Furthermore, the First World War had prompted Russia's allies to advance funds in order to wage the war. The amounts held in a given country varied substantially depending on the form of the claims. According to Paslovsky and Moulton (1924, 21), 80 percent of the prewar government debt was held in France, Great Britain coming second with 14 percent. Industrial securities were more widely distributed: France was first (32 percent), Great Britain second (25 percent), Germany third (16 percent), Belgium fourth (15 percent), and the United States fifth (6 percent). War debts were owed to Great Britain (70 percent), France (19 percent), and the United States (7 percent).[2]

The quantity of Russian bonds held in France in the late nineteenth century may surprise a twenty-first-century reader. Although Russia is still a major economic power, it is inconceivable today that more than 1.6 million French people would own Russian securities worth almost 4.5 percent of national wealth. Yet those were the figures cited in a 1919 inventory of repudiated Russian debt. Some fifty-two Russian government securities were listed on the Paris Bourse, along with a large quantity of industrial paper.[3] While estimates of the nominal value of the debt vary, they are all huge. In a speech to the French National Assembly in January 1918 the deputy Emmanuel Brousse estimated that almost 15 billion francs had been lent to Russia, while in March 1920 the senator Anatole de Monzie advanced a figure of around 14 billion francs.[4] The French National Securities Office (Office National des Valeurs Mobilières) put the figure at between 15 billion and 18 billion francs.[5] According to Raoul Péret, Russian sovereign bonds alone were worth nearly 12 billion francs.[6] Girault (1973, 24), probably the best authority, suggests a similar figure, 11,719,638,166 francs. Although overestimated, because they include bonds held by Russians abroad, these numbers are nevertheless staggering.[7] Niall Fergusson (2001, 289) has argued that the Russian default of 1917 was "perhaps the biggest default in history."[8]

Far from representing commitments by institutional investors, the bulk of Russian bonds were held by small savers all over France. Clerks, shopkeepers, industrial workers, and peasants were holding Russian securities (Feis 1930). The many associations formed to defend the rights of Russian bondholders, such as the National League for Claims of Small Investors in Russian Securities (Ligue nationale de revendication des petits porteurs de valeurs russes), give an indication of the large numbers of retail investors who were not particularly wealthy. In a speech to the senate on 31 May 1919 the finance minister himself, Louis-Lucien Klotz, described the exceptionally wide distribution of Russian bonds, which he said were found in every municipality in France.[9] When the debt was repudiated, the geographical origins of the deputies who raised the question of the bonds in parliament mirrored the scattering of Russian bonds across France. The distribution pattern supports Freymond's claim (1996) that farming regions were hit hardest by the repudiation.

Although the repudiation was felt most keenly in France, investors in other European countries also purchased Russian bonds in large quantities. As in France, Russian bondholders in the United Kingdom lived all over the country.[10] According to Luboff, the majority of British owners of Russian bonds before the First World War were retail investors.[11] Table 0.1 shows the percentage of Russian investment by amount invested, based on holdings recorded by the British Union of Russian Bondholders and the Russian Railway Bondholders' Committee on 10 November 1929.

The amounts in table 0.1 show the predominance of investments of less than 100 pounds. This fact alone does not establish that investments came mainly from individuals who were not wealthy. On the contrary, converted into today's money, the upper limit of 100 pounds would be a tidy sum.[12] According to Luboff, however, the investors registered with Russian bondholder defense organizations included stevedores, servants, barbers, and tailors.

Proportionally to its size, Belgium also lent enormous sums to Russia. During their inventory of Russian bonds in 1919, members of the Committee for the Defense of Belgian Interests in Russia (Comité de défense des intérêts belges en Russie) were astonished to find the amount reached almost 300 million Belgian francs, despite having received only a small number of replies.[13] It is thought that Belgium invested more than 1 billion Belgian francs in Russian bonds.

The types of Russian debt contracted before the October Revolu-

Table 0.1. Percentage of investment in Russian bonds by amount invested

Amount	Individual ratio (% of bondholders)
Under £100	42.3
£100–£500	28.4
£501–£1,000	10
£1,000–£5,000	11.6
Over £5,000	7.7

Source: British Union of Russian Bondholders, 25

tion varied. Most of the Russian debt held in France, the Netherlands, and Switzerland consisted of bonds issued before the war and purchased by retail investors. That was also the case in Belgium, where there was a high percentage of investment in industrial bonds. By contrast, Russian borrowings from the United Kingdom consisted mainly of war debt, representing advances to the Russian ally during the First World War (de Monzie 1931, 256–57; White 1985, 26–28). That debt was so substantial that, as Eliacheff points out (1919, 131), Russia's leading creditor at the end of the war was the United Kingdom, not France.

While it might not seem significant, the type of debt held by the various allies and their citizens would play a decisive role in the subsequent negotiations. Depending on their situations, governments gave prominence to different economic effects of the revolution. For countries whose Russian debt consisted of large quantities of bearer securities owned by the general public, the primary objective of the negotiations with revolutionary Russia was to redeem the bonds. The extremely wide distribution of Russian bonds made redemption a political issue of high priority, since every bondholder was a potential voter. Conversely, in countries that lent money to Russia to support the war effort, the repudiation depleted the government's coffers but had only an indirect impact on taxpayers. Furthermore, whereas the amount to be repaid was fairly easy to determine in the case of bearer bonds, sophisticated calculations were required to determine the respective amounts incurred by each of the parties in the case of war debt. The loans also served disparate purposes. At least some of the debt issued before the war financed

Russia's economic development, but most of the capital raised during the war was spent on American, British, and French contractors.

These differences in the type of Russian debt held would strongly influence countries' demands and attitudes in the negotiations. In addition to their economic positions, the creditor countries had diverse geopolitical concerns. This was not lost on contemporary commentators. As Claude Aulagnon observed on the eve of the Genoa Conference, the goals pursued by London, Berlin, and Rome differed radically from the positions defended by Paris and Brussels.[14] According to White (1985, 28), the Belgian and French positions frequently converged on the priority of repayment. Conversely, for the United Kingdom and Italy, trade considerations rapidly took precedence over debt recognition.

Before analyzing the repudiation of Russian debt, I want to provide some information about the context in which it occurred. Following are descriptions of the conditions in which Russian bonds first appeared in French portfolios, of the trading in Russian debt on the Paris market, and finally of the sequence of events leading to the repudiation in early 1918 and its impact on market prices.

Russian Bonds Make Their Appearance in French Portfolios

Girault (1973) catalogues the reasons that prompted France, and particularly French retail investors, to invest considerable sums in Russian bonds.[15] There was a visible rapprochement between Russia and France in the late nineteenth century, underscored by high-profile events. At the same time, French companies were encouraged to invest in the tsarist empire in order to strengthen the Russian ally and accelerate its industrialization. The appearance of Russian bonds in French portfolios was thus driven primarily by the geopolitical climate. In practice, banks and the press encouraged French investors to buy Russian bonds.

Until the early 1880s the main markets for Russian sovereign bonds were the United Kingdom, the Netherlands, and to a lesser extent Germany. France, which had tense relations with Russia, was only a secondary market.[16] The accession of Alexander III to the Russian throne, combined with difficulties in placing new bond issues in the United Kingdom and Germany, prompted Russia to seek to raise capital in France. Although some Russian debt securities were already listed on the Paris market, the issues of 1888–90 represented the real beginnings of French investors' enthusiastic embrace of Russian bonds. Political factors played a role in the success of the first bond issues, but their popularity in France seems to have been driven initially by purely commercial interest. As Girault (1973) points out, the first large issue of Russian debt in France took place several years before the Franco–Russian Alliance.

To a French saver in the late nineteenth century, Russian bonds seemed a safe investment, promising higher interest than the French alternative—the *rente 3 pour cent,* a 3 percent perpetual bond. Eminent economists confirmed the soundness of Russian bonds. The free-market economist Paul Leroy-Beaulieu considered himself prudent when he advised savers to invest up to 10 percent of their portfolios in Russian bonds (Bainville 1919, 82). As Flandreau (2003) pointed out, most of the capital raised was invested in developing infrastructure and local industry, both of which are revenue generating; therefore the perceived credit quality of the Russian state remained high. At the beginning of the century Russia had an impeccable track record and only a moderate debt (Bignon and Flandreau 2011; Harrison and Markevich 2012). Some sectors of the French economy, such as banks, benefited directly from the issuance of Russian bonds in the Paris market. In addition to the commissions received by brokers for each issue, the Russian treasury deposited a large volume of cash in France, notably with the banks charged with paying the coupons to bondholders (Girault 1973, 34). The banks were paid fees to manage the debt on behalf of the Russian state.

Although investors were probably motivated initially by financial interest, the political ties between France and Russia would soon play an important role in the valuation of Russian bonds. It is difficult to establish a clear causal link between economic investment and political rapprochement, but it appears that financial cooperation may have paved the way for political rapprochement. In the event of a default, lenders could lobby their government to assist the debtor country. Similarly, a government's goodwill toward an ally would facilitate issuance of its bonds. In the case of France and Russia, financial and political factors were probably mutually reinforcing and supported the large-scale placement of bonds with French investors.

Political rapprochement between France and Russia began in 1890, particularly with the appointment of Alexandre Ribot as the French minister of foreign affairs. The rapprochement was driven mainly by strategic concerns. France felt diplomatically isolated compared with the increasingly powerful Germany, especially since the renewal of the Triple Alliance and the Italo–British rapprochement, precisely at a time when the Russian government began receiving less financial support from Germany. The coincidence of these two needs pushed France and Russia into one another's arms. The Franco–Russian rapprochement was rapidly acted out in grand public events, designed to impress. These included the tsar's tour of the French exhibition in Moscow in 1891; a visit by French sailors to Kronstadt in July 1891; a visit by Russian sailors to Toulon in 1893; Tsar Nicholas II's visits to France in 1896, 1901, and 1909; and several French presidents' visits to Russia (Félix Faure in 1897, Emile Loubet in 1902, and Raymond Poincaré in 1912 and 1914). These events triggered a wave of Russophilia in France. Politically, the Franco–Russian rapprochement was reflected in the signing of the Franco–Russian Alliance, "one of the foundations of international diplomacy in the period from 1893 to 1914" (Girault 1961, 67). The Entente Cordiale signed by France and the United Kingdom in 1904 strengthened France's diplomatic position. The integration of the two treaties gave rise to the Triple Entente in August 1907. Patriotic motives probably played a role in investors' decision to lend to Russia. The French public certainly appreciated the security provided by the Franco–Russian Alliance (Renouvin 1959).

The Franco–Russian rapprochement raised the issue of the relative freedom of each party. According to Sontag (1968), Russia retained its financial independence despite the substantial amounts it borrowed. Sontag argues that Russia allied itself with France and sought cordial relations with the United Kingdom solely in order to achieve its goals while safeguarding its interests. Citing Russian foreign trade statistics, Sontag (1968) suggests that Russia did not have to enter into an alliance with France and the United Kingdom to receive a financial lifeline. Given the size of the loans, however, it is doubtful that Russia had much diplomatic independence during the period considered here. Any major crisis would have left the Russian empire with very little room to maneuver. The loans could also be used as a diplomatic weapon in the other direction. Since the French government could not afford to leave the holders of Russian bonds to their fate, the enormous loans to Russia made France practically hostage to Russia. Consequently, the impact of the Russian government's direct or indirect action would be considerable.

From the early 1890s on, the French press was encouraged to take an interest in Russia. Considered an indispensable ally in the event of war, Russia enjoyed the flattering coverage it received in the columns of French newspapers. The press, under the approving eye of the French government, thus fanned the nascent Russophilia in France. As it staged symbolic events and arranged bond issues, the government could count on the support of the French press, whose actions contributed to the success of several issues of Russian debt (Girault 1973, 243–44). To support its strategic aims the French government had no qualms about adopting an attitude that was questionable at best. As Long (1972) indicates, members of the French government encouraged Russian ministers to grease the palms of French journalists to minimize negative coverage of the Russo–Japanese War and the revolution of 1905. The Russian government spent more than 2.5 million francs in 1904–6 alone, the French government acting as a catalyst, to use Long's (1972) term. In fairness to the French, the Russian state did not exactly wait for approval to implement a sweeping campaign of bribery among journalists (Long 1972; Raffalovitch 1931).

Long (1972) attributes the venality of the French press to two factors: fierce competition between newspapers, which had to rely on small print runs, and the limited success of advertising as a source of revenue. Bignon and Flandreau (2011) show that newspapers of lesser reputation exploited the absence of proper libel laws to publish damaging allegations.[17] Their influence was limited by two factors: the existence of serious newspapers investigating the truth of rumors and the emergence of "publicity brokers," whose job was to pool bribes and ensure positive press coverage. As a result, many firms were subsidizing the French press. In 1931 La librairie du Travail published some of the correspondence between the tsarist government and Arthur Raffalovitch, the tsar's representative in Paris and an economist of repute in France. The letters reveal the scale of the corruption. Despite the sensational nature of this revelation, few newspapers reported it at the time. But neither did they refute it, despite the jaw-dropping number of journalists and newspapers that allegedly benefited from tsarist Russia's largesse.[18] Raffalovitch's report for 1896 mentions *Le Journal Officiel, Le Messager de Paris, Le Journal des débats, Le Temps, L'Economiste français, Le Monde économique, Le Petit Parisien, Le Nord, Le Rentier, La Revue économique*, and *La Semaine financière*. Over the years other titles joined the list (*Le Petit Journal, Le Matin, Le Figaro*, etc.), while the least "useful" ones lost their "subsidies" (Raffalovitch 1931). Bignon and Flandreau (2011) show that the so-called Russian subsidies were mostly paid to the high-quality journals. The length of the list suggests wholesale corruption of the press. However, this impression should be qualified because a few relatively more independent newspapers actually ran a campaign against Russian bonds during the events of 1904 and 1905. Surprising as it may seem nowadays, one may also wonder whether Russia could have avoided bribing the press. Bignon and Flandreau (2011, 625) suggest that this was basically impossible when enemies were ready to subsidize negative rumors: "Russia had no choice but to forestall bad press with purchases of publicity and bribes."

The years 1904 and 1905 played a key role in the development of the Russian debt issue. The 1905 revolution can be considered a dress rehearsal for the revolutions of 1917, insofar as in 1905 the revolutionaries made clear their position on tsarist debt. The Russo–Japanese War reinforced the interdependence between the Russian empire and the French financial market. In terms of the political environment and the repudiation, 1905 was what Pipes (1990) calls a foreshock.

Amid domestic political turbulence, Russia found itself engaged in a war with Japan. The origins of the war have been discussed in depth (Pipes 1990, 11). Some authors maintain that "a war could have been avoided if Russia's foreign policy had been in competent hands" (Figes 1996, 168). In any case, Japan's expansionist designs on Korea and Manchuria collided with the Russian presence in the Far East. The surprise attack on the Russian fleet at Port Arthur on 8 February 1904 was the spark that ignited the conflict. The racially prejudiced Russian high command was convinced of its superiority, and this overconfidence resulted in woeful handling of the conflict. Russia became mired in a war initially presented as easily winnable, fueling criticism from the opposition, which denounced the government as incompetent (Figes 1996, 169–70). In July 1904, during the uncertainty of the conflict in the east, Russia's unpopular minister of the interior, Viacheslav Plehve, was assassinated. His reputedly more liberal successor attempted to introduce elected representatives into state institutions. After hesitating momentarily, Tsar Nicholas II rejected the proposed reforms, prompting the minister's resignation and fanning the opposition's discontent (Pipes 1990, 18; Werth 2004, 41).

In early January 1905 a group of workers attempted to deliver a petition and supplication to the tsar. This never reached its intended recipient, as the tsar's soldiers fired on the crowd, resulting in a massacre later called Bloody Sunday (Pipes 1990, 22; Werth 2004, 42). In the following months the protest movements radicalized, and the tsar's uncle, Grand Duke Sergei Alexandrovich, was assassinated. Meanwhile, the Far East campaign went from disaster to disaster. The loss at Mukden in March 1905 was followed by a humiliating naval defeat at Tsushima in May, which forced the tsar to come to the negotiating table. The defeat quashed Nicholas II's hope that a resounding victory would silence the domestic opposition (Pipes 1990, 27). Instead, he was forced to accept major structural reforms, notably the establishment of a parliamentary assembly, the State Duma. Not long afterward, the Treaty of Portsmouth, signed on 5 September 1905, formally ended the Russo–Japanese War, confirming Japanese hegemony over Korea (Pipes 1990, 29).

How did the financial community react to the Russian empire's troubles? The announcement of the outbreak of the Russo–Japanese War depressed market prices for Russian sovereign bonds, both in Saint Petersburg and in Paris. On 11 February 1904 the value of 4 percent bonds fell to 90 percent of par, and the value of 3 percent bonds below 72 percent of par (Raffalovitch 1931, 20). In response to this sudden drop in prices, the chairman of the stockbrokers' syndicate, Maurice de Verneuil, called on the Russian government to intervene, not by buying back bonds on the market, which might have spurred an even bigger sell-off, but by acting to ensure positive press coverage. Russia used two methods to gain the favor of journalists. Regular payments were made under the form of advertising, and in exceptional cases the payments were direct bribes (Bignon and Flandreau, 2011). The war was such a case, and the amounts paid as bribes jumped from 1904 to 1906 (Bignon and Flandreau 2011). This intervention had the approval of the French finance minister. It was not sufficient to stabilize sovereign bond prices, however, and by the end of February another campaign directed at the press was envisaged (Raffalovitch 1931, 24). As pointed out by Bignon and Flandreau (2011), Russian interventions sometimes had a preventive nature. During the Russo–Japanese War, Russia had no choice but to float its bonds in Paris, as Great Britain favored Japan. Indications in the French press that Russia was facing troubles in making ends meet would have weakened the country and increased its borrowing costs. Aware of this, Russia's enemies were ready to subsidize negative rumors about the state of its finances. However, Russian bribes sometimes backfired, as was the case when some newspapers that felt inadequately compensated embarked on retaliatory smear campaigns (Raffalovitch 1931, 32–33). The Russian empire nevertheless succeeded in placing a 5 percent treasury bill on the French market in May 1904 (Girault 1973, 405). Conversely, an issue in 1905 failed because of adverse military developments in Russia. The power of the press—and of those who bribed it—receded temporarily.

At the end of 1905 de Verneuil appealed again to Sergei Witte, by this time the Russian prime minister, to influence the press. Russia's action must have been conspicuous because in 1920 a French senator recalled that Russian bonds had been supported on the Paris Bourse at the behest of the Russian government during the Russo–Japanese War.[19] Paradoxically, the Russian defeat was not presented as casting doubt on Russia's capacity to manage its public finances. Paul Leroy-Beaulieu (1906, 661), one of the most prominent economists of the day, went so far as to claim that the conflict demonstrated Russia's financial preparedness for a major war and its creditworthiness.[20] After the Russo–Japanese War, the Russian government decided to cut back on its monthly payments to the French press. This letup was short-lived. In light of the intense revolutionary activity on Russian soil, a proposal to increase payments to the French press was suggested in November 1905 and acted on in January 1906. In a memorandum to the Russian finance minister, Vladimir Kokovtsov, dated February 1906, Raffalovitch claims that the action taken against the French press convinced the country's investors to hold on to their Russian bonds.[21]

The close ties between French and Russian economic interests did not go uncriticized.[22] The poet and journalist Anatole France took France to task for its financial support of Russia. He deemed France partly responsible "for the follies and cruelties of Tsarism" by "giving it the wherewithal to commit them by lending it the staggering sum of nine billion."[23] Anatole France attacked both the government's wastefulness and the use to which French money was being put. When Russia sought to raise more capital on the Paris market, leftist newspapers and figures mounted a protest campaign. The Socialists called for a boycott of the bond issue.[24] In a speech given on 18 March 1905 Anatole France said that subscribing to the issue was tantamount to "subscribing to the oppression of a people . . . to crime and madness."[25] He echoed voices inside Russia, such as that of the writer Maxim Gorky, who called for the suspension of financial support for the tsar.[26] The German kaiser rejoiced at Russia's problems and made sure no German money went to helping overcome the problem the country was facing (Feis 1930).

In March 1905 Anatole France presciently announced that the tsarist regime in Russia would soon collapse, giving way to a government that would repudiate the debts contracted to suppress the revolution.[27] Quoting Gorky, he predicted that the new popular government would recognize commitments made prior to the events of 22 January 1905 but not "the bonds of massacre and civil war."[28] The Socialist leader Jean Jaurès, too, warned parliament of the dangers to which French lenders were exposed: "You are cheating French lenders. The money Russia is borrowing will never be repaid."[29] These dissenting voices did not succeed in severing the ties between French finance and Russian politics. Conversely, the Russo–Japanese War and the events of 1905 radically altered the balance of power between France and Russia.

By the end of 1905, after the military setbacks against Japan and facing domestic unrest, Russia was left with only limited diplomatic independence. From then on France used its financial clout to gain political leverage (Girault 1961). Criticism from the Socialist opposition did not prevent a bond issue from being floated on the Paris market in April 1906. The French government supported the issue, which saved Russia from imminent bankruptcy, on condition that the Russian government comply with two French demands: the constitutional reorganization of Russia, and Russian support at the Algeciras Conference (Girault 1961). The market reluctantly subscribed the issue, since organized protests and the threat of repudiation drove down the price (Collet and Oosterlinck 2012). Girault (1961) convincingly describes the turnaround that took place in 1906. Until 1904 France had to lobby Russia to be awarded new debt issues, but from 1906 on France positioned itself as a creditor demanding political advantages in exchange for loans. France maintained its role as leading financier until the outbreak of the First World War, in particular by facilitating an enormous 4.5 percent bond issue in 1909. Not long before the start of the First World War, Franco–Russian relations cooled somewhat, mainly because French industrialists were disappointed with Russia's concessions to them (Hogenhuis-Seliverstoff 1981, 15). This cooling did not, however, represent a fundamental threat to Franco–Russian relations.

The Reaction of the French Market in Russian Bonds to War and Revolution

At the outbreak of the First World War, Russia's public finances were closely tied to the French market. Figure 0.1 shows the yields for the Russian 1906 5 percent bond, 1909 4.5 percent bond, and the rente 3 percent from January 1914 to December 1917. The figures shown are the yields to maturity computed on the basis of the opening prices for bonds (published by official brokers in *Cours Authentiques des Agents de Change*).

Several general observations can be made about this figure. First, despite the war the yield to maturity for Russian bonds remained relatively low until 1917. Second, the market seems not to have foreseen the outbreak of hostilities, as yields remained fairly constant right up to the last week of July 1914. Third, the whole market suffered a sudden in-

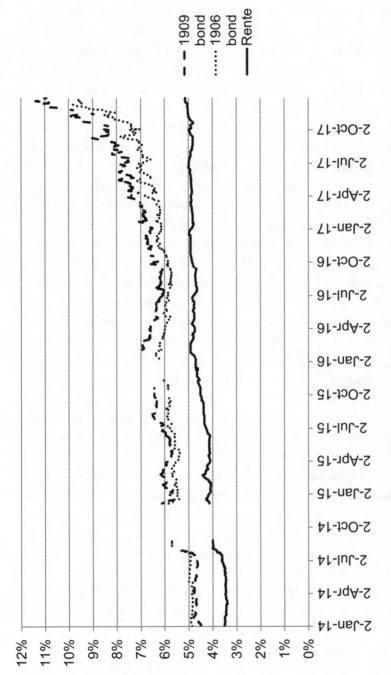

Figure 0.1. Yield to maturity for Russian bonds (5 percent bond of 1906 and 4.5 percent bond of 1909) and the *rente* (French 3 percent perpetual bond) from 1 January 1914 to 31 December 1917. *Source:* Author's calculation on the basis of the *Cours Authentique des Agents de Change.*

terruption during the war—the Bourse was closed from 3 September to 7 December 1914 and when trading resumed volumes were low.[30] Last, Russian bonds moved in lockstep with the rente 3 percent until January 1916, apparently influenced by the same events. Conversely, from January 1916 to February 1917 Russian bonds outperformed the rente. Events on the Russian front did not really affect bond prices.

That Russian bonds were impervious to wartime events is probably owing to French and British financial support of their Russian ally. In hindsight it's clear the resilience of Russian bonds could not have been based solely on the record of Russia's army and public finances. French censorship of news from Russia, which lasted until 1919, also limited price declines (Hogenhuis-Seliverstoff 1981, 15). Whatever the factors influencing trends, Russian bond prices during the war must have seemed reassuring to an outside observer and at least as good as their French counterparts. Such confidence no doubt bolstered many French small investors' faith in the excellent quality of Russian credit.

In March (February) 1917 Russian and French bond yields began to diverge: as yields on Russian bonds increased, yields on the rente firmed up or remained steady.[31] The March (February) demonstrations, the abdication of the tsar, and the October Revolution obviously had a major impact on Russian bond prices. The causes of the 1917 revolutions have been studied in depth elsewhere.[32] I will therefore make only passing reference to the revolution itself, and the analysis will focus on its impact on bond prices.

The February Days of 1917 began with a peaceful workers' demonstration in Saint Petersburg. Since the authorities did not respond, the demonstrators stepped up their action, and the number of strikes increased dramatically. As the movement spread, the government sent in troops to restore order. To the government's astonishment, the soldiers refused to fire on the demonstrators, forcing the officers to do the dirty work in their place. When the soldiers saw the atrocities committed by their commanding officers, they rallied to the demonstrators' cause. The subsequent raid on the arsenal and the distribution of weapons to the crowd precipitated the downfall of the tsar.

In light of developments on the street, the members of the Duma were forced to take a stance. By welcoming revolutionary elements, Alexander Kerensky, the Socialist–revolutionary politician, brought about a rapprochement between insurgents and parliamentarians. This led to the country being governed by two sources of power: the Provisional Committee of the State Duma and the Saint Petersburg Soviet. Misjudging their relative strengths, the two camps sought a compromise solution, which led to the formation of a provisional government on 15 March (Werth 2004, 88–89). In the end, only one member of this government—Kerensky, who accepted the justice portfolio—sympathized with the revolutionary movements. That same evening, on the advice of his army chiefs and ministers, Nicholas II abdicated in favor of his brother, Grand Duke Michael. After receiving threats, Michael signed his own abdication the following day, marking the end of the Romanov dynasty (Figes 1996, 339–45).

The fall of tsarism was not mourned by Russia's allies. The figure of the tsar, popularized at the time of the Franco–Russian Alliance, was not especially missed by French politicians (Hogenhuis-Seliverstoff 1981, 15). In March 1917 the president of the French senate expressed his best wishes to the Russian constitutional government, saying that an era of freedom had opened up in the east and that Germany would now be encircled by a "coalition of democracies."[33] In the United Kingdom the economist John Maynard Keynes wrote to his mother that the revolution was the "sole result of the war . . . worth having."[34]

Russia's new government rapidly sought recognition from the Allies. On 17 March 1917 it undertook to honor the commitments made by the imperial government (Hogenhuis-Seliverstoff 1981, 16). At the time, the Allies' main concern was the provisional government's position on the pursuit of the war. The foreign minister, Pavel Miliukov, reasserted Russia's aims and desire to pursue the war until victory was achieved. This reassured the Allies but drew sharp criticism from members of the Soviet. The clash between the annexationist and anti-imperialist positions led to the April Crisis, which resulted in Miliukov's resignation and a cabinet reshuffle that brought new Socialist ministers into the government (Werth 2004, 103).

With respect to Russia's debt, the provisional government declared it would honor the financial obligations of the previous government, particularly the coupon and amortization payments due on sovereign bonds (Sack 1927; Freymond 1996). Redemption of the bonds did not seem to be much cause for concern at that time. The civil strife in Russia barely dented confidence in its repayment capacity. The political instability and its negative impact on market prices seem to have been perceived as temporary.[35] Russia's vast territory and natural wealth supported the perception that it had the wherewithal to redeem its bonds.[36]

In a decree dated 27 March 1917 the provisional government turned to the bond market by issuing a so-called liberty bond. Trotsky (1995, 325) argued that the new issue enabled the government to demonstrate its intention to honor all its debt. According to Eliacheff (1919, 149), the issue raised more than 4 billion rubles by the end of September 1917. Subscribed by almost nine hundred thousand people, the issue enjoyed the support of French political and social institutions as well as of banks and the press. Werth (2004, 106) says the bonds were unpopular with the Russian bourgeoisie. Conversely, an issue of *Le Rentier* in May 1917 reported that in France "the liberty bond issue seems to be proceeding well," while an undefined number of bonds were purchased in other countries, chiefly the United Kingdom.[37]

Despite the unrest in Russia and falling prices, a section of the French financial press continued to urge its readers not to act in haste. These newspapers argued that a mass sell-off of Russian bonds would only make the situation worse. The main advice given at the beginning of July was to wait and see.[38] It was in this context that the crisis of summer 1917 arose. In June 1917 Kerensky's government began maneuvers in preparation for a major offensive against the German enemy. But after a few short-lived Russian successes, the German counteroffensive broke through Russian lines. Fearing a German advance, the soldiers in the capital mutinied. The mutiny was brutally put down, causing Vladimir Lenin to flee to Finland, undermining the credibility of the far left, and facilitating the rise of the Constitutional Democrat Party (Kadet party). As a result of a reorganization of the army, General Lavr Kornilov was placed in command of the troops. Boosted by his growing popularity, Kornilov attempted a coup but was outmaneuvered by Kerensky with support from the Bolsheviks. This was a turning point in the Russian revolution, as the Kadets, who had supported Kornilov, were eliminated, thereby paving the way for the return of the Bolsheviks.

French investors seem to have been aware of the import of the events in Russia, as yields on Russian bonds increased again in August 1917. The increase can probably be attributed primarily to the worsening political situation in Russia, aggravated by worse-than-anticipated budget estimates and the weakness of the ruble. Despite the fall in prices, the Russian government described the liberty bond as a success in that it had raised 3.5 billion rubles.[39] The veracity of that claim is questionable, however, and the government may simply have been seeking to restore the image of its finances through a positive announcement. In the months that followed the July Days, the Bolsheviks built up their power as the state collapsed. Kerensky's proclamation of a republic in September 1917 failed to lift bond prices. The political and economic uncertainty did influence the price of Russian bonds listed in Paris, since even before the October Revolution Russian bonds had begun to decline on the French market.

In September 1917 Lenin was practically the only leftist leader arguing for a coup d'état (Werth 2004, 122). His repeated attacks on "revolutionary legalism," however, eventually achieved their desired effect, and a majority of the central committee voted for armed insurrection. The uprising began in early November (late October 1917). On 7 November (25 October) the Bolsheviks took power and installed a Provisional Government of Workers and Peasants. Lack of knowledge about the aims of the various revolutionary groups, combined with still-effective censorship, left French investors unable to form a clear opinion regarding the future political evolution in Russia (Hogenhuis-Seliverstoff 1981, 32). The term *Maximalist* was used in reference to the Bolsheviks, but there did not seem to be much awareness of what the name implied. The Bourse did not expect a group sometimes seen as German agents to last long. Some French newspapers advised readers to be patient and not sell their Russian bonds (Freymond 1996, 42). This uncertainty, based on ignorance, naturally increased the perception of risk inherent in investing in Russian bonds. As a result, yields on Russian bonds jumped between late October and December 1917, reflecting the gravity of Russia's domestic political situation.[40]

The Repudiation of Russia's Debt

The repudiation of Russia's debt was on some people's minds well before it happened. On 23 November 1917 an article in *Novaia Zhizn'* criticized the debt. The author, Yuri Larin, said that nonrepayment would
be a choice punishment for the French capitalists he accused of having
brought about the war. Consequently, he described repudiation as "one
of the most natural and necessary conditions for peace" (Noulens 1933,
1:150–51; Mourin 1967, 66). This opinion proved highly popular and
was repeated in the press and in speeches. According to Noulens (1933,
1:150), the repudiation announcement sent jitters through stock exchanges in London, Paris, and Amsterdam. Rumors that the "people's
commissars" would repudiate the debt were circulating in France and
the United Kingdom by late December 1917.[41] The rumors had only
some basis in truth, as what seemed to be an official position, for example, turned out to be only an opinion in *Pravda*.[42] In any case, the market was clearly aware of worrying rumors, even if it was unable to determine whether they were true. The uncertainty about the decisions that
had actually been taken lasted several weeks.

On 27 December 1917 (15 December) a decree on bank nationalization was published in *Izvestiia* (Martin 1921). On 11 January 1918
(29 December 1917) the *Official Journal of the Provisional Government
of Workers and Peasants* published a decree on cessation of payment of
coupons and dividends. The decree suspended all coupon payments and
banned all securities trading.[43] On 8 February (26 January) *Pravda* published a summary of the decree on the cancellation of state debt, adopted on 21 January (8 January) by the Central Executive Committee.[44]
Signed by the chairman of the Central Executive Committee, Iakov
Sverdlov, the decree stipulated:

1. "All state debts contracted by the Russian government are
   cancelled as of 1 December 1917;
2. "Loan guarantees extended by the Russian government
   are also cancelled;
3. "All foreign debt is cancelled unconditionally and without exception;

4. "Short-term bonds and Treasury bills shall be converted into non–interest bearing currency;

5. "Small holders of domestic bonds with a nominal value not exceeding 10,000 rubles may exchange their bonds for registered certificates issued by the Russian Soviet Federative Socialist Republic up to a value of 10,000 rubles;

6. "Deposits in state savings banks and the interest payable on them are inviolable. Cancelled state bonds held by state savings banks shall be replaced by book-entry debt in the name of the Russian Soviet Federative Socialist Republic.

7. "Cooperatives, municipal governments and other democratic or public-interest institutions that owned cancelled debt shall be compensated;

8. "The liquidation of state debt shall be overseen by the Supreme Soviet of the National Economy;

9. "The State Bank is tasked with liquidation of the debt and registration of all holders of securities (cancelled or not);

10. "In agreement with the local Soviets of the National Economy, the Soviets of Soldiers, Workers and Peasants shall form committees to determine which citizens qualify as small savers. The committees are empowered to cancel savings accumulated other than through labor, even if these do not exceed 5,000 rubles."

When the decree was published, the measures introduced by the new regime prompted much speculation in France. There was remarkable confusion about the content, scope, and enforcement of the decree. On 17 February *Pravda* described the repudiation as a blow to the Entente powers "of no less force than Germany's victories on the western front" (Mourin 1967, 67). That said, the blow took some time to hit home. In late February 1918 *Le Rentier* opined that the decree on debt cancellation had not yet been implemented and was only one of several weapons levelled at the Allies.[45] The confusion in France was undoubtedly aided by the French government, which was eager to keep the repudiation a secret for fear that an announcement would trigger panic (Hogenhuis-Seliverstoff 1981, 33).

On 7 March 1918 the *Official Journal of the Provisional Govern-ment of Workers and Peasants* published an additional decision about the practical implementation of the decrees on cancellation of state bonds and other securities.[46] The decision mitigated the repudiation somewhat but only for bonds issued on the Russian domestic market and held in Russia. Holders of bonds with a value between 10,000 and 25,000 rubles would be entitled to an annuity calculated on the basis of a maximum value of 10,000 rubles. Furthermore, all bonds issued prior to 25 October 1917 were canceled, except for liberty bonds with a value of less than 100 rubles. On 11 May 1918 a new decree, undoubtedly motivated by a shortage of money, authorized the use of mature cou-pons of various bonds as paper money.[47]

The measures introduced by the Soviet government had an un-deniable impact on prices on all the markets where Russian bonds were traded. However, as I explain below, the impact was much smaller than what might have been expected, given the radical nature of Russia's decision.

Given the strong correlation between market prices for all the se-curities issued by the same state, it would be largely pointless to examine the price trend for every single bond issued by the Russian empire. My analysis will therefore concentrate on two of the main securities (in terms of volume[48] and liquidity) issued by the Russian empire and listed in France: the 5 percent Russian state bond issued in 1906 (ukase of 17 April [4 April] 1906) and the 4.5 percent Russian state bond issued in 1909 (ukase of 15 January [2 January] 1909). The 5 percent bond was issued to cover the general needs of the treasury, the second to repay treasury bills and meet extraordinary budget expenses in 1909. Both bonds were listed internationally—the 1906 bond in Paris, Amsterdam, Brussels, London, and Vienna; and the 1909 bond in Paris, Amster-dam, and London. Although the bonds were redeemable in various cur-rencies, the exchange rates were fixed at issuance. Fixed exchange rates, which were printed on the bonds, were intended to attract a broader range of investors by eliminating exchange rate risk for the buyer.

Figure 0.2 shows the yields for these bonds for each business day between 1 January 1917 and 31 December 1921, as computed on the basis of the prices recorded in *Cours Authentiques des Agents de Change.*

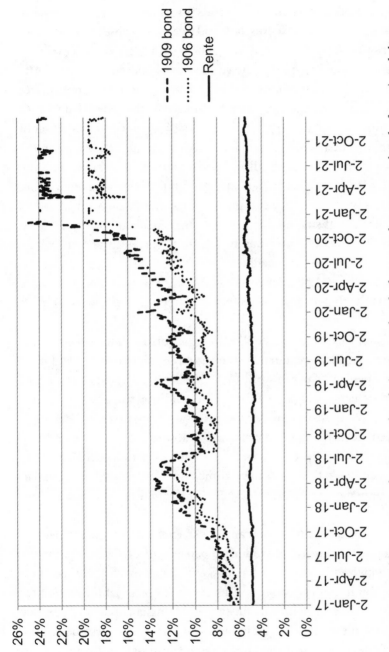

Figure 0.2. Yield to maturity for Russian bonds (5 percent bond of 1906 and 4.5 percent bond of 1909) and the *rente* (French 3 percent perpetual bond) from 1 January 1917 to 31 December 1921. *Source:* Author's calculation on the basis of the *Cours Authentique des Agents de Change*.

The trend in Russian bonds' yields is surprising in several respects (Oosterlinck 2003a). First, Russian yields were very close to French ones at the beginning of the period. In January 1917, after nearly two and a half years of war, the spread between Russian bonds and French rentes was below 170 basis points. Second, although Russian bond prices dropped sharply during 1917, yields stabilized by the end of that year. At the end of December 1917, when rumors of the Soviet repudiation of Russian debt first began to circulate on Western markets, yields on the 1906 5 percent bond were still below 10 percent. The spread with the French rente did not reach even 500 basis points. When the repudiation was officially announced, yields increased only moderately, which seems to indicate that the repudiation rumors had already been priced in and that the repudiation itself was not initially perceived as particularly credible. According to Hogenhuis-Seliverstoff (1981, 72), investors did not expect the Bolshevik regime to last long and were therefore more concerned with nationalizations than with repudiation. The yield trend appears to confirm this view.

Third, Russian bonds continued to perform well for several years, despite having been repudiated. The 1906 5 percent bond was still trading at 45 percent of par in April 1918.[49] This price was the equivalent of an 11.6 percent yield to maturity. Yields did not rise above that level until January 1920. On the contrary, Russian bonds even enjoyed periods of euphoria that pushed yields well below 8.5 percent several times. The relatively modest decline in Russian bond prices was not unique to the French market. In New York, at the end of February 1918, Russian bonds, although at a several-year low, were trading at almost 40 percent of face value.[50]

Even when yields on Russian bonds increased in 1920, the yield on the 1906 bond was still at around 20 percent. Aside from a few jumps yields stabilized in 1921, but the market was mainly characterized by a contraction in trading volumes. To be sure, the fact that the market required a 20 percent yield to maturity to hold Russian bonds is testimony to their riskiness. However, set in historical perspective these yields were relatively low given that the bonds had been in default for more than three years.

Was the resilience of Russian bonds atypical? One way to address this question is to compare the Russian experience with other cases of sovereign debt crisis. The beginning of the twenty-first century has witnessed two dramatic crises: the Argentinean default in 2001 and the eurozone crisis that started in 2007 and affected Portugal, Italy, Ireland, and Greece. After several years of recession Argentina defaulted on its foreign debt in December 2001. The principal of the foreign bonds amounted to close to USD 82 billion, making the Argentine default one of the largest in history. The eurozone crisis followed the 2007 global financial crisis. At the end of 2009 several eurozone countries experienced a severe economic deterioration that prompted investors to question the ability to repay the debt (Lane 2012). Even though several countries were affected, Greece was the most dramatic case. In October 2009 the new government revealed that the fiscal deficit would reach 12.7 percent of GDP, double the original figure. The situation deteriorated so quickly that the country required financial assistance in early 2010. In May 2010 the International Monetary Fund, the European Central Bank, and the European Commission reached an agreement with Greece, which received a €110-billion adjustment loan in exchange for a commitment to lower its fiscal deficit (Gibson, Hall, and Tavlas 2012). This rescue proved to be too small, and in July 2011 eurozone leaders agreed to issue a second rescue package. In October 2011 bondholders were asked to accept a 50 percent reduction in the face value of the bonds as well as a reduction in interest rates. In February 2012 a final agreement was reached, and bonds were exchanged, leading to an estimated loss of 75 percent for private creditors.[51] This agreement prompted the International Swaps and Derivatives Association to trigger credit default swaps on Greek bonds, as the compulsory nature of the exchange was viewed as a credit event.[52]

Both Argentina and Greece make good points of comparison. In a sense the Argentine case is even more compelling than the Greek one. Indeed, in the Argentinean case bondholders had no hope of a bailout. The situation of Greece was more complex. Bondholders could reasonably expect to see the European Union intervene in one way or another to help the country. In this case yields on Greek bonds would have been lower than those on their Argentinean counterparts. I shall therefore usually compare yields with the Greek case. That said, spreads on Argentinean bonds provide very similar results and will also be discussed shortly.

The Russian yields presented earlier offer insights about expectations for Russian bonds. However, spreads with a benchmark are a more traditional yardstick to gauge bonds' riskiness and markets' expectations regarding reimbursement. Figure 0.3 shows the fluctuations in Greek and Russian spreads compared with bonds issued by Germany (in the Greek case) and France (in the Russian case).[53] In order to compare these spreads, the origin date is set at the date of default (the first week of February 1918 for Russian bonds and the last week of October 2011 for Greece), and the figures on the horizontal axis show the number of weeks before or after the default.[54] Figure 0.3 covers three years before the default and slightly less than two years afterward.

The spread movements depicted in figure 0.3 are testimony to the differences between the Russian and Greek cases. Greek spreads increased dramatically well before default was officially declared. Investors were expecting the default more than 75 weeks before it occurred. By contrast, the Russian spread reached only 500 basis points a few weeks before the repudiation was declared. The difference in order of magnitude is also striking. For the period under consideration the Russian spreads remain in the range of 500 basis points, while the Greek spreads are above 1,000 basis points for a very long period, reaching a maximum of 4,400! Due to data constraints, the figure ends 102 weeks after the defaults. By that time both spreads had converged, and thereafter the Russian spread began to increase again. However, even at the end of 1921 it was still below 2,000 basis points.

Greece is just one point of comparison. How do Russian spreads compare to the Argentinean case? Spreads on Argentinean bonds reached even higher values than their Greek counterparts. For instance, the spread between the Argentinean Emerging Market Bond Index (computed by JP Morgan) and US Treasuries was well above 5,000 basis points at the end of 2001 (IMF 2004). Could the difference be explained by the exceptional severity of the Greek and Argentinean cases? or by changes in markets' appreciation of risk? If either is the case, comparing with a less severe episode of default occurring in the past might present additional insights. The Romanian debt crisis of the 1930s, for example,

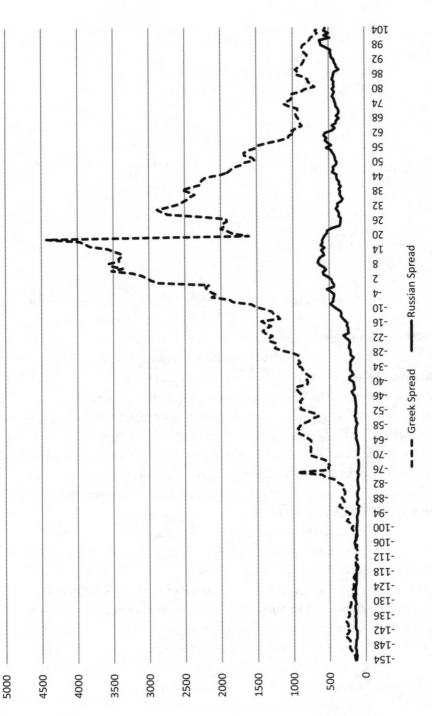

Figure 0.3. Change in Greek and Russian spreads with respect to bonds issued by Germany (in the Greek case) and France (in the Russian case). Values expressed in basis points. Figure centered on the date of default. *Source:* Author's calculation on the basis of the *Cours Authentique des Agents de Change* for Russia's spread and Datastream for Greece's.

Table 0.2. Descriptive statistics during the postcrisis period

	Indicator[a]				Return (%)			
	Mean	SD[b]	High	Low	Mean	SD	High	Low
Russia (1918–20)	104.04	10.48	121.90	83.84	−0.32	3.55	10.24	−6.95
Romania (1933–35)	70.44	12.53	100.00	52.36	−0.44	4.73	15.79	−21.39

[a]The indicator has a value of 100 on the date of the debt crisis (default or repudiation).
[b]Standard deviation.
Source: Oosterlinck and Ureche-Rangau (2005)

is an interesting comparison point. Oosterlinck and Ureche-Rangau (2005) analyzed the behavior of market prices for a basket of Russian and Romanian bonds over a four-year period beginning two years before each country's debt crisis and ending two years afterward in order to compare the effects of repudiation with those of default.

Intuitively, default would appear to be less damaging than repudiation to bondholders. Whereas a defaulting government declares itself financially unable to meet its obligations, a repudiating government refuses to recognize its liabilities. The analysis in table 0.2 nevertheless shows that, regardless of the criterion used (mean price, highest or lowest price, returns or volatility of returns of the two indices), Russian bonds outperformed their Romanian counterparts.[55]

The data in table 0.2 suggest that the market prices of Russian bonds were indeed exceptional. However, there may be several reasons for the differential between the two cases here. First, the validity of the comparison could be questioned. Oosterlinck and Ureche-Rangau (2005) justify their choice of Romanian bonds as a benchmark by the exchanges where they were traded, the types of investors, the bonds' characteristics, the location of the issuers, and the issuance environment.[56] Despite these similarities, prices still might not be comparable because of the microstructure of each market. Second, the high prices for Russian bonds could be due to rational but unmet expectations.

Market prices are an indication of market reality, which is heavily dependent on the specific operation of the individual market. The influence of market microstructure on market prices is well established. The price formation model (that is, order-driven or quote-driven), taxation, the organization of trading, and the liquidity of the securities traded are all factors that can strongly influence prices. It therefore seems relevant to determine whether the resilience of Russian bond prices is only a mirage owing to low trading volumes.

There are practically no statistics on the daily trading volumes of Russian bonds. Trading volumes can be estimated on the basis of taxes paid on transactions or of the number of changes in market prices in the course of a day. The first method cannot be used in the Russian case because of a lack of data. The second method might be possible but would require an enormous amount of data. The estimates of trading volumes used here are therefore derived from comments made by market participants at the time.[57]

The Russian revolution began during the First World War. Its impact on bonds was therefore a combination of the war and the repudiation. During the war, trading on the Paris Bourse was thin. Various laws introduced from 1916 onward further restricted trading on the Paris market, which had shrunk to very low levels by 1918.[58] The contraction in trading volumes of Russian bonds thus needs to be put into the broader context of a sharp decline in all market trading as a result of the First World War.

By December 1917, although trading in Russian bonds had fallen, it was still one of the most active segments when, as the prefect's inspector reported, "trading in the other securities listed on the two indices [was] close to nil."[59] The number of Russian bond trades gradually dwindled because many orders could not be matched. The press attributed this to the difficulty of finding an equilibrium price. Sellers seem to have had a less negative perception of events in Russia than potential buyers did.[60] The situation on the ground was so complex that *Le Rentier* often refrained from making any recommendations to bondholders. Trading was suspended at the end of December 1917, when rumors about the repudiation were in full swing, not because there were no orders but because the mismatch between buy and sell orders was too great.[61] In

January 1918 the opinion of various market professionals was that it was both the wrong time to buy Russian paper and, for those with Russian bonds in their portfolios, the wrong time to sell.[62] Trading in Russian bonds probably reached its lowest point at the end of March 1918, when the press questioned even the representativeness of prices.[63] In August 1918 *Le Rentier* reported a recovery in Russian bonds.[64] Similarly, in September 1918 *La Revue des Valeurs Russes,* a supplement to *La Lettre Hebdomadaire,* noted a pickup in trading in Russian bonds, which it said had been practically nonexistent for many months.[65] But by August 1919 the market was confused again. *Le Rentier* considered prices to be either "too high or too low, depending on whether or not Russia will succeed in ridding itself of Bolshevism."[66]

In all likelihood the profile of typical investors changed over time. The original savers who bought Russian bonds because of their supposed low risk were succeeded by much more risk-hungry investors, who probably viewed Russian bonds as a kind of lottery. Trading in the Russian segment resumed in January 1920.[67] In May 1920 *Le Rentier* commented that prices for Russian bonds in France were meaningless and that bondholders should bide their time.[68] In July of the same year the Russian bond segment was described as inactive once again. Trading in Russian bonds in the United Kingdom, according to several issues of *The Economist,* alternated between periods of renewed activity and dead calm. At the end of 1920 the chairman of the Paris stockbrokers' syndicate decided to suspend trading in Russian bonds for two weeks to avoid quoting rock-bottom prices, despite public opposition to the measure.[69] Trading volumes became smaller and smaller from 1921 on, and large orders could rarely be filled.[70] In October 1922 a senator who lobbied actively for the repayment of Russian bonds nevertheless observed "constant speculation in Russian debt securities."[71]

Although the volume of trade in Russian bonds varied enormously during the period under review, and even though trading practically ceased altogether at times, there generally seemed to be no reason to question the representativeness of prices. Prices usually changed from one day to the next, implying that at least one trade took place per day. Moreover, prices frequently changed several times in the course of a day, which further supports the volume argument. Moreover, according to the descriptions in the contemporary financial press, every pronounced rise in market prices corresponds to an increase in the volume of Russian bonds traded. Finally, when the press refers to problems of volume, these reflect a radical difference in valuation between potential buyers and sellers rather than an inability to sell the securities. By refusing to pay the prices asked by sellers, potential buyers evidently did not assign the same probability to repayment as bondholders. Only on very few occasions did the press mention the influence of trading volumes on quoted prices.[72] On the whole, therefore, the fact that prices remained high does not seem due to a problem of microstructure. In fact, the market seems to have been completely lifeless at the very end of the period under review, by which time prices had already fallen to relatively low levels.

The Russian bondholders' sense of injustice left a deep scar in France, one which was passed from one generation to the next. But, as Szurek (2002) notes, despite this national disaster, "the bondholders—and later their beneficiaries—never gave up completely on their fortunes or modest savings annihilated by the October Revolution."

The behavior of market prices can be explained to some extent by the so-called peso problem. Far from being a sign of irrational behavior, investors' hopes were based on an expectation of one or more extreme events that would lead to repayment. This view is confirmed by witnesses to the events. Léon Martin (1921, 225), the secretary of the General Commission for the Protection of French Interests in Russia (Commission générale pour la protection des intérêts français en Russie), commented that "the Bourse, after weighing up the creditors' chances of recovering their loans, assigns a value to these securities that would not be warranted by an assessment based solely on the actual situation at present."

The variety of grounds for retaining hope reflects the complexity of the military and political situation in Russia, France, and Europe generally. While some of the reasons given below might seem unrealistic in hindsight, contemporary written sources indicate that they were not so at the time. Different reasons for hopefulness were apparent very early on. They are all described in the first communiqué of the General Commission for the Protection of French Interests in Russia in August 1918.[73]

Government bonds might seem straightforward, but the sovereign nature of the issuer bears various implications that actually make them highly complex instruments. The power imbalance between retail investors and the government they have lent to severely limits the action the investors can take to force repayment. The literature identifies four key incentives governments have to repay their debts: fear of a loss of reputation and consequent exclusion from capital markets; fear of armed intervention; trade sanctions; and seizure of collateral. In the Russian case investors remained hopeful for the aforementioned reasons, but they also hoped that a third-party government would stand in for the Russian government and fulfill its obligations.

The possibility of a rapid overthrow of the Bolshevik regime was one of the most obvious reasons to keep hope alive. The possibility that the regime would change its stance was not ruled out by investors either, since they thought the Bolsheviks' extreme position was untenable in the long run. A negotiated settlement therefore also seemed to be a rational expectation. Last, the hope that another government could repay the debt persisted for several years. There are several circumstances in which an alternative administration could intervene. France might have bailed out French investors to mitigate the losses incurred by its citizens. The new countries that emerged from the ruins of the tsarist empire might have taken responsibility for some or all of the debt, in accordance with the succession of states and precedents in international law. And finally, Russia might have demanded that Germany repay some of its debt as compensation for the First World War.

My book seeks to assess the relative weight of each of these reasons to hope. The first chapter describes the financial instrument that is my main focus, namely, sovereign debt. The subsequent chapters have the following structure: a theoretical introduction that provides background with regard to each reason that gave investors hope, followed by an analysis based on the history of Russian bonds.

The second chapter examines reputation and negotiations as reasons people's hope persisted. The third chapter is devoted to the impact of wartime events on market prices for Russian bonds. The fourth chapter describes the hope that French bondholders would be bailed out by their own government. The fifth chapter analyzes expectations of partial repayment, either by the new states that emerged from the ruins of the tsarist empire or by the defeated Germany. The sixth chapter details all the econometric and financial analyses performed on the Russian data to assess the relative importance of each of these factors. The seventh and final chapter summarizes salient points about the Russian case and highlights what the analysis of the Russian repudiation can add to the modern literature on sovereign bonds.

Sovereign Debt

Default and Repudiation

Sovereign debt, or debt issued by a sovereign state, has much in common with debt issued by individuals and private institutions.[1] For example, a state's borrowing capacity depends on its reputation and financial situation. As Baudhuin (1945) points out, "Government credit does not differ essentially from private credit. Both require confidence and are recorded as liabilities; their technique is similar . . . both are valued by the public, as reflected in market prices, and their behavior depends to some extent on the financial market." The perceived risk of debt issued by sovereign states, like that issued by private companies, is monitored by credit rating agencies.

Although sovereign debt is similar to other types of debt, it differs in one essential way: the sovereign nature of the issuer. This unique characteristic may ostensibly seem minor, but it actually has a considerable influence on the valuation of this type of financial instrument.

First, unlike a private company, a sovereign state runs no risk of liquidation. When a state defaults, it is not dismantled; it continues to exist and may seek to borrow again in the future. A company that fails disappears from the scene. Second, in the event of default, there are no bankruptcy laws for countries as there are for private companies. In other words, there are no generally accepted rules on how default should be managed. Last, even if the defaulting state is willing to negotiate, it usually takes a long time to restructure sovereign debt. The creditors are matched against a sovereign state, which they cannot force to repay its debt, or only with difficulty.

In short, as Shleifer (2003) points out, when a sovereign debtor defaults, its creditors are all but powerless, since they cannot seize collateral or force the debtor to negotiate. Moreover, a state can unilaterally declare itself in default. The first research on sovereign debt sought to understand why a rational investor would want to lend to a state (Eaton and Fernandez 1995). Paradoxically, despite the vulnerability of the creditors, sovereign debt continues to be issued, bought, traded—and usually repaid!

A Split Personality in Terms of Risk

The sovereign nature of the issuer has an enormous impact in terms of risk. At the very least, one may argue that sovereign bonds have a split personality in terms of risk. Indeed, debt issued by a government can be considered as either the safest financial asset or one of the riskiest.

Several commonly used financial models refer to the concept of risk-free assets. The capital asset pricing model bases the expected return of an asset on the expected return of a theoretical risk-free asset, plus a premium reflecting the asset's nondiversifiable risk. Although the theory does not stipulate that the risk-free asset must be sovereign debt, government bonds are almost always a benchmark.

That choice of government debt as a risk-free benchmark stems from two prerogatives intrinsic to sovereign states: the power to levy taxes and the power to print money. If required, a state can theoretically always resort to taxation or issue money to repay its debts. Lenders are therefore almost certain they will be repaid at maturity. In view of this unique characteristic, government bonds are used as a benchmark for setting interest rates and are considered the safest debt on the market.

However, the apparent safety of sovereign bonds rests on various assumptions that are not always borne out in practice. Printing money, which is subject to approval by the central bank, can be done only to repay debt denominated in the country's own currency. Massive issuance of local currency is of little use for repaying foreign debt because it has a strongly negative impact on the exchange rate. Similarly, taxation is feasible only up to a point, beyond which it becomes counterproductive. Last, even if theoretically possible, excessive recourse to either of these options would send an extremely negative signal to the markets.

For practical purposes, however, sovereign bonds are still useful as a benchmark for choosing a risk-free asset, especially bonds issued by developed countries, most of which have no recent history of default. By contrast, sovereign bonds issued by developing countries are not reliable benchmarks. Despite the apparent guarantee offered by sovereign powers, many states do actually default. When a default occurs, lenders cannot put their case to any independent legal authority since there is no international court on sovereign failure. Consequently, although sovereign bonds seem safe in theory, the sovereign nature of the borrower creates a highly uneven situation in the event of default. The power relationship between the creditor, an individual, an institutional investor, or even another state, and the debtor, a sovereign state, is heavily weighted in the debtor's favor.

A wealth of economic literature has endeavored to understand why sovereign states—theoretically so safe—go into default. I will outline here the main reasons identified in the literature. Research can be divided into two approaches: one school seeks to understand the reasons for default, while the other aims to identify the incentives a sovereign state has to repay its debts. Although described separately, both approaches clearly go some way toward explaining default, which is rarely attributable to a single cause. In terms of methodology, studies have attempted either to explain why default does or does not occur (for example, by using logit or probit methods) or to analyze the factors influencing the interest rate paid by the borrower. The interest rate is seen as a reliable gauge of perceived default risk, with a higher rate indicating higher perceived risk. The two approaches are obviously complementary and tend to give fairly similar results.

Public debt is one means at a government's disposal for balancing its budget (the other means are taxation and the issuing of money). The literature has therefore sought to determine the influence of macroeconomic imbalances on the probability of default, which is now well established. Manasse, Roubini and Schimmelpfennig (2003) showed that solvency ratios, refinancing risk, and macroeconomic and investor confidence indicators can be used as partial predictors of default. Flandreau and Zumer (2004) demonstrated the influence of indebtedness on the interest rate imposed by lenders when the gold standard was in force.

Eichengreen, Haussman, and Panizza (2003) have suggested that "original sin" plays an important role in the probability of a country's defaulting. Original sin is defined as the impossibility of a country to borrow in its domestic currency. This makes it more sensitive to any depreciation of its currency, since the debt to be repaid is denominated in foreign currency. However, Bordo and Meissner (2006) have shown that original sin is, at best, only one explanatory factor, and that some countries suffering from original sin have been perfectly capable of avoiding default. The authors focus instead on the importance of macroeconomic imbalances.

Reinhart, Rogoff, and Savastano (2003) developed the concept of debt intolerance: countries that have repeatedly defaulted in the past become intolerant to debt and prone to default at levels of debt that other countries find perfectly sustainable, for example, for debt-to-GDP ratios inferior to the 60 percent threshold set by the Maastricht Treaty in 1992. These authors find that such heightened sensitivity to macroeconomic shocks is attributable to the fact that a country's institutions get weaker with each successive crisis. Countries that experience several consecutive defaults enter a vicious circle that leaves them increasingly vulnerable. The authors advance this theory to explain the "serial default" that has plagued many Latin American countries. In a subsequent paper, however, Reinhart and Rogoff (2011) show that when domestic debt is included in the analysis, the serial default anomaly largely disappears.

Given the uniqueness of sovereign debt, specifically the power imbalance between states and their creditors, Eaton and Fernandez (1995) have posited that the main challenge for researchers is to understand why some states do repay their debts. This view is in line with the perception of Feis (1930 [1965], 102), who considered "a loan to a foreign government an act of faith." In the absence of a supranational court dedicated to the management of sovereign debt, individuals have few ways to exert pressure on sovereign states. As seen previously, four main incentives for states to repay international debt have been identified:

1. The wish to maintain a good reputation so as to continue to enjoy access to capital markets;
2. Fear of trade sanctions;
3. Fear of military intervention;
4. Fear that collateral will be seized.

The first three of these played a crucial role in the case of Russian bonds and will be explained in greater detail in the following chapters. Seizure of collateral is often listed as the last incentive for a state to repay its debt. It is conventionally recognized as being inefficient and does not seem to have played much of a role in the Russian case either.[2] In practice, countries repay their debts in order to avoid the first three penalties mentioned above.

In addition to economics and finance, sovereign debt is treated by other disciplines, such as law (particularly international law), political science, and political economy. The decision to default or repay debt is made by a leader, who may or may not be legitimate, acting on motivations of his own. In the past few years researchers have investigated the political impact of defaults and their interaction with repayment decisions. The economic literature analyzes the incentive to repay debt as an effort by the debtor country to avoid military, trade, or other sanctions. In fact, debt repayment decisions are taken by governments, whose members may be pursuing personal ends. Governments have considerable freedom to announce a default given that there is no consensus on the thresholds below which various economic indicators must fall in order to justify a default.

Although governments can in theory repay their debts by levying taxes, some prefer to announce a default rather than introduce such a potentially unpopular measure that could jeopardize their longevity in office. In this regard, an important distinction should be made between domestic and foreign debt defaults. A default on domestic debt could be punished by voters in a democracy or could trigger a coup in an undemocratic regime.[3] Recent literature has sought to determine the role of

political and institutional factors in the probability of default. McGillivray and Smith (2003) suggest that default is less frequent in countries
where the institutional framework facilitates a change of government.
Van Rijckhegem and Weder (2009) have shown the importance of political factors in default decisions. They believe the nature of the political
system—democratic or undemocratic—plays a key role. In democracies
a fixed-term legislature, veto players, and a parliamentary system reduce
the likelihood of a default on foreign debt. In the case of undemocratic
regimes, no political variable emerges with a positive influence. Kohlscheen (2004) partly corroborates these findings. His analyses show that
between 1976 and 2000 countries with a presidential system were five
times more likely to default than those with a parliamentary system.

Political factors thus strongly influence the decision to default. Several default situations exist. A default may be driven by economic reasons. In this situation, the government chooses default over repayment,
which would be either technically impossible or too costly economically
and in terms of the population's welfare. If purely economic reasons predominate, the default may be perceived as excusable. Alternatively, a
regime might decide not to repay its debts by invoking a legal argument
that challenges the legitimacy of the debt. In this situation, the government repudiates its debt. Historical examples of repudiation known at
the time of the Russian revolution are described below because they en-
hance one's understanding of French investors' perceptions at the time.

Repudiation: A Way to Signal Political Change

Given that default and repudiation have the same outcome, namely, nonrepayment, it may seem surprising that a state would elect to repudiate
its debt. Indeed, repudiation raises numerous legal issues and frequently
turns the repudiating country into an international pariah. Until the
Russian bond case, repudiation of international debt was therefore relatively rare. Repudiations, except for those by various American states,
were intended to mark a break, one seen as being permanent, with a
former regime. Repudiation should thus be seen as a political act rather
than an economic decision.

There are several interesting aspects to the debt repudiation by

American states.[4] In the 1840s several of them were in severe crisis (English 1996; Wallis, Grinath, and Sylla 2004). Whereas some states, including Maryland, Pennsylvania, Indiana, Illinois, and Michigan, defaulted without disputing the legitimacy of their debts, others, among them Arkansas, Louisiana, Mississippi, and the Territory of Florida, chose to repudiate their liabilities.[5] These states repudiated only the part of their debt that was incurred primarily to develop banks in the South. They had either given bonds to banks for them to sell in order to raise share capital or guaranteed bonds issued by the banks. The efforts by holders of these bonds to obtain repayment were partly successful in Arkansas and Louisiana but failed in Mississippi and Florida, despite the investors' tenacity, inventiveness, and ingenuity.[6] The long-term consequences of these repudiations have been analyzed in depth by English (1996), who ascribes the partial repayment of the debt to reputational reasons: states wishing to borrow again in the future complied with their debtors' demands. This case of repudiation, one of the first involving international bonds, is an exception because it occurred in a stable political context.

Although most repudiations occur in the context of extreme changes of regime, not all turbulent episodes of government succession have resulted in a questioning of the legality of existing debt. During the French revolution, the liabilities of the ancien régime were not challenged, even though the revolutionary government proved unable to redeem them in full. Given the similarities between the French and Russian revolutions, the French precedent was frequently cited during the 1920s to encourage the Russians to honor their obligations.[7]

A counterexample, however, is provided by the dynastic struggles in nineteenth-century Portugal, which led to repudiation. The death of John VI of Portugal in March 1826 raised the issue of succession. His son Dom Pedro, who had been crowned Pedro I, emperor of Brazil, in 1822, preferred to remain in the colony. He waived his claim to the Portuguese throne and in May 1826 abdicated in favor of his daughter, Dona Maria de Gloria. As she was only seven years old at the time, a regent was appointed. Dom Miguel, Pedro I's younger brother, accepted the regency but soon proclaimed himself king (Wynne 1951 [2000], 361–62). In 1831 Pedro I renounced the Brazilian crown and sailed to Europe to raise an army to defend his daughter's cause. He emerged victorious from a civil war that lasted for several years, and his daughter's claim prevailed. In 1834, as Maria II, she began a reign that was to last almost twenty years.

To finance his armies during the civil war, Dom Miguel raised 40 million francs by issuing debt on the Paris Bourse in October 1832. During the war Maria II announced she would not recognize debt that had been issued illegally by a usurper. She maintained this stance after acceding to the throne (Wynne 1951 [2000], 362–63). French holders of Portuguese bonds protested strenuously against the decision. Despite the announcement, the debt was still listed in Paris and was trading at around 12 percent of par in 1837. After decades of negotiations punctuated by attempts to prevent the issuance of new Portuguese bonds in Paris and by protest campaigns, an agreement was reached in 1891. In this case, the Portuguese government agreed to allocate a percentage of the revenues from the tobacco monopoly to repay the debt issued by Dom Miguel. In the end the bondholders recovered 10 percent of the face value of their bonds (Wynne, 1951 [2000], p. 364).

Other cases of repudiation occurred in the nineteenth century. During the American Civil War the Union states refused to recognize the debts issued by their Confederate counterparts. This repudiation was justified because, in the eyes of the Union, the Confederacy had never been legitimate; the Union states viewed it as a rebellion. According to recent analyses, however, some financial markets believed in southern independence right up until the Confederate defeat at Gettysburg (Oosterlinck and Weidenmier 2007). Mexico also experienced several episodes of repudiation (Sack 1927). In 1867 the Mexican republic refused to recognize the debt contracted by Emperor Maximilian's regime. Later, Gen. Victoriano Huerta (1913) repudiated the debt of President Francisco Madero, President Venustiano Carranza (1915) repudiated the debt of Huerta, and President Alvaro Obregón (1920–24) repudiated the debt of Carranza (Sack 1927)! Although an agreement was negotiated in 1922, it excluded some of the debt.

Repudiation was not confined to debt, as many governments also refused to recognize currency issued by their enemies. The case of Russia is a prime example. There were so many disparate governments and local polities issuing currency at one time or another in Russia that even identifying them all is almost impossible.[8] Last, the emergence of numerous Communist governments in the second half of the twentieth century triggered a new wave of repudiations, similar to the one announced by the Bolsheviks. Currency repudiation in Russia and Communist repudiations after the 1920s, however, are outside the scope of this book.

Several conclusions can be drawn from the cases discussed above. First, repudiation primarily serves political aims, by signifying a clear break with previous governments. Second, decisions to make that break usually occur after a revolution or independence. Repudiations therefore seem unlikely in countries with democratic changes of government.[9] Third, a negotiated solution is unlikely as long as the repudiating authority remains in power. When a negotiated solution is reached, the disputes are usually not resolved until many years after the repudiation.

Last, repudiations have certainly opened a debate about the legality of debt based on its purpose. Indeed, a new type of repudiation emerged in the late nineteenth century, one based on an argument different from the one mentioned above.[10] Instead of debt being considered void because the new government does not recognize the legality of its predecessor, the "odious debt" theory judges the end use to which the debt is put.[11] Khalfan, King, and Thomas (2003) define odious debts as "those contracted against the interests of the population of a state, without its consent and with the full awareness of the creditor." An enormous amount of recent legal literature has analyzed the relevance of the concept of odious debt, particularly after the overthrow of Saddam Hussein in Iraq (Ochoa 2008). Some authors who consider odious debts unjust continue to argue for their outright cancellation.

Lenders and Management of Default

In terms of access to capital markets, the sovereign nature of the issuer encourages lenders of highly diverse types to invest. Today, lenders can be divided into four broad categories: retail investors, institutional investors, governments making intergovernmental loans, and international financial institutions like the International Monetary Fund and the World Bank.[12] Obviously, the motivations of these lenders can differ sharply. While the first two types probably buy sovereign bonds essentially for investment reasons, the latter two types are driven mainly by political concerns.

The relative proportion of debt held by each type of investor has varied considerably from one historical period to another (Oosterlinck 2006). This has been reflected in the form of the bonds. From a contractual viewpoint, sovereign debt is a heterogeneous asset class in that it can take the form of bearer or book entry securities, can be traded on financial markets or over the counter, can be coupled with options to buy, swap, or convert the bond, and can be associated even with lotteries. Governments' ingenuity makes it almost impossible to list all the types of bonds that have existed historically. During the period of the gold standard (1870–1914), sovereign debt mainly existed as bearer securities traded on secondary markets. This type of asset naturally found its way into the portfolios of both private investors and banks. The First World War severely curtailed market activity. At the same time, the financing needs stemming from the war encouraged countries to advance funds to their allies, creating de facto debts between governments. The end of the First World War saw a return to the types of securities issued beforehand. After the Second World War the new financial environment introduced by the Bretton Woods agreements radically altered the terms on which sovereign debt was issued. Until the early 1970s most debt took the form of intergovernmental loans. The end of the Bretton Woods system saw the mass reappearance of private loans, mainly in the form of over-the-counter (OTC) loans from banks to governments. In the 1980s many states found themselves unable to service their debts. To avert a series of bank failures, solutions had to be negotiated between lenders and sovereign governments. The U.S. government, particularly through the intervention of Secretary of the Treasury Nicholas Brady, facilitated the negotiations by proposing to convert these OTC debts into debt that could be traded on secondary markets. The new dollar-denominated bonds, known as Brady bonds, were guaranteed by the U.S. government. Thus, in the space of a century sovereign debt made a comeback in the form of bonds accessible to retail investors.

The variety of lenders plays an important role in the event of default because it brings actors with potentially divergent interests to the negotiating table.[13] Moreover, in the absence of a single supranational body, negotiations require coordination between actors. Today, depending on the debt considered, groups may be entrusted with managing the default negotiations. For example, the Paris Club, an informal group founded in 1956, seeks negotiated solutions between debtor and creditor governments. The London Club, another informal group, brings defaulting countries and groups of bankers or their representatives together. Last, investor associations are set up to defend the interests of bondholders. Their influence, often presented in the late nineteenth and early twentieth centuries as being powerful, gradually dwindled until most of them had disbanded by the end of the twentieth century.

The existence of different types of lenders can raise the problem of group action. The optimum outcome for each debtor is to be repaid in full, if need be at the expense of other creditors (Roubini and Setser 2004, 292–93). Depending on where the debt was issued, group action clauses may or may not be included systematically in bond contracts. That variability makes resolving defaults extremely complex in practice. The disparities between the securities issued on different markets and the huge variety of economic situations at the time of the default explain the extreme range of amounts that holders of the defaulted bonds will recover after the negotiations. Sturzenegger and Zettelmeyer (2006) analyze losses incurred by investors based on debt restructuring agreements in Russia, Ukraine, Pakistan, Ecuador, Argentina, and Uruguay between 1998 and 2006. The authors show that the reduction in net present value ranges from 13 percent of the original debt in the case of Uruguay to 73 percent for Argentina.

Sovereign bonds are thus a complex financial instrument. The motivations to repay, like the reasons to lend, have been at the core of the existing literature on this topic. The Russian case is exceptional in many respects, most notably (as will be argued further) because bondholders had legitimate reasons to hope that something would happen to transform valueless assets into valuable ones.

Reputation, Trade Retaliation, and Recognition

The Hope That the Bolsheviks Would Change Their Position

T he Russian repudiation—an extreme measure—deeply shocked French investors. The predominant mood at the beginning of 1918 nevertheless seems to have been disbelief. There were several reasons for this incredulity and for the expectation that the position on the debt in Russia would soon change. First, Russian bonds enjoyed an excellent reputation in France and were seen as a safe, "gilt-edged" investment (Girault 1961, 67). The repudiation was therefore inconsistent with the perceived quality of the issuer. Furthermore, many people thought the Bolsheviks' extreme position on the Russian debt was untenable in the long term. It was therefore seen as a statement of principle that would not be applied in practice.

The Bolsheviks' position can be seen as essentially pragmatic: though philosophically opposed to repayment, they were willing to negotiate and even pay compensation if the situation required.[1] Far from unbending, the Soviets' position would vary over time, depending on whom they were talking to and what was at stake. The main White Russian governments and military leaders (the Ufa and Omsk governments, Adm. Alexander Kolchak, Gen. Anton Denikin, and Gen. Pyotr Wrangel) always promised repayment. However, it is hard to say whether they considered this a priority commitment or a necessary pledge in order to obtain the financial and military support of the Western powers. In any case it seems unlikely that any government of a country exhausted by civil war would have had the means to service Russia's colossal debt.

Two of the frequently cited incentives sovereign states have to repay their debts were expressed at the very beginning of the repudiation process. Investors had no doubt that Russia would repay the debt in order to maintain its reputation and to avoid trade retaliation. After briefly outlining the theoretical and historical aspects of these incentives, I shall analyze here the negotiations and changes of position on debt repayment. In the Russian case, these two allegedly conventional incentives were superseded by a new one: the Russian revolutionary government's desire for political recognition.

International Relations and Sovereign Debt

Many authors have emphasized reputation as one of the main incentives of sovereign states to repay their debts. Theoretically, a bad reputation has various disadvantages. An ill-reputed state may not be able to raise new loans or may have to pay a higher rate of interest on future debt issuance. Lenders may also demand that previous defaults be resolved before agreeing to make a new loan.

An analysis of historical sources confirms the economic intuition that potential lenders set great store by the reputation of states seeking to borrow. More formal approaches to this phenomenon began to emerge in the 1980s. In particular, Eaton and Gersovitz (1981) show that, assuming a country will be permanently barred from the capital markets if it defaults, creditors would have to set a credit ceiling, or maximum loan size. Conversely, authors such as Bulow and Rogoff (1989, 1989a) maintain that the fear of loss of reputation was not a sufficient incentive in itself for countries to repay their debts. In their view, penalties such as trade sanctions are required to discipline the borrowing country. The authors' findings opened up a debate on how a loss of reputation might influence countries' willingness to repay debt. That debate is far from closed, and a late book describes the wish to maintain a good reputation as the overriding incentive of states to repay their debts (Tomz 2007). However, although reputation was and probably still is important, the role of other incentives should not be overlooked.

More pragmatically, some of the academic literature has sought to ascertain whether countries with a bad reputation were in fact penalized. Jorgensen and Sachs (1989) concentrate on the repayment histories of five Latin American countries: Argentina, Bolivia, Chile, Colombia, and Peru. They calculated the net present value of financial flows related to those countries' sovereign debts. Contrary to what reputation theory would suggest, the authors show that the only borrower to abide by its original borrowing agreements in the 1930s, Argentina, was barely rewarded afterward since it was offered similar borrowing terms to those applicable to countries that had defaulted. The authors attribute this lack of recognition to the poor economic conditions prevailing generally at the time, that is, during the Great Depression. They note that under such extreme conditions bad payers are excused for having defaulted. In other words, in a time of crisis, markets seem to take the same attitude toward good and bad payers alike. Tomz (2007) challenged this proposal, however, by analyzing the cases of Australia and Finland during the same period.

Özler (1993) analyzes the role of reputation by using a sample of more than fifteen hundred bank loans granted to developing countries between 1968 and 1981. Her study shows that there is indeed a reputation effect but that it has a time limit: defaults prior to 1929 seem to have been forgiven whereas those in the 1930s have affected interest rates. Özler (1993) also finds that countries with no credit history, that is, newly established countries (mainly former colonies in her case) suffer from a reputation deficit and are consequently penalized by the market. Mining original data on sixteen countries over thirty-four years (1880–1913), Flandreau and Zumer (2004) found that defaults and the related negotiations influence the interest rates set by the market. When a debt renegotiation process is opened, the interest rate spread (with UK consols as a risk-free benchmark) rises to 500 basis points. Conversely, once an agreement is reached, the spread falls on average to 90 basis points in the first year after the agreement and to around 45 basis points ten years later. Although these values are observable, they do not support the argument that bad reputation has a disastrous impact on the countries concerned. Cruces and Trebesch (2011) take another approach by considering the size of haircuts. In debt restructurings occurring between 1970 and 2010 there was a close relationship between severity of default and the subsequent borrowing terms.

Commentators writing at the time of the events in Russia seem to have perceived the desire to maintain a good reputation as the main reason for countries to repay their debts. Through an analysis of the literature on investment practices written between 1919 and 1929, Tomz (2007) reveals that professionals at the time saw reputation as primordial. According to Fishlow (1985), Britain's dominance of the capital markets in the late nineteenth century dissuaded countries from antagonizing it. Given the importance of the French market at the time, the same argument might apply in the Russian case. The importance of reputation in the early twentieth century has been attributed to bondholders' associations, which were highly active at the turn of the century.

Much attention has been paid to the role of bondholders' associations in getting governments to honor their debts. According to Mauro, Sussman, and Yafeh (2006), the Corporation of Foreign Bondholders (CFB), a British association, played a leading role after the defaults of the gold standard period and the multiple defaults of the 1930s. According to those authors, the fact that agreements were reached with the main defaulting countries is proof of the CFB's success. Esteves (2013) broadens the analysis by comparing the relative success of the main European bondholders' associations. His research shows the enormous institutional variety of the associations, which were far from homogeneous. The first associations were committees formed to resolve a specific case of default. They were widely criticized because they often lacked documentation to support their claims and were prone to manipulation by various financial actors. Given these limitations, the creation of permanent organizations proved indispensable. Within a few decades, bondholders' associations developed in Europe with the purpose of managing all defaults into the long term.[2] The associations were far from united and sometimes in conflict (Esteves 2013). The author's empirical analyses show the benefits of bondholders' associations but also the influence of noncooperation between associations on the final outcome.

Flandreau (2013) has challenged the traditional view that the creation of the CFB in 1868 was a revolution in terms of bondholders' protection. In fact, bondholders' committees were active as early as the 1820s and 1830s. Furthermore, exclusion from the market for sovereign defaulters who refused to come to the negotiation table existed at the end of the 1820s. At the time it was the Committee of the London Stock Exchange which enforced this disposition. Keeping a good reputation was thus important because the stock exchange itself could decide to exclude from its listings sovereigns unwilling to negotiate. Obviously the power of the stock exchange also depended on competition and coordination with other exchanges. If a sovereign excluded from the London Stock Exchange could float a bond in Paris or Berlin, then the threat of exclusion did not carry much weight. Up till the middle of the nineteenth century the London Stock Exchange maintained a dominant position, but by the end of the century other exchanges were vying to attract sovereigns. Besides exchanges other actors played an important role in terms of signaling: underwriters.

The importance of the quality of the underwriter has been emphasized by Flandreau and Flores (2009). They show that in an environment characterized by high asymmetry of information, investors were ready to pay a premium to be able to differentiate bad from good sovereigns. Whereas it was difficult to analyze the credit of each sovereign, investors could easily screen the actions of underwriters. As a result, good underwriters could in a sense grant the benefits of their reputations to sovereigns. In return they exploited their good reputation by serving only what they perceived to be the best sovereigns. The system worked so well that at the beginning of the nineteenth century defaults were not randomly distributed across underwriters (Flandreau et al. 2009). This situation gradually disappeared as the signaling role was taken over by rating agencies.

Several authors have suggested that in addition to avoiding penalties resulting from poor reputation, countries would honor their debts rather than default in order to avoid trade sanctions. The exact mechanism of trade retaliation is not always clearly defined. There are several possibilities. In response to a default, the bondholders' government might decide to amend the regulations on trade with the defaulting country by limiting imports, requiring stricter guarantees, imposing higher tariffs, and so on. Alternatively—and more closely connected with a loss of reputation—investors might decide on their own initiative to suspend dealings with the defaulting country.

Little empirical research has been conducted on this theme to date. Rose (2005) analyzes the impact of debt renegotiation on the foreign trade of the country concerned. On the basis of a gravity model applied to a set of 150 countries over a period of fifty years, Rose (2005) posits that debt renegotiation leads to a statistically significant decline in bilateral trade between creditor and debtor countries. Far from insignificant, the estimated decline was almost 8 percent and lasted for fifteen years. However, applying a similar model to the gold standard period, Mitchener and Weidenmier (2005) do not observe a general decline in bilateral trade relations after a default. They attribute this to the fact that creditor countries preferred more effective types of sanctions at the time. By contrast, the authors do observe a decline in trade when super-sanctions are applied, such as external fiscal control over a country's finances or military intervention. More recent works have attempted to understand the mechanism by which such sanctions would be applied. In case of punishment, bilateral trade should decline mostly with creditor countries. Martinez and Sandleris (2011) find, however, that the decline is of similar magnitude in all countries. Fuentes and Saravia (2010) investigate the impact of sovereign defaults on Foreign Direct Investment (FDI). In the case of FDI, punishment seems more plausible, as FDI declines mostly for the flows originating from defaulters' creditor countries.

The case of the repudiation of Russian debt is unusual in the literature on sanctions applied to defaulting states. Usually, as seen above, the sanctions considered are of two kinds: exclusion from the capital markets and trade retaliation. Although these factors clearly played a part in the Russian case, the most important incentive seems to have been a purely political consideration. The Bolsheviks also sought recognition of their government by the Allies in the apparent hope of reducing Allied support for anti-Bolshevik armed groups.[3] As a consequence, many of the debates and negotiations between the Bolsheviks and the Allied governments centered on diplomatic recognition in exchange for debt recognition or trade concessions.

Moreover, the trade retaliation argument seems to have had the opposite effect in the Russian case, since many industrialists were keen to resume trade relations with resource-rich Russia. The Russian case overturns the traditional logic of sanctions. When the defaulting country is big enough, the threat of trade retaliation carries little weight: the temptation to sever trade relations is blunted by fear of losing a large potential market and access to commodities.

The exchange of political recognition for a debt settlement may seem odd to the twenty-first-century reader. French investors at the end of the nineteenth century would nonetheless probably have viewed this exchange as almost normal. From 1873 on, listing on the official Paris Bourse was subject to the agreement of both the French finance and foreign affairs ministers (Feis 1930 [1965], 120). In the following decades it became common practice to trade admission to the exchange for commercial or diplomatic favors (Gans 1909). As pointed out by Feis (1930 [1965], 133), "Above and beyond all other considerations which induced French official interventions with the movement of French capital abroad was the wish to make the investment serve the political purposes of the state." In some instances loans were exchanged for both political and commercial reasons. French loans to Russia were meant to improve the military capacity of the borrower but on the condition that military spending be done in France. In short, as summarized by Siegel (2014, 103), "If the money was coming from France, the orders should be going to French factories." Linking debts with diplomacy and politics was thus hardly exceptional at the beginning of the twentieth century. France was certainly not the only country to adopt this attitude. In 1908, for instance, Germany refused to recognize the independence of Bulgaria until an agreement was reached to recognize the losses incurred by German nationals following the partial seizure of the Oriental Railway Company. Ivanov and Tooze (2011) also show that diplomatic relations between France and Bulgaria influenced the latter's ability to tap the French capital market. The Soviet demand for political recognition could also be interpreted positively by bondholders who may have hoped that this demand was a first step toward normalizing relations. They could even have hoped that recognition would pave the way to a settlement and future bond issues.[4] The importance of international negotiations and diplomacy on sovereign bond prices has received renewed attention. For example, during the interwar period international diplomacy played a major role in the valuation of the Romanian debt traded in Paris (Oosterlinck and Ureche-Rangau 2012).

In the rest of this chapter I describe developments in the negotiations between France and Russia, which can be outlined as follows. Although the repudiation raised a diplomatic outcry, it was such an extreme measure that it was not perceived as credible. Nevertheless, as early as 1918 associations formed to defend the rights of bondholders in France and other countries. When it became obvious that the Bolsheviks were a serious force, the first attempts at bilateral negotiations took place. On more than one occasion during these talks the Bolshevik government expressed a willingness to repay some of the debt. Simultaneously, other Soviet leaders declared the repudiation inalienable. These contradictory statements left French bondholders in a state of utter confusion. The Russians, adept at exploiting the lack of coordination between creditor countries, succeeded in obtaining separate trade concessions from several governments. They thus managed to circumvent the trade isolation France was hoping to impose on the Soviet Union. Finally, two major multilateral negotiations were opened in 1922. The failure of those initiatives sent the negotiators back to the bilateral sphere. Just as the Soviets made their final repayment proposal, it was refused because of the domestic political situation in France.

A Historically Good Reputation

As mentioned earlier, to a French investor in the early twentieth century, Russian debt was seen as a safe, gilt-edged investment. That view was not unique to France. In the United Kingdom, too, albeit on a smaller scale, Russian bonds were considered prime investments and were purchased by funds set up for the benefit of orphans and widows.[5]

Russian bonds enjoyed such a good reputation for several reasons.

Press manipulation and the corruption of a large part of the French financial elite certainly played major roles in shaping that opinion. The publication of falsified annual accounts and flattering articles about Russia's public finances written by Arthur Raffalovitch, as noted, the personal agent of the Russian finance minister Sergei Witte and an influential figure in French economic circles at the turn of the century, reinforced French investors' positive sentiment (Girault 1961). In addition to these arguments, arguably the most important, factual elements supported Russia's reputation.

To an investor using the past as a guide to the probability of a future default, Russia would have seemed a model of solvency. Indeed, despite several wars and political instability Russia had not defaulted since 1812 (Apostol and Michelson 1922), and even then payment was only suspended, as the creditors' rights were later restored. During the Crimean War, Russia continued even to pay the interest on its debt, including bonds held on enemy financial markets, such as Britain (Raffalovitch 1919, 151; Apostol and Michelson 1922). That position contrasts sharply with that of the warring parties during the First World War, which swiftly passed laws to limit movements of capital and stopped making coupon payments to enemy holders of their bonds. Those restrictions led to a clandestine traffic in coupons. Russia's chivalrous attitude during the Crimean War clearly supported positive sentiment on the markets.

The financial research department of Crédit Lyonnais—something of a private ratings agency ahead of its time—corroborated the reliability of Russian government securities. In 1898, on the basis of several macroeconomic considerations, the department's specialists ranked Russia as "[one of] the countries whose financial management is first rate" (Flandreau 2003). That opinion is especially noteworthy in that it did not stem solely from wheeler-dealers' attempts to promote Russia's image: Crédit Lyonnais's employees took pains to compare and contrast their sources in order to produce new data that would reflect the real situation accurately.

Additionally, though defeated in the Russo–Japanese War, Russia continued to honor its debt.[6] To the surprise of contemporary observers, it did not suspend its stock market during the war (Raffalovitch 1919,

13). Moreover, Russia had overcome an initial episode of revolution in 1905, when the revolutionaries intended to repudiate tsarist debts. Their attempt failed, and the situation returned almost to normal. Although stock market prices were affected by the troubles of 1905–6, they recovered fairly quickly. Most of these factors were known to French investors when the repudiation occurred.[7] It is likely they thought Russia would do everything in its power to maintain the trust it had built up through its numerous past sacrifices.

Russia's good reputation offers an explanation as to why the first rumors of repudiation had so little impact on Western financial markets. Although the market prices of Russian bonds began to head downward at the end of 1917, press commentary and market rumors were not alarming. Many contemporary financial and political figures did not think the repudiation was tenable in the long term because it would jeopardize Russia's future economic development.[8] The French finance minister, Louis-Lucien Klotz, presented this viewpoint in a speech to the lower house of parliament in late January 1918.[9] He pointed to "essential principles that govern international law . . . : if a country diverges from this principle, it would bar itself from ever obtaining foreign credit again."

Some of the past repudiations French investors might have been aware of (see above) ended positively. After years of negotiation, the Portuguese government eventually made concessions in order to regain access to the French capital market. The case of debts declared to be odious seemed less promising, but there was still hope that an agreement would be reached because the repudiation was still recent. Similarly, various actions to obtain repayment by the American states that had repudiated their debts were still progressing in London.

The London Stock Exchange also reacted to the rumors about the proclamation of a decree cancelling all debt issued by Russia. The *Financial Times* for 13 January 1918 shows that the rumor had a negative impact on prices for Russian bonds listed in New York and London.[10] Hopes for a negotiated solution nevertheless persisted. Traders in New York expected that recognition of the Bolshevik government would be contingent on recognition of the debt.

On 18 January 1918 the prefect's agent at the Paris Bourse reported,

"There is much talk of the Russian financial question. Several brokers were heard expressing the opinion that it was both the wrong time to buy Russian paper and, for those with Russian bonds in their portfolios, the wrong time to sell."[11] The possible motives for the repudiation fueled talk at the Paris Bourse. The prefect's agent further reported, "We can see the hand of Germany in the Bolshevik government's decision aimed at triggering panic in France, since our country holds by far the most Russian bonds."[12] The belief that Lenin was a German agent persisted at the Paris Bourse.[13] French newspapers at the time suggested even that Germany had sponsored the dissemination of excessively negative news about the Russian situation in order to sap the morale of the French enemy, which had the largest holdings of Russian debt.[14] In this environment, the actual motives for the repudiation, or even its authenticity, must certainly have seemed complex to an average investor.

The repudiation sparked an almost immediate reaction from diplomats stationed in Russia. On 13 February 1918 the leader of the diplomatic corps, the American ambassador, David Francis, lodged an official protest on behalf of his government and several Allied and neutral countries. According to the protest, the decree canceling the debt was null and void. A few days later France and the United Kingdom signed a joint declaration that stated, "No principle is better established than that which holds a nation responsible for the acts of its government, without a change of government having an effect on pre-existing obligations and that outstanding liabilities are not affected by a change of government. Russia's liabilities remain: they are payable and shall be payable by the new state or the group of states that represent or will represent Russia." Initially, therefore, the repudiation does not seem to have been perceived as credible, although diplomatic missions gave it slightly more credit than the financial markets.

On the basis of past episodes it seems logical that French investors would perceive the desire to maintain a good reputation, and hence access to the capital markets, as paramount. Market participants had not yet fully recognized the revolutionary nature of the Bolshevik experiment. In hindsight, however, it may be wondered whether the Bolsheviks intended the loss of a good reputation with capitalists to be an aim in itself. At the time, little or nothing was known about the ambitions of various factions active in Russia. French economic agents probably viewed the Russian repudiation as a default identical to previous defaults in every respect except size. Consequently, in August 1918 the General Commission for the Protection of French Interests in Russia (*Commission générale pour la protection des intérêts français en Russie*) still thought that Russia would eventually agree to recognize its foreign debt simply in order to reinstate its good reputation.[15] Recognition was far from obvious to observers in Russia, however. In July 1918 Pierre Darcy advised against placing any hopes in the Bolsheviks.[16] Far from maintaining a clearly established position, the Bolsheviks would use debt recognition as a bargaining chip, adding to the confusion already in investors' minds.

The Bolsheviks' Position and the Legal Motivation for the Repudiation

The position of the Bolsheviks on the recognition of debt issued during the tsarist regime was far from unwavering. It shifted from an extreme stance to a negotiating position and even to recognition of the debt, at least on paper. According to Edouard Luboff, leading figures in the Soviet government announced the end of the repudiation. Georgii Chicherin, the people's commissar for foreign affairs, Alexei Ivanovich Rykov, the deputy chairman of the Council of People's Commissars, and Mikhail Kalinin, the president of the All-Russian Central Executive Committee, all apparently admitted on more than one occasion that the Soviet Union was willing to recognize prewar debt and to negotiate an arrangement on certain conditions.[17]

It is hard to determine the sincerity of the Russian representatives' involvement in the negotiations. In hindsight it seems unlikely that the Soviet government genuinely intended to repay Russia's debt in full. What seems more obvious is that promises of recognition soon became a diplomatic weapon and that in the absence of a substantial advantage in exchange, repayment was unthinkable. Even when there did seem to be some progress toward recognition, the amounts to be repaid were debated at length by the Soviets, who were quick to raise some rather unorthodox arguments in order to minimize their liabilities. Lienau (2014,

74) argues that "while Western powers considered the principle of debt recognition central, they showed considerable flexibility on actual payment." Recognition was indeed a prerequisite, and Western governments were certainly eager to make sure the Soviet Union would repay something. Yet they were not ready to agree to just any settlement, as is shown by the debates regarding the amounts to be paid.

At first the Soviet government seems to have viewed the repudiation as permanent and did not envisage resuming trade relations or maintaining diplomatic ties with the rest of the world. Luboff describes the initial attitude of the Soviet leaders as one of isolationism and fierce hostility.[18] In this opening phase, priority was given to the political agenda. Lenin had just published the unabridged version of "Imperialism, the Highest Stage of Capitalism." Reimbursement would indeed have been a direct betrayal of the position expressed in the book. It would also have given support to other parties favoring a less extreme position. The role of bondholders and capitalists in the exploitation of the world had been heavily criticized. The accusation was clear when Lenin (1917 [1952, 9]) stated, "Capitalism has now singled out a *handful* ... of exceptionally rich and powerful states which plunder the whole world simply by 'clipping coupons.'" France was certainly not spared in the attacks. Lenin (1917) contrasted the British and French experiences. According to him, British imperialism took the form of colonial imperialism, with most investments directed toward the colonies. The French case was different, as French capital exports were mostly invested in Europe in the form of government loans. As a result, Lenin (1917 [1952, 77]) said that "French imperialism might be termed 'usury capitalism.'" Profits from investment banks in the framework of government loan issues were also a direct target of the book. In view of all these elements, hostility to repaying the loan in full is easy to understand. In a first phase the repudiation was deemed to be the result of "reasons of principle and political necessity" (Sack 1938). Ironically, the "political necessity" was supposed to be the result of the abandonment of the firms and property by their foreign owners (Sack 1938).

Another element may have played against recognition of the debts. At the end of the nineteenth century several states were forced to accept loss of sovereignty following defaults on their debt. Mitchener and

Weidenmier (2010) list the states which were supersanctioned and forced to relinquish control of part of their fiscal apparatus to international bodies. If the Soviets recognized the liabilities but were unable to pay, they may have feared that such sanctions would be imposed on Russia. When Egypt suspended payment on its debts, Great Britain eventually took control of the country (Feis 1930 [1965], 108). France did the same with Morocco. There was thus a risk, should the Soviets recognize the debts, of seeing part of the empire fall under the sphere of influence of European powers.

Shortly after the publication of the cancellation decree, however, dissension was heard in Russia, even within prorevolutionary movements. Opposition to the repudiation was mainly grounded in a fear of being excluded from international capital markets in the future. In an article published in *Novaia Zhizn'* on 27 March 1918 Boris Avilov suggested the government start by "revoking the decree on debt cancellation" and seeking common ground with Russia's creditors.[19]

The revolutionaries had to justify a measure as extreme as debt repudiation in one way or another. Initially they found grounds for nonrepayment in traditional legal doctrines, such as "the occurrence of an event—the Revolution—that either prevents the execution of obligations (force majeure) or radically alters them (*rebus sic stantibus*); the *ab initio* illegality of the debt; or compensation for damage caused by foreign intervention in Russia" (Eisemann 2002, 61–62). The justification of their position was crucial because, as pointed out by Lienau (2014), deciding to repudiate the debt was in fact costly: the regime could have chosen to rely on cheap talk (that is, promises to repay the debt) instead of embracing the intransigent repudiation stance.

Francis Delaisi, a financial adviser to a Russian bondholders' association, explained the argument of the purported illegality of the debt. The Soviets made a sharp distinction between debt issued before and after 1906. They considered debt contracted after 1906 as illegal because it was issued without the approval of the Duma (Delaisi 1930, 10). That legal aspect was raised at the time of the bond issue in April 1906, when the French minister of finance, Raymond Poincaré, was reluctant to authorize it to take place on the Paris market for that very reason (Girault

1961, 75). Opposition to this issue was such that the lead underwriter, the Crédit Lyonnais, met secretly with the tsar's agents to decide if it was reasonable to go on with the bond issue (Bayle 1997). For several years after its flotation, investors required a premium to hold this specific bond (Collet and Oosterlinck 2012). According to Girault (1961), two factors prompted Poincaré to change his mind: the opinion of Russian lawyers and pressure from the finance minister, Kokovtsov, who demanded a fair reward for Russia's support of France at the Algeciras Conference.

The arguments developed subsequently in Russia took a less traditional turn. The Russian lawyer Evgenii Korovin considered that "the succession of debt does not take place in the case of political transformation; the previous government had personal debts, which are *res inter alios acta* as far as the new government is concerned."[20] According to Delaisi (1930), the Soviets refused to recognize these debts because they considered that the tsar had plundered and oppressed the people. In this, the Soviet argument was close to the concept of odious debt. Indeed, it emphasized the oppressive nature of the issuing government and the fact that the debt did not benefit the people who were supposed to repay it. To undermine this argument, associations of Russian bondholders rejected the description of the debt or bonds as tsarist, which might imply that the capital had been raised to satisfy the tsar's personal wishes.[21] Instead, the bonds were always described as part of the imperial debt. This argument was, however, supported and expanded by the French opposition, particularly the Socialist Party. Marius Moutet accused the French creditors—and the government that encouraged them to lend to Russia—of having "enriched an entire corrupt aristocracy" and of having "fuelled the corruption of a whole system."[22]

The legal arguments developed by the Soviets gave rise to numerous debates and interpretations by international lawyers. The outcome of this exercise in international law was that a fairly objective justification was found for the repudiation, but the Soviet government adopted a much more pragmatic approach to its debt. The debts, unfair or not, would plague all subsequent negotiations between France and Russia. But before that, the debt had to be addressed as part of Russia's withdrawal from the First World War.

The Hope of Brest-Litovsk and the
Treatment of the Germans

Despite the accession to power of the Bolsheviks, some of whom were keen to sue for peace, the war with Germany did not end immediately. Bilateral negotiations between the Soviets and the Central Powers began in December 1917. Unable to agree on which territories should be assigned to each of the parties, the negotiators postponed the talks. In Russia itself, opinions diverged: should Russia sign a separate peace to ensure the survival of the revolution? or should it continue fighting and launch an all-out revolutionary war? Because of these disagreements, a policy of obstruction was adopted: the negotiations were pursued, but the real aim was to procrastinate (Werth 2004, 140–41). The peace treaty signed between Germany and the Ukrainian Congress (the Rada) radically changed this approach. Leon Trotsky was forced to fall back on a third path he had described earlier, namely, a unilateral declaration of the end of the war between the Central Powers and Russia. Unmoved, the Central Powers launched a massive offensive against Russia.

The outcome of the offensive was particularly unfortunate for the Bolsheviks. The German army had advanced so deeply that the Bolshevik leaders saw a peace treaty with Germany as a condition essential to the survival of the revolution (Figes 1997, 547). The talks led to the Treaty of Brest-Litovsk, signed on 3 March 1918. The treaty had an immediate and disastrous effect on Russia by formalizing the loss of a huge swathe of territory belonging to the former Russian empire. The ceded regions accounted for 26 percent of the population of the empire, 23 percent of its industrial output, and 75 percent of its iron and coal production (Werth 2004, 142).

In addition to territorial concessions to Germany, Bolshevik Russia was forced to accept conditions on the repayment of the debt. On 27 August 1918 Russia and Germany added a financial agreement to the peace treaty (Eliacheff 1919, 234–35). Under the additional clauses, Russia was to pay Germany a portion of the gold from the Russian State Bank's reserves, along with Russian currency and 2.5 billion marks in securities and 1 billion marks in goods (Raffalovitch 1919, 80). Eliacheff (1919, 234) writes that the total amount paid to Germany was 6 billion marks (a billion of which might have been payable by new independent states established on the territory of the former empire, such as Ukraine and Finland).

The gold mentioned in the financial agreement between Germany and Russia kindled as much greed as hope. The agreement provided for the payment of 245.564 tons of gold in five successive tranches. According to Eliacheff (1919, 235), the first payment was to include 42.86 tons of pure gold and was payable on 10 September 1918; the next four payments, amounting to 50.676 tons, were scheduled for 30 September, 31 October, 30 November, and 31 December 1918. The Armistice of 11 November 1918 interrupted the transfers. Burdeau (2002) believes the equivalent of almost 240 million marks had been paid to Germany by that date. In March 1919, even before its final destination had been decided legally, the Bolsheviks suggested that the gold transferred to Germany be deducted from its outstanding prewar debt (Burdeau 2002). The fate of the gold was decided by the Treaty of Versailles: it was to be paid to the main Allied Powers, who would determine how it would be appropriated. A total of 94 tons of gold was shipped to the Banque de France, half of which was transferred to the United Kingdom in 1924 (Szurek 2002). The final appropriation of the bullion that remained in France has been the subject of much discussion. It appears to have been sold over a period from 1921 to 1937 (Burdeau 2002). Freymond (1996, 157) argues even now that it should have been used to repay French holders of Russian bonds.

The Treaty of Brest-Litovsk had an immediate positive impact, not only on the price of Russian bonds traded in Germany but also on the foreign exchange market. Although the treaty covered only Russian bonds held in Germany, the *Frankfurter Handelsblatt* attributed the appreciation of the mark on the foreign exchange market to the improvement in Germany's creditworthiness as a result of the treaty.[23] The sections of the treaty concerning the repudiation attracted the attention of French holders of Russian bonds and the associations formed to defend them.[24] Simultaneously with this interest in the treatment of German holders of Russian bonds, rumors began to circulate about the destination of bonds purchased on the Paris Bourse. In May 1918 market participants suspected that many of the securities were bought on behalf of

Swiss citizens who intended to take them to Germany in order to benefit from the favorable treatment given to Russian bonds there.[25] They believed the sudden interest in Russian securities coincided with the end of the inventory period for Russian securities holdings in Germany. The treatment reserved for German holdings of Russian bonds was indeed perceived as a crucial precedent in potential negotiations with Russia.[26] In September 1918 a short item in the *Messager de Paris* suggested that Austria had succeeded in extracting from the Soviet government a promise of repayment of the debt held by its citizens.[27] By September 1918 France seemed to be losing the race on Russian repayment.

Action Taken by Associations of Russian Bondholders

Although many refused to believe that the repudiation of Russian debt would last, associations were quickly formed to defend the interests of Russian bondholders. There were huge differences in the activities and political clout of these associations. Their priorities also differed: securities redemption was a primary aim of some, while others saw the recovery of assets nationalized in Russia as more urgent.

THE GENERAL COMMISSION FOR THE PROTECTION OF FRENCH INTERESTS IN RUSSIA: ACTION INITIALLY FOCUSED ON FRANCE

After the repudiation, numerous committees appeared in defense of Russian bondholders. At the end of January 1918 the National Securities Office (*Office National des Valeurs Mobilières*) studied the feasibility of setting up a committee to protect French interests in Russia.[28] It did not think a decision taken by a "terrorist government, not recognized by the Allied Powers" called for any action from investors since the Bolshevik position seemed untenable. The report concluded that it would be premature to form an association for the protection of Russian bondholders.

In July 1918 French financial institutions and companies with interests in Russia discussed establishing an entity to defend those interests. Many dubious committees were formed, precipitating the decision to set up a body specifically to defend French economic interests in Russia.[29] The first such initiative, the French Committee on Russian Bonds (*Comité français des fonds russes*), ended in disaster when the chairman was arrested for fraud in September 1918.[30] In August 1918 the appointment of the General Commission for the Protection of French Interests in Russia (*Commission Générale pour la protection des Intérêts français en Russie*), comprising forty-one members representing industrial companies, banks, and other lending institutions, the stockbrokers' syndicate, and the National Securities Office, was officially announced.[31] The commission would be tasked with researching four key areas: issues of concern to bondholders (a key source of my analysis here) as well as industrial, financial, and trade issues. The commission had a very broad remit since it sought to centralize the "defense of any assets and interests owned or represented by French citizens in any territory now belonging to or having belonged to the Russian state before war was declared."

To fulfill its mandate the General Commission endeavored to inventory the Russian securities held by French citizens and established an archive of information about the situation in Russia, including eyewitness accounts and translations from the contemporary Russian press.[32] By appointing the former chairman of the stockbrokers' syndicate, Maurice de Verneuil, as its chair, and by setting up a Committee of Holders of Russian Government Bonds, Securities Guaranteed by the Russian State and Municipal Debt (Comité de Porteurs de Fonds d'Etat Russes, de Valeurs Garanties par l'Etat Russe et d'Emprunts Municipaux) in September 1918, the General Commission signaled the central role it intended to play in the defense of bondholders.[33] On 24 September 1918 the commission held its first meeting, chaired by de Verneuil and attended by representatives of the French government. Three other noteworthy events occurred at that time: a similar committee, chaired by a Frenchman, was founded in Russia; the commission contacted the representatives of associations of Russian bondholders in other countries; and an archive on the Russian question was established.[34]

In April 1919 a second committee, the Defense Committee of French Holders of Russian Industrial and Banking Stocks (Comité de Défense des porteurs français de valeurs industrielles et bancaires russes), performed a role similar to that of the General Commission with respect to industrial and banking stocks.[35] The two committees were formed to attract the interest of small investors, and both were chaired by Fernand des Closières, the director of the National Securities Office and formerly the representative of French holders of Bulgarian debt.[36] The committee evidently fulfilled the wish of Pierre Darcy, who, in July 1918, had advised forming an association of holders of Russian private bonds in France.[37]

Other organizations offering to support holders of Russian securities appeared in Paris. The Russian Securities Union (Union des Valeurs Russes), founded under the auspices of the French and Russian Industrial Cooperation Organization (Coopération industrielle française et russe), proposed a program of direct action to "facilitate price stabilization" and "stop speculation driven by enthusiasm or panic." Its plan was to publish regular information about Russia as well as to facilitate the sale of or reinvestment in securities in France and Russia.[38] Numerous other associations and committees were set up later, leading to a plethora of initiatives that suffered from an obvious lack of coordination.[39] Among the groups defending French interests in Russia, the General Commission enjoyed a preeminent position, probably reflecting the social status of its members and its inclusion in the National Association of Securities Holders (Association Nationale des Porteurs de Valeurs Mobilières). In the 1920s the press directed Russian bondholders toward the National Association of Securities Holders, cautioning readers against bogus associations.

The success of the associations can be measured not so much by bond repayments as by the size of their membership base. According to Le Rentier, several hundred thousand bondholders belonged to the National Association of Securities Holders.[40] By the late 1920s the General Commission boasted of having approximately 275,000 members who owned government bonds and almost 43,300 members holding industrial and banking paper.[41]

INTERNATIONAL ACTION

Although the actions of the other national committees for the defense of Russian bondholders were watched with great interest in France, it was not until 1920 that real synergy developed between committees in different countries.[42] As early as 1918 the Dutch government attempted to group the various demands within a single association, but the proposal was rejected by the French government, which claimed a special relationship with Russia (Hogenhuis-Seliverstoff 1981, 77). In the other main creditor countries, too, national associations formed rapidly to defend the interests of their citizens in Russia. The list of countries with an association defending its nationals' Russian interests is impressive.[43] Similarly, the existence of several competing associations in small countries like Belgium and the Netherlands is an indication of their perceived importance in the negotiation process. In many countries the bondholders' associations counted high-ranking political and business figures as their chairmen and as members, including the governor of the Bank of England and a former finance minister in the Netherlands.

In the United Kingdom in June 1918 the Corporation of Foreign Bondholders convened an assembly of Russian state and municipal bondholders in order to decide on a course of action to defend their interests. The assembly agreed on the need to set up an ad hoc committee for that purpose.[44] The corporation's annual reports in the following years do not give the impression that the corporation was very active, however.[45] In the early 1920s a newspaper called the *British Russian Gazette* was published and presented as the official mouthpiece of the Association of British Creditors of Russia, Ltd. The actions of this association also seem to have been fairly limited.

On the initiative of the Belgian government in exile, in February 1918 a Committee for the Defense of Belgian Interests in Russia (Comité de défense des intérêts belges en Russie) was founded in Paris, with branches in London and The Hague.[46] As soon as the situation allowed, the association's first act was to inventory Russian securities held in Belgium. Given Belgium's colossal investment in Russia, the committee found itself in the unenviable position of being charged with the largest interests ever defended by the Belgian Association for the Defense of Government Bondholders (Association belge pour la défense des détenteurs de fonds publics).[47] The leadership of the committee indicates the importance of these interests: it was chaired by Félicien Cattier, a leading figure in Belgian capitalism.[48] Other committees with a similar purpose, such as the Committee of Belgian Interests in Russia (Comité des intérêts belges en Russie), coexisted, apparently on good terms, with the first committee.

The first international conference of defense committees, held from 12 to 17 April 1920 in Geneva, was attended by representatives of national defense associations from Denmark, the Netherlands, Norway, Sweden, and Switzerland.[49] This was followed by a larger international meeting from 10 to 12 June 1920 in Paris, called by the General Commission for the Protection of French Interests in Russia.[50] The conference was attended by representatives of the Belgian, British, Danish, Dutch, Italian, Norwegian, Spanish, Swedish, and Swiss national associations. After a debate, several resolutions were passed. All negotiations would be subject to acceptance of the following conditions: the recognition of all treaties and commitments entered into by the central or local Russian authorities prior to 25 October/7 November 1917; the return of the assets, rights, and interests of the plaintiffs; the payment of "fair" compensation; and the creation of an international body to carry out this last task.[51]

Following on from the success of the meeting in June 1920, an international conference on the protection of private interests in Russia was held in early 1921.[52] According to the conference minutes, the aim of the meeting was to work out guidelines for governments. In other words, the meeting seemed to be dedicated to drafting a common agreement that each association would then defend in its own country. The question of the guarantees to be demanded of Russia occupied a central place in the discussions. To avoid the eventuality of the creditors of the most powerful countries being the only ones repaid, the commission expressed the wish that any agreement with Russia be signed within the framework of an international treaty. The General Commission also agreed to support the mobilization of claims and not their consolidation in the form of a "consolidated bond." The creation of a consolidated bond with a benchmark interest rate of 5 percent and a board to manage the bond had been suggested back in 1920.[53]

At the general assembly in 1921 the General Commission stressed its close relations with bondholders' associations from other countries, particularly the Committee for the Defense of Belgian Interests in Russia, the Association for Mutual Assistance and the Protection of Swiss

Interests in Russia, and the Association of British Creditors on Russia as well as measures taken to establish closer relations with American bond-holders associations.[54]

The outcome of the talks was that the Belgian, British, Dutch, and French associations of Russian bondholders agreed unanimously on several resolutions.[55] These stated that it was in Russia's interest to recognize its debts because otherwise it would permanently be denied access to the international capital market. Furthermore, recognition left no room for Russia to unilaterally reduce the amounts payable. The practical terms of repayment would not be discussed until Russia renounced repudiation. In any case, it was agreed that the principal of the debt should be repaid, given that Russia's per capita debt was lower than that of other nations striving to honor their obligations. In other words, the only room for negotiation on the schedule and facilities would concern coupons in arrears and outstanding. Last, the committees said they would oppose any attempts to drive a wedge between the creditors. The General Commission was still referring to the close ties between the various national associations in the late 1920s.[56] According to the commission's members, the Bolsheviks' attempts to destabilize this entente proved vain. However, despite the apparent agreement between them, some associations counseled that unconcerted action should be considered to accelerate the repayment process (British Union of Russian Bond-holders, 8).

Debt Recognition and Trade Relations in Exchange for Legal Recognition

In the early stages of the revolution, securing official recognition of the Russian government was hardly a priority for the Bolshevik leaders (Hogenhuis-Seliverstoff 1981, 37). Gradually, however, the revolutionaries began to see recognition as desirable. For instance, as early as 1919 the Soviet government opened an office in Washington in order to gain diplomatic recognition from the United States but also to increase international trade (Siegel 1996, 6). However, in view of the repudiation of the Russian debts, the nationalization of property, and the propaganda waged by the Soviet government, recognition by the United States was out of the question (Siegel 1996, 39). In France, recognition was quickly made contingent on the prior recognition of its financial obligations.[57] In theory, France would also consider a resumption of trade relations only once the dispute over the debt had been resolved. Because of a lack of coordination and sometimes divergent interests, however, the European states adopted positions of varying flexibility toward the Soviet regime. The Bolsheviks took advantage of this dissent to win recognition as the legitimate government of Russia and resume trade relations with France. Several milestones punctuated developments in the relations with Russia and revived the hopes of Russian bondholders. These included the Anglo–Soviet Trade Agreement (March 1921), the Genoa Conference (1922), and the work of the Russian Affairs Commission, headed by Anatole de Monzie (1925). The latter two negotiations formed the basis for fresh hopes of repayment.

The question of the recognition of the Soviet government was raised as soon as it became clear that the Bolsheviks were likely to remain in power. Meanwhile, the Bolshevik government attempted to establish contact with the main Western nations relatively quickly. The Soviets tried several times to make peace with the Allied nations that were intervening militarily on Russian soil. The debt issue was raised in some of these diplomatic exchanges. For example, in an interview for the London *Daily News* in December 1918, Maksim Litvinov, the Soviet government's roving ambassador, suggested offering trade concessions in exchange for a moratorium on Russian debt (Thomson 1966, 89). The Bolsheviks' promises did not seem to be enough to reassure market participants in Paris.[58]

With the civil war still raging between the White Russian armies and the Bolsheviks, the issue of Russian representation was raised during the peace negotiations at the end of the First World War. Not only were the Allies split on their attitude toward the Bolsheviks and the other parties claiming to represent Russia, but even within countries, positions diverged strongly. Disunity over Russian representation fueled a number of debates. Eventually, the Allies proposed a meeting to be held on Prinkipo, the largest of the Princes' Island in the sea of Marmara, in early 1919 at which all the Russian parties would be represented (Thomson 1966, 80–81).

The proposal was the first attempt by Western diplomacy to take the Bolsheviks seriously. It was criticized by the representatives of the White Russian armies and seen by many as a betrayal. The real intentions of the Bolsheviks about the Princes' Island proposal gave rise to diverse interpretations. The Soviet response of 4 February 1919 included various concessions the government was prepared to make to facilitate the peace talks. One of these was related to the sovereign debt: the Soviet government was willing to recognize the Russian debts but, owing to its financial difficulties, requested to be allowed to pay the coupons in commodities (Thomson 1966, 114). This announcement was perceived as credible by the financial markets. *The Economist* linked the increase in prices for Russian bonds listed in London in February 1919 to the expectation that the situation in Russia would improve and to the Soviets' changed attitude to the debt.[59] However, many diplomats criticized the wording of the Bolsheviks' proposal, which they found insulting because it implied that diplomatic recognition could simply be bought. Given the position of the various representatives of the White armies, the purportedly insulting nature of the Bolshevik proposal, and French opposition to the Princes' Island proposal, the planned conference was abandoned in late February 1919.

The failure of Princes' Island rekindled interest in sending a secret investigative mission to Russia. The mission was eventually led by William C. Bullitt, the chief of the Division of Current Intelligence Summaries with the American Commission to Negotiate Peace (Siegel 1996). It was criticized for several reasons. Bullitt was only twenty-eight years old at the time and had little experience of diplomacy. Like him, his companions were opposed to Allied intervention in Russia, did not hide their sympathy for the Bolshevik experiment, and had barely any negotiating experience (Thomson 1966, 160–61). Bullitt met several of the main Bolshevik leaders in early March 1919. The Soviet proposal that resulted from those meetings contained an offer to repay the Russian debt (Thomson 1966, 165), one of the first in a series of many.

Between 1919 and 1921 there were many announcements that the Bolsheviks would recognize the debt or resume negotiations. On the financial markets these announcements were greeted variously with skepticism or enthusiasm. Some observers criticized the market for being gullible enough to believe the Bolshevik announcements (Eliacheff 1919, 229). In a statement issued on 18 October 1919 the Russian minister for trade and industry announced he would exercise "great prudence in granting concessions and admitting foreign capital."[60] Despite the aggressive tone, the statement did not totally rule out concessions and was therefore seen by some as a step forward. For holders of Russian securities listed in France, the possibility that trade relations with Russia would resume was indeed a reason to be optimistic.[61] The proposals to recognize the debt also seem to have been strongly influenced by the military situation in Russia. In March 1920 Litvinov stressed the desire to repay the debt and resume trade relations once the Polish–Soviet War was over (Carley 2000). De Monzie viewed the Bolsheviks' proposal in early 1920 as motivated solely by the wish not to alienate France during that conflict. As soon as the Polish military threat had receded, the proposal was dropped.[62] After bond prices rose, in February 1920 a *New York Times* journalist lampooned the optimistic reaction by portraying Lenin and Trotsky playing at influencing the Russian bond market by announcing debt recognition or a peace treaty.[63] Ironically, a peace proposal from the Bolsheviks, who agreed to repay 60 percent of the principal as well as coupon arrears, was mentioned in the same issue of the newspaper.[64]

In August 1920 *Le Matin* referred to a debt recognition proposal from a member of the politburo, Lev Kamenev.[65] The newspaper reported that the Allies would initially advance new amounts to Russia to convert and exchange the old debt into new bonds. The deal would take place under the supervision of a debt council headquartered in Paris, and the principal and coupons of the new bonds would be guaranteed jointly by France and Russia, with the United Kingdom undertaking only to cover the interest in the event of a default by the other two countries. In fact, the French trade minister's representative in London, Joseph de Poulpiquet du Halgouët, had met the people's commissar for foreign trade, Leonid Krasin, on 9 August.[66] Krasin conveyed the Soviets' wish to reach a negotiated solution to the debt issue and had even outlined a plan. The discussion between the two parties shows that the Soviets believed the French government would give in to public opinion and be forced to negotiate with them.

The Bolsheviks' changes of position caused enormous confusion in France. It would be difficult to compile a list of all the announcements made in one direction or another. Lenin's categorical statement, published in *Izvestiia* in late March 1920, that "any agreement with the Entente must include the outright rejection of the claims of holders of Russian bonds and stocks" was considered on the Bourse to be "pure bluff."[67] Several Bolshevik leaders nevertheless reasserted the same line shortly afterward.[68] Even so, less than a month later the Bourse was enthusiastic about Russian bonds again, on the expectation that Krasin would recognize Russia's foreign debt as part of the Anglo–Soviet debt negotiations.[69]

An extract from an article in *Le Rentier* captures how disoriented investors were by the Bolsheviks' continuously changing stance: "Statements by Krasin on behalf of the Soviet economic delegation appear randomly in the foreign press at the same time as contrary proposals by Litvinov, which are in turn disavowed by Chicherin and Kreghan."[70] In September 1920 the situation was so confusing that *Le Rentier* urged the markets to stop circulating unverifiable news that raised false hopes. The newspaper referred explicitly to the Copenhagen talks on the recovery of the debt and Krasin's statements.[71]

From 1920 on, several observers in France began to think that recognition of the Soviet government might precede the discussion of the repudiated debt. Faure (1920) noted that de facto recognition was inevitable given the Bolsheviks' position on the ground in Russia. In his view, Alexandre Millerand, the prime minister when Faure's article was published, was willing to recognize the Bolshevik government as early as July 1919 provided it undertook to honor the liabilities of previous governments. The Soviet government obviously wanted the position reversed, so that recognition of its authority preceded recognition of the debt. In a speech to the lower house of parliament on 24 June 1920 Prime Minister Millerand reasserted his position: recognition of the Soviets can be envisaged only if they "accept liability for all the international commitments contracted by previous governments" (Mourin 1967, 128). At the end of 1920 the French position was inflexible: an agreement with Russia would be considered only after the debt had been recognized.[72] The argument over prior recognition would be shunted back and forth between the parties until 1924.

The French position was reinforced by the fact that other tactics had failed to achieve repayment. These included an attempt at direct action when France asked Sweden and the United Kingdom to seize any Russian gold in their countries. The request was consistent with the French position, which sought to prevent recognition or trade until the Russian debt issue had been settled.[73] The Belgian bondholders' associations seemed to accept seizure as a matter of course since, in their view, "treasury gold is the collateral of the creditors of the Russian state, including holders of state bonds."[74] Seizure was deemed illegal in the United Kingdom, however, even though the gold probably came from the imperial bullion reserve.[75] Not until 1986, under a broader agreement with the Soviet Union, was the gold deposited with Barings used to compensate British holders of Russian bonds (Szurek 2002).

The year 1921 began amid rumors that the negotiations would resume.[76] In France, interest in trading with Russia was growing. This sentiment was confirmed by the many parliamentary questions aimed at clarifying the French government's official position.[77] The government's response, based on an opinion published in the *Journal Officiel* on 16 December 1920, was hardly encouraging. Although trade was not prohibited, it was to be conducted entirely at the traders' own risk since France had virtually no diplomatic relations with the government in power in Russia. The British government's position was much clearer. Most of the Russian debt in the United Kingdom was war debt. Even though a portion of public opinion still opposed concessions to the Bolsheviks, industry largely backed a resumption of trade relations with Russia. The balance tipped in favor of the business community, leading to the signing of the Anglo–Soviet Trade Agreement in March 1921. The agreement not only sealed the end of the policy of isolation advocated by France; it was the first chink in the collective effort to resolve the default.

THE ANGLO–SOVIET TRADE AGREEMENT

Russia's interest in renewing international ties coincided with the New Economic Policy introduced in early 1921. British bondholders' associations saw the resumption of trade with the United Kingdom as a factor that would encourage the Soviet government to recognize the debts of its predecessors (British Union of Russian Bondholders, 9). The Soviet government could thus restore confidence in Russia and simultaneously resolve its economic problems. The Russian debt issue was discussed during negotiations leading to the signing of the Anglo–Soviet Trade Agreement in March 1921.[78] Glenny (1970) describes the obstacles encountered during the talks, which ultimately delivered only one point of agreement, trade.

In the negotiations the two parties focused on the recognition of Russia's debt and the Bolsheviks' use of the gold in the imperial State Bank. Krasin laid down five reasons the Soviet government should not repay the Russian debt:

1. If state debts to private persons were given priority over other classes of debt, Russia would be the loser because it could not counterclaim *pari passu,* having by nationalization turned all private claims into state claims;

2. Private debts were only one class of debts, and there was no good reason that class should rank over others;

3. It was false reasoning to contend, as the British government did, that recognition of private debts was essential in order to restore confidence in Russian trade among business firms: it was, on the contrary, business people who were readiest to write off their bad Russian debts in order to get back to trading and hence to recoup past losses;

4. Russia, devastated by war and intervention, refused to regard the reimbursement of foreign capitalists as a first charge on her shattered economy; on the contrary, it felt entitled to present the Allies with a massive bill of indemnity for the vast losses in life and property sustained as a result of Allied intervention in the Civil War;

5. The Soviet government regarded itself as absolved from all tsarist debts, etc., owing to the Allies' warlike acts of intervention and blockade. Any Soviet recognition of such debts

could now be negotiated only by formal agreement and
could not be obtained as of right. A formal peace treaty
with Soviet Russia was therefore essential.[79]

Numerous drafts of the treaty were discussed by the United Kingdom
and Russia between January and March 1921.[80] Some of them included
recognition of prerevolutionary debt.[81] When the agreement was finally
signed in March 1921, however, recognition of the Russian debt was
conspicuously absent.

France intervened several times in the Anglo–Russian talks.[82] The
diplomatic effort to ensure France's privileged creditor status paid off, at
least on paper. In a statement to the House of Commons, Prime Minister David Lloyd George acknowledged France's special rights over Russia's assets and pledged Britain's support when a solution was reached.[83]
Despite these assurances, France expressed strong misgivings about
certain clauses in the agreement, particularly one authorizing the Soviet
government to use the imperial State Bank's bullion reserves. The French
business press roundly criticized Anglo–Russian rapprochement.[84] The
purported sale of Russian bonds by the Soviets on the London market
provoked tensions between France and the United Kingdom. In late
March 1921 the chairman of the General Commission for the Protection
of French Interests in Russia questioned the French foreign minister
about the sale of bonds by the Soviets on the London stock exchange.
The fear was that bonds confiscated by the Soviets were being resold
on the London market, forestalling any attempts by their legitimate
owners to reclaim them. The French government asked the British government to intervene, especially when Chinese bonds that seemed to
come from Bolshevik confiscations were sold. The French request was
dismissed out of hand.[85]

Not wishing to settle for a trade agreement with the British alone,
Soviet diplomats made overtures to the Germans. A trade agreement
between the Soviet Union and Germany was signed in May 1921. This
stoked the fears expressed by Poincaré (1921, 476), who declared that he
was "inclined to assume that England and Germany had started talks
with a view to coming to an agreement on the economic exploitation of
Russia." In Poincaré's view (1921), the signing of the agreements with

the Soviets buried the policy of isolation. A fear that French industry would be beaten by its English and German rivals in the race for Russia is manifest in his article. Once again, France seemed to have been overtaken by the other European nations.

French public opinion nevertheless seemed to believe that France still enjoyed a privileged status with Russia. In June 1921 the market rose on persistent rumors that the Soviets were going to recognize the debts of the former Russian regime during a secret meeting between Krasin and the Prime Minister Aristide Briand. The rumors held that, acting on inside information, friends of Louis Loucheur, at that time the minister of the liberated regions, had allegedly purchased Russian bonds.[86] *Le Rentier,* usually wary of Soviet declarations, nevertheless responded enthusiastically to a wire from Helsinki announcing Krasin's recognition of the debt and a resumption of coupon payments in 1925.[87] By the end of 1921, however, enthusiasm had waned, and skepticism about a Bolshevik change of attitude prevailed in both Paris and London.[88]

Despite the bilateral arrangements, Senator de Monzie continued to push for a multilateral solution and called on the French government to convene an intergovernment conference to resolve the Russian debt issue.[89] The conference finally took place in 1922, although as a result of events external to France.

CONFERENCES IN GENOA (APRIL–MAY 1922) AND THE HAGUE (JUNE–JULY 1922)

Famine and a simultaneous epidemic of typhus and cholera broke out in Russia in the spring of 1921. The United States intervened in the summer. The American government's action did not go unnoticed on the financial markets, and in August, in response to an agreement organizing a food shipment to Russia in exchange for the release of American prisoners, the Russian bond market in America enjoyed "a little boom."[90] It soon became apparent, however, that action by the United States alone would be insufficient to stop the Russian famine. Without consulting Russia, a conference on the famine was held in Brussels in early October 1921 and was attended by no fewer than twenty-one countries (Fink 1993, 5–6). The conference advocated an increase in private and public aid but set two preconditions that Russia had to meet: the Bolshevik government had to commit to recognizing the Russian debt and to providing adequate security for future obligations (White 1985, 34–36).

Naturally the Russian government was displeased that it had not been invited to the conference. In a memo to the British government on 28 October 1921 People's Commissar for Foreign Affairs Chicherin acknowledged that he had not followed protocol in stating his government's position on the matter. According to Chicherin, the Russian state was willing, on certain conditions, to recognize debts predating the revolution (White 1985, 34). At the same time, he strongly criticized the attitude of the participants in the Brussels Conference, which in his opinion exploited the famine for political ends. He cited a speech by Prime Minister Lloyd George on 16 August of the same year describing as a "devilish scheme" the proposal to use the famine in Russia to force it to recognize the tsarist government's debts.[91] Chicherin also claimed that the Soviet government had "always declared its willingness to provide an adequate return for foreign capitalists who might wish to develop Russia's natural resources and to re-establish its economic administration" and that legal guarantees were offered to those same capitalists.[92] The irony of this statement was undoubtedly not lost on the holders of Russian industrial bonds, whose property was confiscated in the early months of the regime.

Chicherin's memo is both contradictory and subtle. It promises a bright future for foreign capitalists while simultaneously attacking their firmly held beliefs. In the memo, debt recognition is a concession the Soviet government could grant rather than the consequence of an element of law. Chicherin stresses that "the Soviet Government is firmly convinced that no people is obliged to pay the cost of the chains it has worn for centuries."[93] Moreover, recognition of the debts is contingent on the cessation of activities hostile to Soviet Russia, on the de jure recognition of the Bolshevik regime, and on the granting of conditions that would make repayment a real possibility. The demand for special payment terms would become a constant in the debate and was vigorously refuted in France.

The French government expressed considerable skepticism about Chicherin's claims. In a letter to the British embassy, the French foreign minister clarified France's position.[94] Despite the positive aspects of Chicherin's statement, the French government remained firmly convinced that Russia would be unable to recover economically unless it abandoned the Bolshevik experiment. The foreign minister heatedly attacked Chicherin's arguments about debt recognition. For France, recognition of the debt was simply the application of a principle of international law and therefore could not be used as a bargaining chip to obtain recognition of the Soviet government. Moreover, the French government criticized the limited scope of the proposed recognition, which excluded war debts, municipal bonds, and compensation for confiscated property. It nevertheless agreed to discuss guarantees and payment conditions. The French government wanted guarantees that the Soviets would cease their support of Bolshevik agitation abroad. This was presented as a nonnegotiable precondition to any direct talks with Russia. In the meantime, the institutions established at the Brussels Conference would act as an intermediary.

The newsletter of the General Commission printed extracts from the Bolshevik press. According to *Pravda*, only prewar Russian debt would be recognized, a sacrifice justified by the famine. *Izvestiia* quoted its editor, Yuri Steklov, and Karl Radek, who were certain that once the debts were recognized, foreign governments would be forced to concede favorable payment terms to Russia. They saw this as a positive development since recognition of the debt, by removing the main grounds for excluding it, would enable Russia to return to the fold of nations.[95] Recognition of the debt had allegedly been put on the agenda by French maneuvering, precipitated by talks about issuing a Russian bond in the United Kingdom. The article refers only to recognition of prewar debt, most of which was held in France. *Novyi Put'*, a Bolshevik newspaper published in Riga, accused France of acting "like Shylock."[96]

The definition of the Soviet position was the subject of lengthy debates in Russia. At its meeting of 13 September 1921, the politburo decided to recognize the debt due to some countries, excluding war debt, on the condition that Russia receive compensation for the Allied interventions on its territory. In light of the international situation, Chicherin in mid-October suggested recognizing all tsarist debt. Lenin's opposition to any additional concessions resulted in the memo of 28 October

1921. Krasin, in a letter to Chicherin, proposed that municipal and railway bonds should also be recognized (White 1985, 39). This was again rejected, and the politburo decided that any negotiations on the debt should take place as part of an international conference, notifying its decision to the British government. The financial markets barely reacted to the announcement of this Soviet turnaround because the credibility of the government in Moscow was already seriously compromised.[97]

Given the Bolsheviks' stance, the establishment of an organization to take control of Russian assets in Europe and ensure the repayment of the Russian debt was proposed in parallel to the negotiations (White 1985, 39). The organization would be part of a broader scheme to restore trade with Russia. A meeting was held in Cannes to discuss how the scheme could be put into practice. This culminated in a resolution announcing an international economic and financial conference, to be convened shortly afterward in Genoa, with a view to reaching a solution that would enable the economic reconstruction of central and eastern Europe. The Cannes meeting also set six essential conditions for the resumption of talks, one of which was the recognition by Soviet Russia of all public debt and obligations.

In February 1922 the Bolsheviks criticized the fact that attendance at the Genoa Conference had been made conditional on acceptance of the points made at Cannes. Since those conditions had been set unilaterally, the Russian representatives asked to postpone the negotiations. The reprieve was put to good use in Russia, and a period of intense discussion about the upcoming conference ensued. By late February an initial position was decided: Russia would recognize the debts if the other governments acknowledged the damages and losses caused by their actions. If this resolution was accepted, the Russian government would consider that its counterclaims for damage caused by Allied action covered Russia's outstanding debt (White 1985, 108). If the parties failed to agree on this point, the Russian delegation would quit the negotiating table. Simultaneously, a massive press campaign to accredit the idea of bilateral talks between France and Russia was deployed, apparently by the Soviets (Hogenhuis-Seliverstoff 1981, 209–10). The scale of the endeavor prompted Poincaré to order an investigation into its origin.

The lead-up to the Genoa Conference saw renewed activity on the

markets. The main British association, the Corporation of Foreign Bondholders, found that the situation was generally perceived as better and
hoped that a modus vivendi could be found between the Great Powers
and Russia.[98] Investors nevertheless seem to have anticipated a sharp
reduction in the British debt. The *British Russian Gazette* refers to a sug-
gestion to cancel Russia's war debt and replace the remaining debt with
bonds that would bear interest for just five years.[99]

In France, too, the announcement of the Genoa Conference pushed
the bondholders' associations into action again. The French government
invited members of the General Commission to send unofficial delegates
to the meeting.[100] In this capacity, Claude Aulagnon outlined his view
of the French position on the Russian debt in March 1922. The United
Kingdom did not see recognition of the Soviet government as economically profitable at the time. According to Aulagnon, France should support Russia's economic recovery in order to counter Germany's eastern
ambitions.[101] Economic recovery should not, however, be achieved at
the expense of the rights of French and Belgian citizens. In other words,
Aulagnon was not advocating helping the Bolshevik government but
rather making aid conditional on democratization of the regime. Extending credit without conditions would only make the problem worse
or at least delay a happy ending to the Bolshevik episode. In Aulagnon's
opinion the failure of the Genoa Conference would be problematic
mainly for the Soviets, who would have to face an increasingly discon-
tented population. On the basis of this view, he opposed any compromise with the Bolshevik regime.

The Genoa Conference began on 10 April 1922, and the proceed-
ings were split between four commissions: political, financial, economic,
and transport (Fink 1993, 154). The debt was obviously on the agenda.
Certain that the Russian delegates would demand a reduction in the
debt, the Allied representatives did not take the trouble to calculate
the amounts they considered due to them. When the Soviet delegation,
represented by Litvinov, demanded 50 billion gold rubles in compensation for the damage caused by Allies in Russia, it sent a chill through
the assembly since that amount exceeded the Allies' claims (Fink 1993,
167). The Allied governments withdrew to discuss this development:
the United Kingdom was willing to concede a 50 percent reduction in

the war debt, whereas France refused to accept a reduction of more than 33 percent (Fink 1993, 168). Given these divergences, it became clear that a compromise would not be easy. The talks nevertheless continued.

It is hard to say whether an agreement signed by the Soviets would have been honored. The archives of the discussions between the Soviet negotiators at the conference and the leadership in Moscow are enlightening in this respect. According to the correspondence between the politburo and Chicherin, the Soviet delegates were given little leeway to negotiate. The war debts and interest on prewar debt were to be covered by the counterclaims for damage caused by the Allied intervention in Russia (Pipes 1998, 159). Restitutions were excluded, and repayment of recognized prewar debt would start only after a fifteen-year moratorium (which could be lowered to ten years if a concession were necessary). Dispossessed property owners could be granted concessions or a preferential right to lease their former factories. In exchange, Russia would be permitted to raise capital—approximately 1 billion dollars—through a major bond issue.

The Treaty of Rapallo, signed on 16 April 1922 on the margins of the Genoa Conference, disrupted the negotiations. Under the treaty Germany and Russia renounced all territorial and financial claims against one other as a result of the First World War. Diplomatic ties were established between the two countries, since Germany recognized the Soviet government. After the signing of the Rapallo Treaty, talks between the Allied powers and Russia resumed, but the outlook was gloomy. Chicherin reopened the negotiations by claiming that Lenin had authorized him to accept the Allies' conditions. Chicherin's announcement was probably interpreted too enthusiastically by some Allies, who believed that a final agreement was about to be signed. On 21 April Chicherin took one step forward—by accepting some of the Allied demands—and one step backward—by making any agreement conditional on de jure recognition of Russia and immediate material and financial aid (Fink 1993, 188).

Even as the Genoa Conference was still under way, hopes of repayment were starting to wane. Doubts about the sincerity of the Russian proposals, combined with a Soviet attitude described as unbelievable, sent Russian bond prices plummeting to rock-bottom levels.[102] By contrast, the announcement in April 1922 that Prime Minister Lloyd George would do everything in his power to recognize the Soviet government had a positive price impact on Russian bonds traded in London.[103] The conference continued against all odds until May. On 11 May the Russians refused the proposed memorandum. This still left the door open for future negotiations. Despite the failure of the Genoa Conference, adjourned on 19 May 1922, a resumption of the negotiations was soon proposed. This was to take the form of a meeting of a committee of experts in The Hague in July 1922.

Even before The Hague Conference began, the resolutions adopted jointly by the British, Belgian, Dutch, and French bondholders' committees were published in the press.[104] The Hague Conference, which took place in June–July 1922, sparked renewed activity on the Paris Bourse and the London Stock Exchange, chiefly because the British delegate seemed willing to grant credits to Russia, but also because Russia was believed to be cornered.[105] On the Soviet side, recognition of pre-1914 debt and its repayment rescheduled over the long term and interest-free would be considered only in exchange for a loan of almost 3,220 million gold rubles (Szurek 2002). The Allies deemed the Russian demands to be exorbitant, and the talks foundered. Russian bond prices in the United Kingdom plunged at the end of July because of the lack of concrete results for bondholders.[106] The Hague Conference was the last attempt at a multilateral solution to the Russian debt issue (Szurek 2002).

Despite the failure of the Genoa and The Hague conferences, Russian bond prices rose again on the much-publicized announcement in September–October 1922 of a visit to Russia by the Radical Party deputies Edouard Herriot, Edouard Daladier, and a consortium of French industrialists. According to *Le Rentier*, the visit signaled a new development in relations with the Soviets, and Russian bondholders "had not had as much reason to expect more and hope since the war."[107] In the United Kingdom, Herriot's visit raised fears that France would overtake Britain in trade relations.[108] Following his trip to Russia, Herriot became one of the chief advocates of Franco–Soviet rapprochement and asked Prime Minister Poincaré and President Millerand to reverse the French position on the Soviet Union (Carley 2000). According to the Soviet government, the obstacle of repudiation could be lifted in exchange for

French credit. The Soviets were quick to support the newfound enthusi-asm for Russia by using the same methods as its predecessors working for the tsar. Between August 1922 and January 1923 the Soviet Union "subsidized" the French press, including such leading newspapers as *Le Temps* and *Le Petit Parisien,* and indirectly even Herriot himself (Carley 2000, 2006). The Bolsheviks' sincerity and the reliability of information from Russia were criticized at the time by Senator Gaudin de Villaine who, in a draft resolution on the Russian bonds, wondered whether the Bolsheviks' promises "did not emanate from a news agency with a hand in the incessant market fluctuations in Russian bonds."[109]

The failure of multilateral negotiations put France in a new posi-tion. After 1922, talks would take place within a bilateral framework. Discussions between the Soviet Union and other Western countries were closely monitored in France. As other governments signed trade agree-ments, France's position became increasingly isolated. A turning point came in 1924 when, like many other countries, France finally decided to recognize the Soviet Union, partly in the hope of launching negotiations about the debt. These were to be conducted by a commission set up for that purpose.

RECOGNITION OF THE SOVIET UNION (1924)

Until 1924 recognition of the Soviet Union, in the eyes of many coun-tries, was conditional on recognition of the debts of the former Russian regime. With the exception of the main signatory countries to the Treaty of Brest-Litovsk and former territories of the Russian empire, no large nation legally recognized Soviet Russia before 1924. That year marked a definite turning point: China, Italy, Great Britain, Mexico, and finally France all recognized the Soviet Union de jure in 1924 (Anderson 1934). As for the United States, Anderson (1934) considers that two major issues stood in the way of recognition: Russia's refusal to respect its in-ternational obligations and the fact that its government did not truly represent the Russian people. The United States refused to compromise for a long time. Loath to barter their principles cheaply, the Americans held that the repudiation decree had to be rescinded before negotiations of any kind could begin (Siegel 1996, 90). As long as the Soviet govern-

ment went unrecognized, the representatives of the Kerensky government were still considered the legitimate representatives of the country.[110] That situation lasted until 1933, when the United States finally
recognized the Soviet Union.

The United Kingdom and France saw recognition as paving the
way for bilateral negotiations over the Russian bonds, among other
issues. Those recognition agreements did stipulate the cessation of all
Soviet propaganda in Western countries and their colonies, one of the
main concerns of their governments (Poincaré 1921). British recognition of the Soviet administration resulted from the election of a Labour
Party government at the end of 1923. In exchange for recognition, an
agreement on repayment was settled. The British Association of Bondholders positioned itself in favor of de jure recognition of the Soviet
government (British Union of Russian Bondholders, 8). British recognition obviously influenced the French position. If the United Kingdom
succeeded in negotiating a resumption of coupon payments, this would
set a precedent for future negotiations. At the same time, recognition by
one of the large nations put Russia in a strong bargaining position.

Carley (2000) has analyzed the Soviet viewpoint. Chicherin apparently divided the defenders of French interests into two groups: those
for whom the strategic dimension of recognition took precedence (Herriot and Paul Painlevé), and those for whom the economic aspect came
first (notably de Monzie). According to Carley, the first group could be
satisfied with a compromise under which something would be paid to
France. The second group would settle for economic concessions, which
Chicherin saw as an easier option. The election of the Cartel des Gauches
catapulted Herriot to the French premiership on 14 June 1924. As prime
minister, he began making direct moves to settle the issue of the Russian
debt and recognize the Soviet Union.

In August 1924 Le Rentier devoted an entire article to the subject of
Russian bonds. Recognition of bonds owned by British subjects hinted
at a possible settlement for French bondholders. According to the article
in Le Rentier, credits from the British government were apparently conditional on an agreement between the Russian government and at least
50 percent of Russian bondholders.[111] Spurred by political developments
in France and the United Kingdom, the French government decided to

recognize the Soviet Union on 28 October 1924 (Carley 2000). Following recognition, diplomatic relations were less tense, with France welcoming Krasin as Russian ambassador while Russia received Jean Herbette.[112] According to Delaisi (1930, 9), three main issues were raised in short order: Russian debt, nationalized property of French citizens, and resumption of trade between the two countries. The action taken by Russian bondholders' associations may well have contributed to the emphasis on Russian debt repayment. According to the members of the General Commission, the presence of their chairman, Joseph Noulens, ensured the inclusion of clauses designed to protect their interests.[113] Ironically, the repayment agreement obtained by the British, which probably precipitated French recognition of the Soviet Union, was not ultimately ratified: it was denounced on 21 November 1924 by the Conservatives, who had come to power (Szurek 2002).

Even before it recognized the Soviet Union, France took the initiative by setting up a consultative commission on Russian state debts. The commission submitted a report in February 1923 estimating the amount of Russia's outstanding debt and interest arrears since 1918 (Szurek 2002).

The Russian Affairs Commission and the de Monzie Commission (1925–1927)

After the recognition of the Soviet Union, a joint Franco–Russian commission was established, in which Krasin and de Monzie were to play a leading role. The question of the Russian debt was hardly new to de Monzie, who had already raised the issue in the Senate in 1920. Favorable to recognition of the Soviet Union, de Monzie had met Chicherin and other Soviet officials in Moscow in the summer of 1923 (Carley 2000).

The resumption of negotiations with Russia had the unexpected effect of causing a sharp decline in prices for Russian government bonds in December 1924. Contemporary observers attributed the slump to several factors, including the liquidation of a large speculative position; a bear movement orchestrated to enable the purchase of bonds cheaply in the hope of substantial gains after the negotiations; and even covert action by the Soviet government aimed at strengthening its position in the negotiations.[114] Talks on the repayment of the Russian debt took place between Herbette and Chicherin, Litvinov, and Krasin in January 1925. During the discussions the Soviet negotiators reiterated their demand for credit prior to any satisfaction of claims (Carley 2000). From April 1925 on, de Monzie held various ministerial portfolios and was therefore replaced by Victor Dalbiez as chairman of the consultative committee on Russian affairs. At the same time, given the disagreements between the various associations of Russian bondholders, a consultative committee on Russian debt, established by decree and chaired by Louis Dausset, was authorized to represent Russian bondholders (de Monzie 1931, 258).

An analysis of the correspondence between the various Soviet leaders shows the way in which debt recognition was used as a diplomatic weapon. According to Carley (2000), who bases his findings on internal Soviet correspondence between January and April 1925, the Russian negotiators decided to make a few concessions with the aim of favorably influencing French public opinion. In September 1925 France received an initial proposal of repayment from Krasin. The money was to come mainly from Russian assets in France, the Brest-Litovsk gold, and, more broadly, from reparations paid to Germany by the Soviet Union in 1918 that were taken over by the Allies at the end of the First World War (Carley 2000). In exchange, Krasin asked for loans. Krasin's offer was rejected by Joseph Caillaux, then finance minister, who considered it too low (de Monzie 1931, 258). Caillaux preferred to hold the Brest-Litovsk gold as collateral against the Russian war debt to the Allies (Carley 2000). Two months later Chicherin proposed to resume the talks within the broader framework of a conference to settle the disputes between France and the Soviet Union.

A Franco–Soviet Conference opened in Paris on 26 February 1926. Delaisi (1930) describes the formation of the de Monzie commission. Its members were de Monzie, minister of public works, Paul Bastid, a member of parliament, Senator Dausset, and three senior civil servants: Philippe Berthelot from the Ministry of Foreign Affairs, one Serruys from the Ministry of Trade, and one Chasles from the Ministry of Finance. Their Soviet counterparts were directors of banks and industry, and the delegation was led by Ambassador Christian Rakovski. According to Delaisi (1930, 16), the de Monzie commission initially sidelined the issue of nationalized property in order to concentrate on Russian bonds. The first key point in the discussion was to determine the actual amounts owed by Russia. The French and Soviet viewpoints differed sharply on this point. In fact, during the negotiations with the creditor governments, the Soviet negotiators played on two levels: recognition of the debt (see above) and the amount owed by Russia. After lengthy negotiations about exactly how much Russia owed, the Soviet delegation proposed a lump settlement comprising sixty-two annuities of 40 million gold francs (de Monzie 1931, 260). On 17 July 1926 Briand's government collapsed. De Monzie returned as finance minister in the new administration. The extremely short-lived term—19 to 23 July 1926—of Herriot's government did not leave it enough time to craft an ambitious policy toward Russia. According to Carley (2000), political instability and the change of finance minister in France halted the negotiations. Several external factors made relations between the two countries extremely tense afterward. The return of Poincaré as prime minister on 23 July 1926 had a major impact on the negotiations. Poincaré also took the finance portfolio in his own cabinet. He refused to limit the negotiations to prewar debt, believing they should cover all Russia's debts (Carley 2000).

Despite Poincaré's appointment as finance minister, Rakovski and de Monzie continued to negotiate. In April 1927 rumors of an agreement began to circulate. On the French side, the relationship between de Monzie and Poincaré was characterized by increasing disagreement. The talks resumed in June 1927, and de Monzie and Rakovski were in frequent contact in July 1927. When he met Rakovski on 23 July 1927, Poincaré, concerned about the upcoming elections, was compromising over France's position on extending credit. Despite Poincaré's refusal, Rakovski and de Monzie continued to work toward an agreement. In August 1927 the Soviets offered to repay 60 million gold francs a year in exchange for trade credits of 120 million francs per year. Franco–Soviet relations deteriorated in the summer of 1927 (Carley 2000). The Soviet government issued fresh proposals at a meeting between the chairmen of the two delegations on 21 September 1927. The Soviet Union announced its willingness to repay sixty-two annuities of 60 million gold francs and to confer most-favored-nation status on France (de Monzie 1931, 261).[115] In exchange, France was asked to extend trade credits of 120 million francs for six years (Carley and Debo 1997). Poincaré did not change his position in response to these proposals, as he was seeking a way to break off the negotiations. His wish was fulfilled when Rakovski was recalled to Moscow. According to Carley (2000), the Russian bond-holders' interests were ruthlessly sacrificed by Poincaré and civil servants from the French ministry of finance, who wanted to avoid enhancing the prestige and credibility of the Soviet Union at all costs.

The negotiations were not limited to debt recognition; the amounts actually due by Russia were also the subject of conflicting interpretations. At the end of June 1920 Prime Minister Millerand set up an interministerial commission, the Russian liquidation commission, in order to "determine the total amount that the former Russian state owes to the French state."[116] Broadly, France wanted the Soviet Union to repay the Russian debt and to reinstate the rights of French citizens dispossessed by nationalizations. The Soviets wanted two other issues to be taken into account when discussing repayment, namely, counterclaims for the Allied intervention on Russian territory and the use of the gold paid to the Germans under the Treaty of Brest-Litovsk (as well as Admiral Alexander Kolchak's gold) to repay French holders of Russian bonds (see below).

There seems to have been no dispute about the amount of the annuities paid before the war, and it was agreed that 400 million francs would be allocated annually to repayment of the debt (Delaisi 1930, 17). Some 25 percent of the debt was considered as payable by other states that emerged from the ruins of the Russian empire (see below), thus reducing the Soviet Union's annuity to 300 million francs. The inventory of the Russian debts determined a nominal amount equivalent to an annuity of 240 million francs (Delaisi 1930, 17). The difference between the two amounts—20 percent—is substantial. There are several possible reasons for this, such as the material disappearance of bonds during the First World War and the export of Russian bonds from France to Germany after the Treaty of Brest-Litovsk. The most likely reason, however, is that some of the bonds were deliberately hidden during the inventory of 1919 in order to avoid taxation. One well-placed witness said, "Everyone believes it is only for tax purposes" and "The banks are overwhelmed with requests for information and many customers have said they will not declare their bonds."[117] Given the additional workload, the banks also seem to have decided not to declare the unidentified bonds deposited with them, unless their customers expressly requested it.

The Russian negotiators agreed only to repay an annuity of 60 million, or one-quarter of the amount declared. They did not see why the Soviet Union should treat French savers any better than France did. The Soviets considered that by devaluing the franc, the French government had robbed its own citizens of four-fifths of their investments, since they had lent "Germinal" francs but were repaid in "Poincaré" francs.[118] The Soviets therefore "generously" offered to apply a discount of only 75 percent, compared with the 80 percent loss incurred by holders of francs (Delaisi 1930, 18). The question of repayment included the war debt. A section of Russian opinion considered this irrelevant. Since Russia had not claimed reparations from Germany, the Soviet negotiators considered that the Soviet Union was entitled to cancel its liabilities unilaterally.[119] The French position regarding its interallied debts was also viewed as an argument not to pay in full. Indeed, France was reluctant to repay to its Allies the debts it had incurred to wage the First World War. Chicherin noticed the inconsistency of the French government. As expressed by Carley (2006, 301), "The French jibbed at paying British and American war debts, but demanded payment from the Soviet Union."

From 1924 on, the French press circulated the view that full repayment was unlikely and that the bondholders would have to make concessions. It seemed to go without saying that coupon arrears were lost forever. Similarly, bondholders would have to give up on the exchange options offered with many bonds. Gradually the press supported the idea of accepting minimal repayment. *Le Rentier* repeated the Soviet argument about the devaluation of the franc to show that the losses incurred by bondholders would not be so severe, relatively speaking, even if Russia decided to repay only 20 percent of its debts.[120] On the basis of these elements, *Le Rentier* considered Russian bonds to be underpriced.

It was of the opinion that "overall, Russian bondholders have more chance of gain than risk of loss by holding onto their bonds."[121]

To determine the exact amount of the claims, French bondholders were asked again in 1924 to provide details of their bonds to the Committee of Action for the Settlement of French Interests in Russia (Comité d'action pour le règlement des intérêts français en Russie).[122] To counter harmful speculation in Russian bonds on the Paris Bourse, it was suggested that only those purchased in gold francs before the war would be eligible for repayment (Delaisi 1930, 19).[123] To my knowledge, this kind of discrimination, based on the date of purchase, had never previously been posed in a renegotiation of sovereign debt. The Paris Bourse soon expressed its discontent, and the financial press carried on the protest.[124] The French government does not seem to have objected to the proposal that created two distinct categories of bondholders (Delaisi 1930, 19). However, since neither the stockbrokers' syndicate nor the French government stopped discriminating between stamped and unstamped securities on 27 March 1923, these measures seemed hard to implement in practice.[125]

Protracted discussions over the amount to be repaid were not unique to France. Describing the situation in the United Kingdom in the late 1920s, Luboff observed that every previous offer made by the Soviet Union had contained arbitrary provisions about debt repayment.[126] He describes two of those conditions in more detail. First, Russia systematically refused to consider repaying debt denominated in rubles, thus establishing remarkable inequality of treatment between bondholders. Second, the Soviets suggested, as in the French case, excluding from the repayment process any bonds purchased after the signing of the Anglo–Soviet Trade Agreement (March 1921). As Luboff notes, this can be seen as the Soviet government awarding itself a premium on dishonesty. Indeed, the decision to repudiate the bonds triggered sales by investors, who feared losing their entire investment. The exclusion of bonds purchased after a certain date would drastically reduce the amount to be repaid, since only those original investors in a position to sustain a supposedly temporary loss would have held on to their bonds.

Last, after the Genoa Conference, the Soviet negotiators introduced a counterclaim against the amounts it owed. Claiming that Allied intervention had caused considerable damage to Russia's infrastructure and economy, the representatives of the Soviet government considered they were entitled to compensation. As Cosnard (2002) points out, it is more than likely that the sole purpose of this counterclaim was to obtain an alleviation of the debt. It was nevertheless part of the legal arsenal deployed by the Soviets during the negotiations. The French representatives were extremely skeptical. Even in the extraordinary event that French liability were admitted, the actual cost of damage by Western military action would remain in dispute. The amounts presented unilaterally by the Soviets would need to undergo a critical assessment, which would be difficult to undertake in practice.

The Soviet Union's Repayment Capacity

Alongside the issue of debt recognition was the question of Russia's ability to pay. Even before the repudiation was announced, sentiment was predominantly positive about the country's long-term economic potential but extremely negative about its short-term capabilities.[127] Financial incapability was one of the first reasons cited by the Bolsheviks to justify the default. Already at the end of February 1918 the Russian ambassador to Paris had declared that the "maximalists" were "absolutely unable, for want of resources, to service the debt."[128] Assessing the situation as the war drew to a close, Stéphen Pichon noted that the annuity due by Russia had tripled in relation to the prewar situation because of the numerous advances made by the Allies during the war.[129] At the same time, the country suffered mass destruction of its industrial infrastructure, especially in Ukraine. In October 1918 the resumption of coupon payments by a Russia eager to recognize its debts seemed conceivable in the medium term at best. Given the general conditions in Russia, the French foreign minister considered that recognition alone was insufficient and that macroeconomic and tax measures would also be needed to restore the country's economy.[130] Skepticism about Russia's capacity to meet its liabilities was shared by the historian Jacques Bainville, an Action Française sympathizer who in a book on postwar financial investments wrote, "Under the most favorable hypothesis, regular servicing of the Russian debt will not resume for a long time, if ever" (Bainville 1919, 81).

The British press was scarcely any more enthusiastic about Russia's ability to cover its short-term needs.[131] The repayment capacity of the Russian state was still considered severely diminished in May 1920, a situation reflected on the market by a preference for Russian industrial bonds.[132] The reports submitted to the Genoa Conference by the Russian Financial, Industrial and Trade Association and the Committee of Representatives of Russian Banks in Paris, both fiercely opposed to Socialist experiments, described the situation in Russia as disastrous. In their opinion the country's economic and financial conditions ruled out any resumption of public debt service. The outlook had changed little by 1924, when repayment capacity was still divided into the short term and the long term, and Russia was seen as a country with considerable potential, especially because of its geological resources.[133] Paslovsky and Moulton (1924) nevertheless thought that Russia would be able to meet its liabilities only if it first received loans enabling it to rebuild its economy. Less optimistic than many of their contemporaries, Paslovsky and Moulton in their analysis hinted at an extremely lengthy process before repayment could be assured.

It would have been hard for Western countries to paint a picture other than one that distinguished between short term and long term. Assessing the current situation as satisfactory would have amounted to acknowledging that the Soviet experiment was a success. On the other hand, too much emphasis on the Soviet Union's inability to pay was likely to legitimize a future default. The associations of Russian bondholders saw the problem from another angle. According to Luboff, relative to the country's population, the amount of Russian debt was extremely low. Russia's per capita debt was actually lower than that of any industrialized nation.[134] That measure, which evades any assessment of the country's state of economic development, is open to much criticism, and even at the time of Luboff's claim it was not used in the apportionment of debt between countries. In the late 1920s the Soviet government made several announcements about the healthy state of its economy. Basing his position on official Soviet reports that spoke in particular of a large budget surplus in 1929, Luboff said that Russia was perfectly able to meet its obligations and that measures to alleviate the debt were unwarranted.[135]

AFTER DE MONZIE

Despite the breakdown of negotiations between the Soviet Union and the de Monzie commission, French investors refused to abandon hope of repayment. Detailing all of the negotiations that followed this failure is outside the scope of this volume. Readers who are interested in developments in Franco–Soviet relations in the late 1920s can refer to Carley and Debo (1997). Only a few salient moments, mainly cited in Freymond (1996, 2002) and Bayle (1997), will therefore be presented here.

The final deadlock in de Monzie's endeavors to reach an agreement with the Soviets did not snuff out French investors' hopes. Their claims were taken up on a regular basis by various political groupings. Bayle (1997, 81) notes that in May 1933, Charles Baron, an SFIO (the French Section of the Workers' International) member of parliament, blamed the French government for the failure of the negotiations. His speech to parliament immediately attracted sharp criticism from the French right. In August 1933 the negotiations ahead of a Franco–Soviet trade agreement mentioned the need to resolve in the near future all the outstanding economic and financial issues between the parties (Bayle 1997, 82). Although the settlement of the disputes never went beyond intentions, this did not prevent a trade agreement from being signed in January 1934.

After the Second World War the Russian bond segment of the Paris Bourse saw periods of excitement. Freymond (1996, 99) refers to major price fluctuations in the 1950s. The fate of the Russian bondholders in France returned to the fore in March 1954, with a settlement proposal demanding the resumption of negotiations with the Soviet Union to reach an agreement (Bayle 1997, 84). A year later a new bondholders' group, the Association des Porteurs de Titres Russes, was established by Marcel Grizey and Elie Charnoz (Freymond 1996, 100; Bayle 1997, 86). The association lobbied members of parliament, thereby probably maintaining interest in the issue but failing to secure the hoped-for repayment. An indirect effect may have been the buyback of defaulted bonds at low prices on the market by the Communist Party on behalf of the Soviet Union. Rumors about this circulated at the time (Freymond 1996, 102). Speeches and bills in parliament kept the debate alive in the 1960s. Market prices for Russian bonds would sometimes spike in response, only to fall again subsequently. Political lobbying continued into the 1980s, but the French government did not manage to obtain any results from its Soviet counterpart.

Military Intervention and the Impact of War Events

Hopes for "White" Repayment

W ars can have a significant impact on sovereign bond prices. The literature deals with two aspects of the relationship between military intervention and debt. One part of the literature looks at the role of military intervention in forcing defaulting states to honor their obligations. Put simply, does sending troops or threatening to do so expedite repayment of defaulted sovereign debt? The other part of the literature examines the impact of war events on market prices for sovereign debt. Both issues are relevant here because of foreign military intervention in Russia and because Russia was involved in a civil war until 1921. Since almost all of the White governments had pledged to repay the Russian debt, the outcome of these conflicts must have been of interest to French investors. After a brief literature review, I describe here developments in the Russian civil war and the impact of various war events on prices for Russian bonds, as perceived by the press and market participants. I shall then outline the position of the White armies and their governments on debt repayment.

Military Threats, Conflicts, and Sovereign Bond Prices

The decision to intervene militarily to force a country to repay debt held by its nationals is a matter of international law. It is also a political decision, however, and may therefore be influenced by domestic concerns and geostrategic motives. In the nineteenth century most military interventions were directed at small countries, while the largest countries were mostly left alone. Independently of the decision to intervene, investors were interested in the efficacy of such a measure. In the next section I describe several historical examples of intervention and then discuss more recent analyses that seek to determine whether intervention—or the threat of it—is effective.

DEFAULT AND MILITARY INTERVENTION

The legitimacy of military intervention to force a defaulting state to honor its debts is mentioned in writings dating back to the seventeenth and eighteenth centuries. According to Borchard (1913, 9), legal theorists such as Hugo Grotius and Emer de Vattel considered intervention in such cases to be legitimate if all other avenues had been exhausted. In practice, the actions of creditor governments in relation to a defaulting state have varied considerably depending on the defaulter, and they have been inconsistent over time. The default of some American states raised fears that Britain would intervene militarily because it was home to most of the bondholders (English 1996), but those fears proved unfounded.[1] A few years later, in 1861, Spain, France, and the United Kingdom decided to intervene militarily in Mexico when that country defaulted. Five years later Britain refused to intervene in Venezuela in a similar case (Borchard 1951 [2000], 242) but then did intervene in Egypt in 1880. Default therefore does not seem to be an automatic trigger for intervention, an act which is decided in a broader political context.

Despite some examples to the contrary, continental European nations generally seem to have been more eager to intervene militarily than the United Kingdom and the United States. In the latter two countries, the fact that their citizens voluntarily and knowingly entered into a contractual relationship with a foreign government has usually been considered enough to discharge their governments of any liability (Borchard 1913, 10–12). In the nineteenth and early twentieth centuries several European countries used force on a number of occasions to scare small Latin American countries into repaying their debts (Borchard

1951 [2000], 269). Military threats or actual intervention influenced negotiations with Guatemala, Haiti, Nicaragua, Saint-Domingue, and Venezuela between 1890 and 1925. The most striking example seems to have been the intervention against Venezuela in 1902–3.

For almost two years (1898–1900) Venezuela was in the throes of a revolution that resulted in substantial losses for citizens of several Western nations and in a default on its foreign debt. In 1902 British holders of Venezuelan bonds unsuccessfully petitioned the local government to negotiate a solution (Mitchener and Weidenmier 2005). Given the Venezuelan government's unwillingness to cooperate, Britain, Germany, and Italy imposed a naval blockade on two cities, then seized the customs service in December 1902. Germany went as far as bombarding Fort San Carlos. These actions paid off, as the Venezuelan president, Cipriano Castro, agreed to sit down at the negotiating table to discuss terms for repayment of the debt. The Permanent Court of Arbitration in The Hague eventually settled the dispute and awarded the blockading nations the right to preferential treatment amounting to 30 percent of their claims. Claims from nations that did not intervene were deemed subordinate.

The use of force to expedite repayment was increasingly criticized. Taking the view that investors are aware of the risks when they purchase bonds issued by foreign states and demand remuneration proportional to that risk, some commentators found it illogical to engage in military conflict simply in response to default. Drawing on this argument, in 1902 Argentina's foreign minister, Luis María Drago, wrote a doctrine that has since been named after him. The Drago Doctrine stated that default on public debt by an American nation cannot be grounds for armed intervention or occupation of part of its territory by the United States or Europe (Borchard 1913, 37). In the early twentieth century most lawyers shared this opinion and, in general, considered the use of force unjustified in cases of sovereign default (Borchard 1913, 40). This position suffered from a major exception, however: if the defaulting country refuses in bad faith to pay, then intervention can be justified. In short, lawyers at the time seem to have made a distinction between inability and unwillingness to pay.

EFFICACY OF MILITARY INTERVENTION

What exactly does the efficacy of military intervention mean? Bondholders will perceive intervention as effectual if it results in the recognition of their claims. However, an effectual operation for bondholders may be viewed negatively by the intervening government if, for example, the military or diplomatic costs exceed the material benefits for some of its citizens.

In several cases (Tunisia in 1868, Egypt in 1880, and Greece in 1897) military intervention led to the takeover of some of the defaulting country's tax administration (Borchard 1913, 42). According to Eichengreen and Portes (1989), military intervention was infrequently used to recover debts in the nineteenth century and became rare by the 1930s. The authors argue that intervention primarily pursued military or strategic aims. Tomz (2007) considers that, given the military balance of power between some creditor and debtor countries, the threat of military intervention could not be regarded as credible. Conversely, Mitchener and Weidenmier (2005, 2010) demonstrate convincingly that the threat of military action could alter the position of debtor countries.

Rather than looking only at military operations actually engaged in to force defaulting countries to repay their debt, Mitchener and Weidenmier (2005) analyze the impact of the threat of intervention on market prices for that debt. Their study is based on the announcement effect of the Roosevelt Corollary to the Monroe Doctrine, which stipulates that the United States reserves the right to intervene to ensure that defaulted debt of Central American and Caribbean nations is repaid. The study shows that in the year after the Roosevelt Corollary was proclaimed, prices for bonds issued by the countries concerned rose by an average 74 percent, an increase that was not observed for other sovereign debt. Mitchener and Weidenmier (2005) consequently attribute this sharp rise to the credibility of the American threat.[2] The importance and the complexity of the impact of military interventions on sovereign bonds are illustrated by the French situation after Waterloo. Oosterlinck, Ureche-Rangau, and Vaslin (2014) show that British bankers were ready to lend to France because they viewed their loan as guaranteed by the troops present on French soil. When the troops departed in 1818, the price of French sovereign bonds nosedived!

Mitchener and Weidenmier (2010) look at how supersanctions such as military intervention, takeover of tax collection, seizure of collateral by private creditors, and trade sanctions affected repayment during the gold standard period (1870–1913). On the basis of defaults and supersanctions observed during that period, the authors show the importance of the latter, which were applied in almost 42 percent of cases of default. It is therefore possible that the threat of both military sanctions and supersanctions played a role in the pricing of Russian bonds.

IMPACT OF WAR EVENTS ON MARKET PRICES

The threat of military intervention probably influenced the position of several debtor countries during the gold standard period. Moreover, aside from military intervention aimed specifically at achieving repayment, any conflict should intuitively have an impact on market prices for debt issued by the warring parties.

The announcement of a war tends to have a negative impact on market prices for the bonds of the warring parties. This effect can be attributed to concerns about the cost and financing of the conflict. Note, however, that bond prices do not fall in cases where investors are required or strongly encouraged to buy bonds, as was the case in Belgium, France, and the Netherlands during the Second World War.[3] Within the general trend observed during the war, several studies have attempted to understand the impact on bond prices of specific news from the front. In an efficient market, the impact of an event, in wartime or not, depends on its announcement. Several econometric studies have shown that some events now recognized as key had a strong impact on prices but also that some battles, seen in hindsight as less important by historians, were considered important when they occurred.[4]

In the Russian case, additional factors indicate why the announcement of war events would have triggered significant reactions. In international wars, reactions stem from fears, either about the duration of the conflict or about its outcome and hence the country's solvency. In a civil war the outcome is particularly important insofar as the ultimate victory of one party is likely to result in repudiation of the debt issued by the opposing party, as happened during the American Civil War (Oosterlinck and Weidenmier 2007) and also during the Chinese civil war (Mitchener, Oosterlinck, Weidenmier, and Haber 2015). A civil war also excludes the possibility of demanding reparations from the defeated party. Finally, in a civil war any worsening or extension of the conflict erodes the resources available for repayment, since war damage affects the country's productive base.

Before examining the positions of the representatives of the various armies opposed to the Bolsheviks, I want to outline the war events that influenced the prices of Russian bonds listed in Paris. Since news from the Russian front sometimes took a long time to reach France, the market's reactions, when there were any, did not coincide with the actual dates of victories or defeats. The analysis therefore needs to take into account not the date of the battle but the date of its announcement in Paris.

Civil War and Allied Intervention (1917–1921)

The Bolsheviks' military position clearly influenced prices of Russian bonds, as a defeat would probably have resulted in cancellation of the repudiation. The Russian Civil War involved numerous armed groups above and beyond the traditional divide between Whites and Bolsheviks. However, I focus here exclusively on those two groups and will not refer to other participants—the Green Army, anarchists, local liberation movements, and so on—unless their actions might have influenced the perceptions of French investors. Meanwhile, special attention will be paid to action announced or undertaken by Allied troops in Russia, to which the Paris Bourse was also highly responsive. The belief that foreign troops would be more efficient at toppling the Bolshevik regime appears to have persisted for a long time.

The events of the Russian Civil War until the final defeat of the White armies have been analyzed by many authors. Pipes (1995) maintains that, in hindsight, the White armies did not stand a chance given the mismatch of forces and resources. At the outset of the war, however, the Bolsheviks' final victory seemed far from certain. The Soviet victory has been attributed variously to a lack of coordination between the White armies, the divergent interests of the various counterrevolutionary armed groups, the enormous human and material resources at the Bolsheviks' disposal, and military inefficiency on the part of the White generals. I do not suggest any new ideas in this regard. Instead I shall concentrate on changing perceptions in France of the military situation in Russia. The periodization used here, based on Pipes (1995, 7), is divided into three phases: the initial phase from the revolution to the Armistice, the decisive phase from March to November 1919, and the final phase in 1920.

Initial Phase (1917–1918)

The Russian Civil War involved large numbers of actors on three main fronts: a southern front (the Volunteer Army and the Southern Army), a northern front (led by Gen. Nicolai Yudenich) and a Siberian front (led by Adm. Alexander Kolchak). Chronologically, the first armed opposition movements were formed in the south of the country. Pipes (1995, 15) attributes the emergence of White armies to the frustration of army commanders who felt dishonored by the Bolsheviks' withdrawal from the First World War and therefore by the "betrayal" of the promise to the Allies. One of the principal White military forces, the Volunteer Army led by Gen. Mikhail Alekseev, emerged in this context. The movement was soon joined by a number of officers and generals, such as Lavr Kornilov, who refused to back the Bolshevik regime.

The Paris Bourse initially expressed confidence in Kornilov's and Kerensky's ability to restore order and subsequently in General Alekseev.[5] Rumors of the death of various Bolshevik leaders circulated on the Paris market for several years, boosting prices for Russian bonds. On 6 December 1917 it was rumored that Lenin and Trotsky had been assassinated.[6] From December 1917 on, the market expected the Allied nations to assist Kerensky and Kornilov. The Japanese landing in Vladivostok, the Chinese intervention in Harbin, and a possible Romanian intervention were cited in this context.[7] Japan's intervention in Siberia sparked lengthy debates, particularly with the United States, which distrusted it (Carley 1976). Despite these divergences, the Allied interventions fostered renewed confidence in Russian securities.

The reasons for the Allied military intervention in Russia have been the subject of a long-running debate (Carley 1976). The need to reopen the eastern front has long been posited as the main motivation. Furthermore, every country involved also had its own reasons for becoming militarily involved.

Hogenhuis-Seliverstoff (1981, 42) maintains that the settlement of debts was initially only a minor consideration for France. Not all contemporary observers shared that view, however. US Secretary of State Robert Lansing appears to have questioned the real motives of the French, as he thought their support for the Japanese intervention was a way to achieve debt repayment (Hogenhuis-Seliverstoff 1981, 62). The reasons for France's intervention in Russia therefore seem to have been complex. Moreover, France's support of the White armies was far from immediate. In early 1918 the French generals in Russia had a low opinion of their Russian counterparts, doubting their ability to overthrow the Bolshevik regime. In Paris, support for a policy of accommodation with the Soviets soon emerged (Carley 1976). Opposed to this idea as early as March 1918, the French ambassador to Russia, Joseph Noulens, proposed a forceful interventionist policy. This position, shared by Gen. Henri Berthelot, the commander of the French military mission in Romania, eventually prevailed in April 1918. Protecting French economic interests in Russia therefore also played a role in the decision to intervene.

Britain's intervention in Russia until November 1918 was part of the First World War. Once the Armistice was signed, however, the underlying motives became less clear. Leading statesmen advocated a very different policy. Prime Minister Lloyd George held that the end of the war meant the withdrawal of British troops. But Winston Churchill, vehemently anti-Bolshevik, was in favor of increasing the British presence. Leaving aside the nature of the Bolshevik regime, the Russian revolution gave Britain a free hand in the Middle East. There seems to have been no clear policy behind the American intervention, which was mainly passive. Japan made no secret of its territorial ambitions in the Far East, which justified its intervention (Pipes 1995, 65).

The Russian case presents a crucial difference from other instances of military action taken after a default. The aim of armed intervention is usually to force the government in power to agree to repay its debts. The

Allied intervention in Russia, by contrast, seems to have been aimed not at convincing the Bolsheviks to change their position but at overthrowing the government in order to replace it with a more accommodating one. Hogenhuis-Seliverstoff (1981, 42) assert that the French placed their hopes of repayment in the counterrevolutionary movements. In the first few hours after the repudiation, the Bolsheviks considered, then dismissed, the possibility of Allied intervention. In an article published in *Novaia Zhizn'* on 23 November 1917 Yuri Larin wrote "They [England, Germany, and France] will not go to war against Russia solely because we have cancelled the foreign debt" (Noulens 1933, 1:150). Larin would soon be proved wrong by actual events, however. The option of intervening militarily to recoup the debt would enjoy support for a long time. As late as 1920 Faure (1920) maintained that war, beginning with the bombardment of various cities, could force the Bolsheviks to repay.

The anti-Bolshevik movements began to get organized in January 1918. The Volunteer Army was placed under the command of Kornilov, with Alexeev in charge of political and financial aspects. The destiny of the Volunteer Army was closely linked to the Cossack troops, who hailed from the territories where the army was founded (Pipes 1995, 18). Although opposed to the Bolshevik regime, the Cossacks had their own agenda, which was to protect their homelands rather than to defend the rest of Russia.

Although there were no major battles, the Western press in early January 1918 did not expect the Bolshevik government to remain in power for long. That view held sway in New York, London, and Paris.[8] On 17 January 1918 the *Financial Times* reported only a slight decline in prices for Russian bonds owing to the fact that market participants believed the Bolshevik regime was unlikely to survive.[9] Some investors on the Paris Bourse placed their hopes in military action commanded by Grand Duke Nikolai Nikolaevich, who was thought to be in the Caucasus.[10] More broadly, in early 1918 many investors saw the Bolshevik takeover as a temporary episode in Russia's tumultuous political life, one which would come to an end sooner or later when order was restored in Russia.[11]

The White armies did not face the Bolsheviks alone for long. Keen to reopen the eastern front, the French government made contact with

Czech troops stationed in Siberia. Those soldiers were originally part of the Austro-Hungarian army but chose to defect when the Allies promised to back the creation of an independent Czech state. This led to the formation of a Czechoslovak Legion incorporated into the French army. Given these developments, it must have seemed logical to redeploy the troops stationed in Siberia to support France's war effort in the west. An agreement with the Russian troops would guarantee them safe passage to Vladivostok on the condition that they disarmed first (Mourin 1967, 80–81). Refusing to disarm, some of the Czech soldiers clashed with Bolshevik troops in May 1918. According to Pipes (1994), the Czechs were the only competent combat unit on the eastern front between May and October 1918. The quality of these troops undoubtedly explains why the British government opportunistically decided, after the clashes between Czech and Red soldiers, to use the Czechs to mount an attack against the Bolshevik government. Given this change in target, the Czechs marched westward and took control of a vast swathe of territory along the Trans-Siberian railway line.

The Allied intervention in Russia took place in several stages. While the First World War raged on, the Allies sent troops to Russia chiefly to fight the Germans. The British dispatched soldiers to Murmansk in March 1918 (Werth 2004, 149). Shortly afterward, the Supreme War Council in London approved the assignment of Japanese troops to Russia, where they set up a base in Vladivostok in April 1918 (Mourin 1967, 89). In June 1918 French investors seemed convinced that the Japanese would intervene in Siberia, with American support.[12] In fact, the Japanese intervention was met with alarm rather than endorsement in the United States.[13] Nevertheless, according to market watchers, those expectations precipitated a sharp rise in Russian bond prices. Although the Japanese intervention was considered relatively unimportant in itself, in July 1918 investors came to the conclusion that Japan would not have intervened unless it believed in the overthrow of the Bolsheviks.[14] In June 1918 the Bourse thus rated the Bolshevik government's chances of survival as extremely slim.[15] In late June 1918 French and British forces landed in Murmansk (Mourin 1967, 85) and soon secured a larger area, which included Arkhangelsk. By the summer of 1918 Allied troops seemed to have established a firm foothold in Russia.

In the south the fortunes of the White armies, which in April 1918 had suffered heavy losses, including that of their charismatic leader General Kornilov, improved considerably. Gen. Anton Denikin, Kornilov's successor, launched a major offensive in May 1918. While some of the military command was in favor of attacking Tsaritsyn to link up with the eastern troops, Denikin decided to concentrate on Kuban in the south in order to wipe out the enemy troops to his rear (Pipes 1995, 35).[16] Although outnumbered, Denikin's forces won a string of victories that led to the capture of Krasnodar (Ekaterinodar at the time) on 15 August and Novorossiisk on 26 August. These victories made the Bolsheviks' position seem so uncertain that the first communiqué from the General Commission for the Protection of French Interests in Russia told investors not to attach too much importance to the repudiation because "the Soviet government has established only precarious authority over a part of Russia."[17] The same view prevailed on the Bourse, encouraging investors to purchase Russian bonds.[18] That mood can probably be ascribed to General Denikin's successes in Kuban between June and September 1918. By the end of that campaign, according to Pipes (1994, 36), the Volunteer Army seemed stronger than ever.

In September 1918 *La Revue des Valeurs russes* also predicted the demise of the Bolshevik government under the combined effects of an internal revolt and Allied military action in Siberia.[19] The enthusiasm of the press can be attributed to the arrival of an American expeditionary corps in August 1918. The market's optimism seems exaggerated in light of the small numbers of Allied soldiers actually on the ground in Russia. Given the military situation on the western front at the end of summer 1918, the Allied governments were hardly eager to sacrifice troops to take control of more territory or to overthrow the Bolsheviks (Mourin 1967, 88). However, coordinated Allied action was considered, especially after the appointment of the French general Maurice Janin as commander of all the Allied troops in Russia. The French government expected Janin to quickly link up the forces in Siberia with those active in southern Russia.

The action of the Russian factions opposed to the Bolsheviks changed General Janin's role. The State Conference, bringing together all the anti-Bolshevik Siberian governments, met in Ufa from 8 to 15 September 1918. The meeting led to the formation of the Ufa Directory, based in Omsk, on 22 September.[20] Consisting of members of the Socialist-Revolutionary Party as well as career soldiers such as Admiral Kolchak, the directory (also named the Provisional All-Russian Government) was recognized by the Allied governments (Mourin 1967, 94). During this period the White armies enjoyed several military successes, but dissension soon emerged among their generals. Relations between Kolchak and Janin were also fraught, and tensions between them increased when Kolchak proclaimed himself supreme ruler on 19 November 1918, scuttling the already fragile authority of the directory. There have been many interpretations of Kolchak's takeover. Britain soon showed its support for him by supplying substantial military aid, which made Janin even more suspicious of the admiral, whom he saw as a British puppet.

The Armistice radically changed the situation in Russia. Many troops that had been deployed during the First World War questioned why they were still stationed in Siberia. The creation of a Czech state obviated the Czech Legion's presence on Russian soil (Mourin 1967, 95). At the French government's request, the Czech troops delayed their departure in order to guard the line of communications along the Trans-Siberian between Omsk and Irkutsk. However, their attitude became essentially defensive (Pipes 1994, 33). Strong opposition to keeping troops in Russia was manifested in several other European countries. That sentiment soon spread to the soldiers themselves since those who had survived the war were hardly willing to risk their lives in Russia (Thomson 1966, 12–13).

Despite increasingly fierce opposition to pursuing any intervention, there were rumors at the end of 1918 that each Allied nation would contribute fifty thousand men to an expedition to Russia. These rumors rekindled interest in Russian bonds, a mood that immediately subsided when the United Kingdom denied any expedition on that scale was in the cards.[21] Rumors and conflicting news about armed intervention frequently circulated on the Bourse. In December 1918 France sent troops to Russia to prevent the spread of Bolshevism. They were quickly stationed near Odessa. Concurrently, the Royal Navy fought to secure Baku and assumed control of the Caspian Sea, while other British ships blockaded the eastern Baltic (Pipes 1995, 73). In January 1919 a British battalion was sent to Omsk to reinforce Admiral Kolchak. Many Bolshevik leaders saw these moves as the beginnings of a larger-scale military action. The succession of announcements caused confusion on the Bourse as positive news stories were often followed by negative ones. For example, contemporary commentaries reported that on 7 January 1919 forty thousand Frenchmen volunteered for the expedition to Russia, but the next day a severe Allied defeat near Arkhangelsk was announced.[22]

THE DECISIVE PHASE (MARCH–NOVEMBER 1919)

The successes of General Denikin in Kuban encouraged the Bolshevik government to radically adjust its troop numbers and create a regular army. Severely disadvantaged by a lack of officers, the Soviet leaders reconciled themselves to enlisting former officers from the imperial army. To ensure their loyalty Trotsky introduced a system of hostage taking (Werth 2004, 151). He eventually succeeded in overhauling the Bolshevik defenses and creating an army worthy of the name. The introduction of conscription supplied a sufficient number of soldiers to fight the White armies.

The fate of the counterrevolutionary movements was decided in the space of a few months from spring to autumn 1919. In March 1919 Kolchak launched a major offensive in the east aimed chiefly at joining up with the Allied armies stationed in Arkhangelsk, conquering the cities of Ufa and Kazan, and taking control of Samara and Saratov and thereby unite with the White troops in southern Russia while isolating the Red forces in Central Asia (Pipes 1995, 77). At first Kolchak's advance was spectacular. Within a few weeks, by mid-April, the front line had been pushed back more than six hundred kilometers, an area of almost three hundred thousand square kilometers was under his control, and the Volga lay less than one hundred kilometers away.

The announcement of positive news from the Russian front in late April 1919 had an impact not only on Russian bonds but also on the market in general. The Paris prefect's agent at the Bourse reported, "The news from the Romanian and Polish fronts has been met with enthusiasm. The market believes Russian Bolshevism has been exterminated and it is expecting the front to collapse, from Arkhangelsk to the Black

Sea."[23] Rumors of total victory and Bolshevik despair spread like wildfire for several days and included some highly fanciful variants. It was rumored, for example, that the Bolsheviks were so desperate they had reopened negotiations on repayment with France; that Lenin had fled to Budapest with 15 million rubles and no hope of ever returning to Russia; that the Bolsheviks had evacuated Petrograd.[24] The role of the Allies in the successes in Russia also aroused considerable interest. The real impact of the Allied troops in the fighting with the Bolsheviks should not be exaggerated, however. Foreign troops were, in fact, only sporadically involved in the fighting, and skirmishes strongly undermined the morale of the French detachment in southern Russia. Faced with threats of mutiny, the French government preferred to withdraw its troops and ordered the evacuation of Odessa in early April 1919. The withdrawal coincided with expectations of British action on the Murmansk Coast.[25] The Bourse then saw that intervention as the decisive factor that would produce a favorable outcome.[26] Russian bond prices in Britain were also influenced by military news. At the beginning of May the announcement of the first Bolshevik setbacks and the hope that the regime would be short-lived pushed up Russian bond prices.[27] The prospect that Petrograd would be evacuated in late May 1919 renewed interest in Russian bonds, as the market thought a defeat there would force the Bolsheviks to revise their position.[28]

Kolchak's advance eventually elicited a forceful reaction from the Bolshevik leaders, who concentrated their forces on eliminating him. As Kolchak continued to advance, probably hoping to be the first to reach Moscow, he chose not to link up with the southern Russian armies before pushing on to the capital. The decision was strongly criticized subsequently because it enabled the Red forces to fight the White armies one after the other instead of having to face them together. From the beginning of June 1919 the Red forces fighting Kolchak began to enjoy the advantage of superior numbers, which swelled as the conflict progressed (Pipes 1995, 78). On 9 June 1919 the Bolsheviks retook Ufa after bitter fighting. By the end of June the Bolsheviks had crossed the Urals. Kolchak's troops held out from mid-August until mid-October but never managed to regain the offensive. The withdrawal of Admiral Kolchak from the Volga in June 1919 had a negative impact on market prices for

Russian securities listed in London.[29] The market rapidly switched its attention to the other front and the armies commanded by Denikin.

While June 1919 was synonymous with retreat for Kolchak, a major offensive was launched in southern Russia that month. The assignment of Red troops to combat Kolchak facilitated the advance of Denikin's forces. On 21 June 1919 Kharkov was taken, and on 30 June 1919 Volgograd fell to Gen. Pyotr Wrangel's army (Pipes 1995, 82). Once Tsaritsyn had fallen, Wrangel and Denikin disagreed on whether operations should continue. Wrangel thought the forces should be concentrated on taking Saratov, whereas Denikin had a more ambitious plan to significantly broaden the front (Wrangel 1930, 118). Denikin's choice prevailed but has been much criticized since. His defeat is attributed to having insufficient troops to maintain such a broad front. The initial attacks, however, proved Denikin right by enabling him to enlarge the area under his control in August and September 1919. On 7 October 1919 Denikin's army reached the city of Orel, less than three hundred kilometers from Moscow. Denikin's military successes in September and October 1919 pushed Russian bond prices up in London as rumors circulated about a Bolshevik demand for an armistice.[30] That price rise offset the decline that followed the announcement of the withdrawal of British troops from northern Russia.[31] The withdrawal, paradoxically just as the Russian troops were advancing, can be explained by the extremely negative impact of Kolchak's retreat in the east, which many observers felt heralded the inevitable defeat of the White armies.

As Denikin moved ever closer to Moscow, another White attack was mounted in the north. On 11 October 1919 General Yudenich launched a major offensive from the Baltics to retake Petrograd. His troops advanced swiftly, reaching the outskirts of the city by 16 October 1919. In response to these developments, Lenin prepared to evacuate the city. Opposing evacuation, Trotsky went to the front in person to galvanize the troops. His presence and actions boosted the morale of the Red soldiers, who, given their superior numbers, eventually repulsed Yudenich's offensive. Hopes of taking Petrograd had evaporated by the end of October. Yudenich's army was forced to retreat to Estonia, where it was demobilized. Despite the ultimate failure of the offensive, the announcement of the initial successes near Petrograd was followed in Paris by a rise in market prices for Russian bonds.[32] When Yudenich's armies suffered their first reverses, prices fell.[33]

Further south, Denikin's advance was halted. On 24 October 1919 Voronezh fell to the Red forces, and the southern White armies began a general retreat. At the same time Lloyd George announced the end of Britain's intervention in Russia (Pipes 1995, 128). On 17 November Kursk was evacuated, followed by withdrawals at Kharkov and Kiev in mid-December. Denikin had asked Wrangel to resume command of the Volunteer Army in late November. In December 1919 Wrangel was forced to observe that the army no longer existed (Wrangel 1930, 115–22). In the meantime Kolchak's army had also been practically wiped off the map. Omsk was evacuated on 14 November without fighting, and Kolchak retreated to Irkutsk, where he was deposed. On 14 January 1920 Kolchak was handed over to the Red armies, who executed him after a sham trial on 6 February 1920.

THE FINAL PHASE (1920–1921)

To contemporary observers the White armies' ultimate defeat seemed certain at the beginning of 1920. Yudenich's offensive had been driven back in the north, Kolchak had been executed in Siberia, and Denikin's southern army was in tatters and had evacuated Odessa in disastrous conditions. It was therefore only logical that in March 1920, peace with Russia was seen as certain on the Paris Bourse.[34] Despite the pitiful state of the White forces, there were still critical moments in the civil war in 1920.

The routing of the White armies in the south finally convinced the Allied governments that there was no point in continuing to back them. Strongly criticized for his management of events, Denikin was forced to give up his post. Supported by the other officers, Wrangel agreed to take command of the White armies on 4 April 1920 (Wrangel 1930, 155). He soon managed to restore discipline and, unlike his predecessors, created a credible government made up of competent people. Despite those qualities, the longevity of Wrangel's command in Crimea can be attributed solely to the fact that large numbers of Soviet troops were diverted to a new front at the start of the Russo–Polish War.

The Poles had been in conflict with the Russians since the start of the revolution, but full-scale war did not break out until 1920. The Russo–Polish War followed bilateral talks aimed at establishing a common border. Eager for peace, the Russian government offered Poland a more generous eastern border than the one proposed under the Versailles Treaty. The offer was nevertheless rejected by the Polish prime minister, Jozef Pilsudski, who had set his sights on restoring the country to its former glory by rebuilding a "greater Poland." Polish troops entered Ukraine in April 1920. Advancing at an unexpectedly rapid pace, they captured Kiev at the end of April (Pipes 1995, 133). The announcement of the outbreak of war between Poland and Russia was met with enthusiasm on the Paris Bourse. The first Polish successes revived hopes that the Bolshevik government would be ousted.[35]

The Polish advance was welcomed in France because it offered Wrangel an opportunity to mount a counteroffensive in the south. In early June 1920 he was able to take control of the territories north of the Azov Sea, notably the city of Melitopol (Wrangel 1930, 204). Those initial actions under Wrangel's command raised fresh hopes, as his chances of success were perceived as being good in early 1920.[36] In fact, those chances depended chiefly on the outcome of the Russo–Polish War. The Polish front began to collapse in mid-June, and Kiev was evacuated on 17 June (Werth 1994, 168). From then on, the Red forces made rapid progress against the Poles and invaded Poland at the end of July. Meanwhile, in southern Russia Wrangel launched an expedition in Kuban in July–August 1920. Those actions boosted the Russian bond segment. The Bourse remained confident in the White armies under Wrangel's command and thought they would receive Hungarian and Romanian support.[37] France's recognition of Wrangel's government on 11 August 1920 was undoubtedly also seen as crucial (Sack 1927).

On the Polish front, the advance of the Red armies seemed unstoppable. In addition to their military strength, the Bolshevik leaders were counting on the outbreak of a Socialist revolution in Poland and possibly even in Germany. In the end a different popular movement prevailed and, in an upsurge of patriotism, the Russian invasion was repelled at the gates of Warsaw after fierce fighting in mid-August. This brilliant, unexpected counterattack of 16 August 1920 became known as "the

Miracle on the Vistula" (Fiddick 1973). On 22 August Wrangel became aware of the Polish army's success, as his Polish counterpart talked of the collapse "of the Bolshevist attack" (Wrangel 1930, 243). The victory, quickly followed by other battles that increased the advantage of the Poles, proved decisive to the future of Poland and led to a general withdrawal of Russian troops. In France the brilliant success of the Battle of Warsaw was attributed to the French general Maxime Weygand. An adviser to the Polish chiefs of staff, Weygand in reality played only a minor role in the conflict. His return was celebrated triumphantly in Paris on 28 August (Davies 1972, 221–22). Peace talks between Poland and Russia began in September 1920. Wrangel tried to convince his temporary Polish allies to keep fighting but failed to do so. The warring parties signed a peace treaty in Riga, Latvia, on 12 October 1920. The announcement of the Polish victories of August and September 1920 had a positive impact on Russian and Polish bonds, according to the agent at the Bourse.[38]

On the southern front Wrangel mounted a series of victorious offensives on the Dnieper in October. These triumphs prompted lively trading in Russian bonds on the Paris Bourse. In a burst of enthusiasm, *Le Rentier* exclaimed, "Our savers have invested too much capital in Russian state bonds and perpetual bonds to be abandoned without defense!" and recommended a resumption of Allied military intervention.[39] But the signing of the Russo–Polish peace left Wrangel no chance. On 20 October large numbers of Red troops were redeployed to take part in a major offensive in Crimea. Aware that defeat was inevitable, Wrangel prepared to evacuate his troops. On 14 November the last White troops left Russian soil in orderly fashion, but with no hope of ever returning (Wrangel 1930, 299–305). Although predictable in hindsight, Wrangel's defeat does not seem to have been anticipated by the markets since its announcement triggered a steep decline in prices for Russian bonds, especially industrial bonds.[40]

The French intervention in Russia and France's recognition of Wrangel's government were criticized at the end of 1920. Jacques Bonzon raised the issue of the cost of French support for Pilsudski, Wrangel, Yudenich, Kolchak, and Denikin.[41] In any case, it seems the French government permanently buried any hope of Wrangel's returning when in

December 1920 it set up a special section of the Commission on the Liquidation of the Russian Debt called Section for the Liquidation of Russian Assets Pertaining to the Account of General Wrangel.[42] At the end of December 1920 Ernest Lafont, a Communist member of parliament, challenged the government over the real cost and results of France's policy in Russia, particularly with regard to Wrangel.[43]

In March 1921, as the main White generals were finally succumbing to defeat, hope returned briefly during the Kronstadt rebellion, an uprising which began with the mutiny of the crews of two battleships. French financial circles viewed the event as noteworthy because the rebels were sailors from the fleet that had started the 1917 revolution.[44] The Bourse hoped still that their actions would lead to the end of Bolshevism.[45] Like the others, that hope would also prove to be vain.

The Positions of the White Army Leaders on the Debt

Notwithstanding the diversity of the movements claiming to represent Russia, most disagreed with the Bolshevik position on the debt. As Eisemann (2002) reports, the opponents to the Bolshevik regime disavowed the Bolsheviks' unilateral decision to repudiate the debt, if only to benefit from the creditor governments' support. Harboring disparate ambitions, the Russian governments opposed to the Bolsheviks failed to speak with one voice. Some groups wanted to restore the Russian empire within its original borders, others pressed for democratization, and still others campaigned only for the independence of a specific territory. In general the military commanders distanced themselves from political matters, even though a stronger commitment from them would undoubtedly have benefited their cause. As Pipes points out (1995, 14), most saw their duty as consisting solely in waging war. This explains the dearth of statements about the debt by White soldiers. Given the many governments, I will examine the political evolution of the main groups only and their position on the debt.

The Ufa and Omsk governments agreed to recognize the debts issued by the Russian government. That position was formally confirmed in several telegrams sent in early October 1918 from Omsk to Russia's diplomatic and financial representatives in Paris, London, and Washington (Sack 1927). Admiral Kolchak took a similar position. On 21 November 1918 he published a statement to the effect that, once a unified Russia had been restored, he would honor all the financial liabilities of the Russian treasury, including servicing and repaying the state's domestic and foreign debt (Sack 1927; Raffalovitch 1919, 152). He reasserted that stance on 28 November 1918 (Pipes 1994, 48). Still not completely reassured, the Allied governments asked for further confirmation in May 1919. This was given by Kolchak on 12 June 1919 (Szurek 2002).

Denikin also recognized the Russian liabilities in 1918 (Hogenhuis-Seliverstoff 1981, 82). The finance minister of the high command of the armed forces of southern Russia under the command of General Denikin, and then of General Wrangel, expressed the same willingness. A letter dated 13 July 1920 sent by the head of the diplomatic office of the commander in chief of the southern Russian armed forces to the French president, Alexandre Millerand, confirmed that Wrangel's government intended to honor Russia's international commitments.[46] General Wrangel's acceptance of responsibility for Russian debts of the former regime was symbolic at best. The Committee for the Defense of Belgian Interests in Russia was skeptical of the Wrangel government's ability to pay, given that "one million Wrangel rubles could be exchanged for 1,200 francs" at the time. At best, the committee saw Wrangel's declaration of recognition as "an act of courage and fundamental honesty."[47] In fact, the recognition was part of a broader context and was a precondition for France's recognition of the Wrangel government (Hogenhuis-Seliverstoff 1981, 181).

Despite the White armies' gestures of goodwill, repayment was far from assured. Even though the majority of White governments declared their opposition to the repudiation, the major risk for investors at the time was that repudiation would turn into default. While that development may have been seen as an improvement, it was nonetheless a qualified one. In reality, a French investor had next to no chance of recovering anything from Russia in the short term, no matter how small the amount, since repayment by a White government was dependent on a budget surplus.

Precisely how various governments in Russia were funded is hard to establish even now. As well as material, moral, and military aid, the

White armies received some financial support from the West.[48] Even some private investors were willing to risk lending money to the White governments. In October 1919, for example, the *New York Times* reported that a short-term loan of almost $40 million, backed by ingots and currencies deposited in Hong Kong, was extended to the Omsk government by a consortium consisting of Kidder, Peabody & Co., Guaranty Trust Company, and National City Bank.[49] The opacity of the situation in Russia was fertile ground for rumors, and there was frequent speculation about the payment capacity of the White governments. The fantasies of French investors eager to believe in White repayment were stoked by gold and other precious metals.

French investors' expectations were not groundless. While it is impossible to say whether the victorious White governments would have used gold to repay holders of Russian bonds, the existence of the gold does not seem to have been in doubt. Prior to the outbreak of the First World War, the Russian State Bank had increased its bullion reserves considerably. Estimated at almost 100 million pounds and kept in Petrograd, the gold was transferred to Kazan under the threat of the advance of German troops in autumn 1917 (Burdeau 2002). After several detours, the reserve came into the possession of the Omsk government, then, when that government was overthrown, fell into Kolchak's hands. The gold was providential for Kolchak at a time when his application to launch a bond issue on the Paris market had just been refused. "Kolchak's gold" experienced numerous vicissitudes. A fraction was used to purchase equipment. The fate of the gold after Kolchak's demise has given rise to many theories. Some believe the Czech Legion helped themselves to it after handing Kolchak over to the Bolsheviks in return for an amnesty. Other authors maintain that the gold remained in the hands of the Soviets. The murky fate of the gold enabled the Soviets to claim that it had been seized by the Allies, in order to demand a reduction in the size of the debt repayment (Burdeau 2002).

The White governments did honor some of Russia's foreign liabilities. Unable to meet all the obligations, however, they implemented a de facto selective default by endeavoring to maintain their credit rating with lenders perceived as vital. A 6.5 percent bond issued by the imperial government in 1916 for 50 million dollars had been placed by a consortium of American banks. In June 1919 Serge Ughet, chargé d'affaires ad interim and financial attaché at the Russian embassy, announced Russia's incapacity to repay the bond. By contrast, the coupons on another Russian bond, worth 25 million dollars, were paid on the due date of 1 June 1919.[50] It thus seems that the representatives of the Omsk government continued to honor some debt long after the Bolshevik repudiation. That decision may be linked to military orders by the Omsk government, most of which were with the United States. The Omsk government thus had a reason to honor its obligations toward that country for as long as possible. Shortly after the announcement of the default, the bankers who placed the issue met to discuss possible measures in favor of the creditors.[51]

A French Bailout?

The nationality of bondholders is rarely considered a relevant criterion for pricing sovereign debt. Yet history has shown that issuing governments do not always treat bondholders of different nationalities equally. Several Latin American countries entered selective default, which affected European countries without altering the defaulters' capacity to borrow from America (Esteves 2013). European countries have also demonstrated discriminatory behavior. Under the Treaty of Versailles, for example, Swiss, Dutch, Belgian, and French investors were treated more favorably than Americans (Eichengreen and Portes 1986). Erce and Diaz-Cassou (2011) show that eventually sovereigns often discriminate bondholders on the basis of their residency. While defaulting countries have adopted varying positions depending on the bondholders' country of origin, the governments of the bondholders have also responded very differently to the announcement of default.

Default and Governments' Responses to Citizens' Losses

As Borchard (1951 [2000], 239) observes, the attitudes of bondholders' governments range from total indifference to military intervention. In any event, the decision to intervene, diplomatically or otherwise, is guided primarily by political factors. According to Eichengreen and Portes (1989, 13), the French and German governments felt less compelled to remain neutral than their British counterparts did. Britain was instead radically opposed to bailing out its citizens, arguing that their imprudent investments ought not to be made good by public funds. Lord Palmerston, the future foreign minister, said, "British subjects who buy foreign bonds do so at their own risk and must abide the consequences" (English 1996, citing McGrane 1935). Toning down that rather harsh statement, however, Palmerston said in an 1848 circular that the government was entitled to take any action it deemed useful (Borchard 1951 [2000], 240). The view that the British government should not interfere with foreign sovereign borrowing was stressed again in 1906 by Edward Grey, the British foreign secretary (Siegel 2014, 106). What might the expectations of Russian bondholders be in light of France's response to previous defaults?

One of the most striking examples of intervention in France's past was the action taken in defense of French holders of Mexican bonds when these were repudiated by the republican government of Benito Juárez. Proclaiming Emperor Maximilian's rule illegitimate, Juárez announced the repudiation of the debt issued by him. In practice, however, the Juárez government repudiated only the 6 percent bonds issued by Maximilian in Paris in 1861 and in London in 1865 but agreed to service the 3 percent bond worth 4,864,800 pounds issued by him in 1864.[1] After the repudiation the French government decided to intervene to bail out French holders of the bonds. The Mexican bonds had been heavily subscribed in France, as investors were egged on by Emperor Napoleon III, who saw the issue as a means to support his ally in Mexico while furthering his own ambitions there.[2] The French budget of 2 August 1868 earmarked almost 4 million francs in 3 percent French perpetual bonds as well as more than 1.7 million pounds from the capital raised by the 1864 bond issue, for holders of Mexican bonds. Given the complexity of the matter, payment of the indemnity was difficult to arrange, and problems were still being reported in 1869.[3]

Although opposed in principle to a bailout by the bondholders' governments, Neymarck (1872, 9), who believed his position reflected the general sentiment, described the compensation offered to the holders of Mexican bonds as being far too small. In 1915 a small extra payment was added to the amounts already paid out to the French holders of Mexican bonds (Sack 1927). In the end the bondholders recovered almost 50 percent of the face value of their investment (Wynne 1951 [2000], 30). In France the Mexican precedent remained in people's minds for a long time. In June 1921 *Le Rentier* drew a parallel with the Mexican bailout by calling on the government to act in favor of bondholders, given its even greater involvement in the case of the Russian bonds.[4] It would be a mistake, however, to think that France always bailed out its investors. During the Cuban debt crisis of 1898, for example, France saw no reason to compensate French bondholders (Feilchenfeld 1931, 331).

In the case in point, France intervened on several occasions to assist either Russia or its own investors. The interventions were always limited, however, and consisted in advancing funds to Russia and making modest arrangements for French holders of Russian bonds.[5] France sent aid to Russia during the First World War; these advances were presented as the temporary bolstering of a war ally. The action to support French bondholders raised the issue of the French government's liability toward them.

French Interventions
AGREEMENT ON ADVANCES TO TSARIST RUSSIA

As shown above (see fig. 0.1), although yields on Russian bonds increased with the outbreak of the First World War, they did not suffer a dramatic rise until the events of February 1917. That can be attributed partly to French advances to Russia, which boosted Russian bonds during the war.

At the beginning of the war Russia appears to have been in a sufficiently strong financial position to cover the cost of the coupons on its bonds held in France (Barnett 2001).[6] Subsequently, however, in order to cover payment of the coupons, assist an ally, and avoid transfers of cash between Russia and France, two secret agreements were signed by the French finance minister, Alexandre Ribot, and his Russian counterpart, Piotr Bark, on 5 February and 4 October 1915.[7] The first agreement provided for advances of 500 million francs, and the second a monthly advance of 125 million francs for twelve months from the date of signing, mainly through the Banque de France.[8] According to Eliacheff (1919, 140), a third agreement, signed in 1916, stipulated that France would continue to pay advances for the duration of the war, with no mention of a ceiling. Parliamentary speeches in early 1918 do not refer to the agreement, but, whether it was extended or not, the advances apparently continued to be paid. In January 1918 the total amount spent on payment of coupons and repayment of the principal of the Russian bonds had already reached almost 1.5 billion francs.

Britain also advanced considerable sums to its Russian ally to support the latter's war effort (Raffalovitch 1919, 18). The question of credits had been raised at an interallied conference on funding for the war in 1915. Britain borrowed a large share of the amounts pledged from the United States and subsequently lent them to Russia (Barnett 2001). Given Russia's substantial gold reserves, Keynes suggested some of the gold be transferred to the United Kingdom. Bark opposed this measure on the grounds that Russia had adequate credit to secure additional loans and that the physical transfer of tons of gold during the war was far too dangerous (Barnett 2001). He was not inflexible, however, and arranged for a modest shipment of bullion. Despite attempts made to ensure the actors' discretion, it appears the public already knew of the gold shipments in 1915. In 1922 the *British Russian Gazette* estimated the total advances at 800 million pounds.[9] In the late 1920s Luboff posited a similar figure, valuing Russia's war debt to Britain at close to 765 million pounds.[10] The practical terms of the loans were obscure: Luboff finds no public record of them.

Although theoretically secret, the advances to Russia do not seem to have been at all confidential. The Allies' financial backing was mentioned even before the Russian debt was repudiated. In May 1917 an article in *Le Temps,* responding to questions from readers, reported that French and British intervention had enabled the coupons on Russian bonds to be paid during the crisis period.[11] Even more surprisingly, according to Albert Grodet, an independent Socialist MP, the complete list of the bonds whose coupons were paid with advances from France, as well as their amount and the list of banks that handled the payments, was published in full in the directory of the Paris stockbrokers' syndicate (1915–17).[12] Grodet criticized the secrecy of the agreement, not because the supposed secret had been divulged but because neither the senate nor the lower house had been informed of it before payments began.

Between mid-December 1917 and the end of January 1918 there was talk on the Bourse that France would continue to pay the coupons after the repudiation.[13] The rumors pushed up prices for Russian bonds. At the end of December 1917 there was uncertainty on the Bourse about whether the Russian coupons would be paid in January, despite reassurances from *Le Rentier*.[14] Even before the repudiation had been officially confirmed in Russia, the deputy Henri Roulleaux-Dugage asked what steps the French government would take to defend French interests in Russia should the need arise.[15] The finance minister said that useful measures would be adopted jointly with the Allies to safeguard those interests and that a government commission had been set up to gather information and assess the situation.

THE REPUDIATION, THE "ADVANCES TO AN ALLY," AND FRANCE'S ACTIONS DURING THE WAR

The French government was just as surprised as investors were at the repudiation of Russian bonds. The advances paid in the name of mutual assistance between allies put France in an extremely delicate position. Some factors argued in favor of continuing the advances. In political terms, their suspension could have been perceived as recognition of the Bolshevik takeover, with no hope of seeing a more moderate government come to power in the near term. In economic terms, the partial or total coverage of the losses incurred by bondholders could be warranted in the event of a risk of a spate of bank failures. In ethical terms, the payment of coupons could be justified by the French government's attitude when the bonds were issued. While legally the French government had never underwritten these bonds, it had vaunted their reliability and attractiveness.

On the other hand, advancing coupon payments was very costly for a country at war. Furthermore, if the Bolshevik regime were to remain in power for the long term, financial intervention by the French government would result in an irredeemable loss. Moreover, the assumption of foreign debts could fuel a sense of injustice among holders of other defaulted bonds.[16] Large-scale financial intervention also risked creating a double moral hazard, for investors and for foreign governments. First, a bailout by France might encourage French investors to lend more readily to countries with troubled finances. If France were to take over from the defaulting country, this kind of investment would become extremely attractive given the relatively high rates of interest for the debt of high-risk countries. For foreign governments, there would be little incentive to maintain fiscal discipline or to repay bonds if France assumed their debts in the event of default.

When the repudiation was announced, there was nevertheless hope of repayment by France. The French government soon declared its opposition in principle on the grounds that, since it had not guaranteed the bonds, it had no liability for them. At best, the government could intervene temporarily.[17] Paying the first coupons falling due was a problematic move because an initial move would undoubtedly be seen as a precedent for the payment of subsequent coupons or even repayment of principal. Although most of the Russian bonds were held in France, it was not the only country facing this dilemma. The French government noted the positions of the Allied countries.

The British government's decision to pay the coupons on Russian treasury bonds falling due on 28 January 1918 attracted attention. Despite this operation, thought to apply to almost 10 million pounds' worth of treasury bonds, the chancellor of the exchequer, Andrew Bonar Law, was keen to point out that this should in no way be considered an admission of British liability.[18] The decision was widely commented on. On 21 January 1918 the Paris prefect's agent at the Bourse reported, "People are talking less about the political situation there [in Russia] than about last week's decision by the British government to pay the coupons on Russian Treasury bonds owned by British nationals," and "even though France has a much bigger commitment than Britain, we hope the French government will follow the example set by London."[19]

After a speech to the lower house on 31 January 1918 the French finance minister, Louis-Lucien Klotz, made clear that France had reaffirmed Russia's liability for the debt in December 1917. The French government nevertheless proceeded to pay the coupons for January and February.[20] Those payments were to be understood as temporary, since the Allies had yet to reach a joint decision.[21] In the face of fierce opposition from some politicians, a vote in the lower house yielded a large majority in favor of paying the coupons for January.[22] The French government therefore decided to advance the first Russian coupons due in 1918. According to Noulens (1933, 1:152), that action supported the Bolsheviks' position because they saw it as evidence of France's ability to "assume Russia's debt without it being too heavy a burden." The moral hazard described above had just become a reality.

Its assertions notwithstanding, the government's attitude toward covering the payment of the coupons in January and February 1918 was in fact highly ambivalent. The financial intervention during the war under the Bark–Ribot agreement reinforced a sense that France had some liability for the Russian bond affair. The finance minister's contradictory statements were resented by some of France's politicians. While the government gave the impression that it would intervene only temporarily, if at all, some of the finance minister's statements in January 1918 implied that the government did not intend to change its policy. The decision to pay the Russian coupons came in for criticism in the lower house of parliament. Grodet denounced it on the grounds that the Bark–Ribot agreement had not been submitted to parliament for approval, that the agreement had not been renewed, and that France had never guaranteed the Russian bonds. Grodet's speech was applauded by the left-wing parties.[23] The positions on France's payment of the Russian coupons reflected a political and philosophical divide. Overall, the conservative and right-wing parties were in favor, while the left-wing and Socialist parties were against. The Socialists' intense opposition to the Russian bonds dated from the 1905 revolution and the campaign against the issuance of Russian bonds. In the Socialists' opinion, French financial support at the time had enabled the tsarist regime to quell the revolution.[24]

Strongly opposed to payment of the coupons, some Socialist politicians argued that liability lay not with France but with the ministers who had encouraged French investors to buy Russian bonds. Marius

Moutet criticized the reassuring tone at the time of issuance, particularly the fact that the government's financial policy had "consisted in presenting foreign bonds as a safe-haven investment, when in fact no other investment has lost French savers more money."[25] The other target of criticism was the banks. Accusing them of having grown rich by placing the Russian bonds, Moutet considered the banks to be liable. Emmanuel Brousse asked Finance Minister Klotz whether the banks might take on some of the losses given that they had received substantial commissions when the bonds were placed.[26] The minister rejected that solution out of hand because it could give the impression that France had lost confidence in its Russian ally. It was nevertheless thought to be one of the proposals that encouraged new investors to purchase Russian bonds as late as August 1918.[27] There were various other repayment proposals, for example, that France pay a fraction of the coupons and that payment be reserved for small investors.

As well as by the so-called British example, France's position was probably influenced by uncertainty about the situation in Russia, particularly how long the Bolshevik government would last. There was discussion of "exit conditions" that would enable the government to terminate an intervention once begun. In March 1918 the Brest-Litovsk Treaty provided the French government with a justification for ceasing to pay the Russian coupons. By signing a separate peace, Russia's status in the world war changed from ally to nonbelligerent or even to enemy.[28] Since the official reason for France to advance funds was to support an ally, the payments were therefore no longer justified, and the French government suspended them.[29] That decision would later be the subject of heated debate, particularly in 1920. At first, the market did not seem to believe the payments would be suspended for this reason. In early April 1918 the Bourse was on tenterhooks.[30] In mid-April 1918 *Le Rentier* reported that neither France nor the United Kingdom would pay the April coupons but attributed this to a vote on the issue pending in the two countries.[31] The news barely made waves, however, because attention was focused on war events in France.[32] Although the coupons were not paid in April, market participants still placed their hopes in French government intervention. An article in *La Cote Vidal* challenging the usefulness of an intervention triggered no reactions. On the contrary, demand for Russian perpetual bonds actually increased.[33] Hope for an intervention remained fairly steady for the next several months.[34]

A lobbying campaign gradually developed to persuade the government that action was important. In May 1918 *Le Rentier* advised readers to write to their representatives in the lower house and the senate, stressing that the bulk of the Russian debt was held by small investors.[35] In fact, that advice came after many individuals had already done so. Some investors even indicated the serial numbers of their bonds to their representatives in the hope of being refunded.

In late July 1918 there were rumors that the French government would resume the payments. The first rumors were not specific about the terms; then it was suggested that France would either pay the Russian coupons or accept them in exchange for subscription to a future French bond.[36] The rumors boosted prices for Russian bonds and were still circulating in September 1918.[37] Despite the government's stated position, in August 1918 the General Commission for the Protection of French Interests in Russia still hoped that some or all of the Allied governments would intervene, given the political motivations surrounding the issuance of Russian bonds.[38] That position was soon adopted by a section of the press and the public, who felt it was perfectly legitimate. A large percentage of the general public thought the French government had implicitly guaranteed the Russian bonds by encouraging investors to buy them in the name of the sacrosanct Franco–Russian Alliance.[39] According to *Le Rentier*, which probably represented a widely held opinion, "without the Russian Alliance, the Russian bonds would never have been subscribed and supported in France as much as they were."[40]

In late August 1918 Raoul Péret, then chairman of the budget commission, propounded a twofold solution: first, an exchange of Russian coupons for French securities as part of the fourth National Bond issue and, second, the repurchase of Russian securities by the French government at a given rate.[41] Those proposals were hard to implement not only because the First World War was still raging but also because they could be perceived as being unfair: Why make all taxpayers bear the cost of the Russian debt? Interestingly, Péret, who was strongly opposed to recognition of French liability, fails to offer any justification for such generous interventions.[42] At most, in a later article he claims that France had given a moral guarantee to the issuance of Russian bonds.[43]

In September 1918 *La Revue des Valeurs Russes* proposed that the advances should continue until a new government was appointed in Russia.[44] According to that newspaper, the French government would be taking only a limited risk, given military developments in Russia. At the end of 1918 the French government made a minor concession by admitting the coupons as 50 percent payment for subscription for the next French bond. The finance minister suggested compiling an inventory of all Russian securities in France. The Bourse clearly appreciated the gesture, even if this gratitude was reflected not in an immediate increase in prices but in a medium-term effect.[45] The need to provide 50 percent of the subscription payment in cash spurred the emergence of a parallel market in Russian coupons. The finance minister deemed the operation a success, since almost 265 million francs' worth of coupons were exchanged.[46] Although that was a large amount, it represented the coupons of bonds with a total face value of 5.3 billion (assuming a coupon rate of 5 percent). The exchange therefore concerned barely 45 percent of the total estimated funds lent to Russia (if one considers a conservative value of 12 billion francs).

Despite the operation in September 1918, in a letter to the chairman of the National Securities Office (Office National des Valeurs Mobilières) the French foreign minister reasserted that the French government bore no liability and said the action of the Defense Committee of Holders of Russian Bonds should not focus solely on the public authorities.[47] The minister's position appeared to be unequivocal: the French government did not consider itself liable in any way for the Russian bonds. Nonetheless, the French government showed itself willing to find a solution. At one of the first meetings of the General Commission, in response to a question from Maurice de Verneuil, one of the finance minister's undersecretaries stressed the importance of the commission's action while assuring it of the "benevolent support of the French government."[48] Foreign Minister Stéphen Pichon reaffirmed that support in a letter to the chairman of the National Securities Office in October 1918.[49]

THE WAR AND INDUSTRIAL INTERESTS IN RUSSIA

Far from consisting solely of government bonds, investments in Russian securities spanned vast sectors of the economy. Although apparently similar, French industrial interests in Russia were in fact extremely diverse. Some companies were established under French law, others under Russian law but with French capital, and yet others were equivalent to the modern concept of joint ventures. In some cases French involvement was limited to ownership of shares in Russian companies. Given these differences, French investors probably soon realized that a single solution was not possible. Nevertheless, hopes of a bailout by the French government extended beyond holders of government bonds to holders of Russian shares as well.

Pierre Darcy describes investors' expectations in a letter dated July 1918.[50] Cynicism and calculations transpire in the reports: "Again today I heard support for the opinion that the most enviable fate for our industries in Ukraine would be to be taken over by the Germans, because the French shareholders would certainly be generously compensated when peace is signed and be able to realize their assets." In the case of industrial investments, France could have provided aid preventively to forestall French interests from ending up in German hands.

As early as May 1918 the French ambassador to Sweden, Emile Thiébaut, informed Foreign Minister Pichon of attempts to buy Russian securities transiting through Sweden.[51] According to the ambassador's informants, "various Russian Israelites, including a relative of Trotsky," had offered to channel Russian gold and securities to Germany for sale via Nya Bank.[52] The advantage for buyers was the supposed favorable treatment granted to Germany under the Brest-Litovsk Treaty. According to Thiébaut, a clause in the treaty exempted "German capital from the confiscation measures imposed on bourgeois capital." After a portion of the Russian securities held in Russia were sold, the ambassador feared that attention would shift to Russian industrial and banking securities held in France. Sick of receiving no dividends, French investors would likely be tempted to sell their securities.

The concern expressed by the French ambassador to Sweden at the time is easy to understand. If the transactions he describes were to begin in France, the country would lose heavily. First, one can assume that in order to limit their losses French retail investors would have sold their securities at a price that did not represent their real value. Second, the sale of the securities to Germany would result in the enemy acquiring ownership stakes in a region formerly dominated by French interests. Curiously, there is no mention anywhere of the possibility that the Bolsheviks might renege on the Brest-Litovsk conditions, even though the whole operation depended on their good faith.

In any case, the threat was considered serious enough for Thiébaut to urge, with respect to a French guarantee of Russian securities, "the French government to consider . . . the wisdom of altering its policy in light of the interests at stake."[53] The legal acquisition by the enemy— Germany or Austria—of companies in Russia would remain a cause for worry until the end of the war. In July 1918, for example, Darcy reported attempts to appropriate French investments in the Donbas (Ukraine).[54] Financial difficulties made these companies easy pickings for the Germans and Austrians. The Central Powers saw the companies' financial fragility as an opportunity to infiltrate their management by offering them loans. When successful, this action had two effects: participation in management and control over production for the war effort. In light of that threat, Darcy advised forming a French financial consortium for the purpose of assisting the French-owned companies. The fate of French interests in Ukraine continued to preoccupy French investors even after the Armistice. In January 1919 the fear that Germans would take over French industries gave way to fears that Ukraine would come under the sway of the Bolsheviks.[55]

FRENCH GOVERNMENT LIABILITY?

After the First World War any hope that France would advance money to Russia to cover the costs of war vanished. France would need another reason to intervene financially. The French government's liability in the placement of Russian bonds with its citizens became the main argument for demanding financial compensation from France.

As described above, the involvement of successive French governments and a broad swathe of the French political class in the issuance of

Russian bonds on the Paris Bourse was undeniable. Girault (1961) notes that from 1895 on, a section of the French government began to express misgivings about public enthusiasm for Russian bonds. There were even some attempts to prevent bond issues at the turn of the century, but these were unsuccessful. According to Adrien Gaudin de Villaine, every French finance minister except Georges Cochery and every head of state said that the loans to Russia were vital.[56]

The French government's liability toward holders of Russian bonds could be invoked on three grounds: first, the legal obligations of the state; second, the public recommendations made by the state; and, third, the unofficial action, legal or illegal, of the state.

In the period under discussion here, the prerogatives of the government included the power to refuse to admit foreign debt to the market. The decision to admit or refuse a foreign bond issue was considered as a factor that could influence relations between the borrower country and France. Consequently, admission of foreign securities to trading could be decided only with the express authorization of the finance minister, in practice after a favorable opinion from the foreign minister (Boissière 1925, 173–74). The success of a large security emission thus depended directly on the French government's favors (Feis 1930). In turn, these favors were directly linked to the political and economic advantages France could gain from the issue. The military alliance with France was the main counterpart for the loans, even though in some instances specific demands were made, for example, an increase in military strength and the construction of strategic railways.[57] In some cases the French government demanded explicitly that Russia buy exclusively from France (Siegel 2014, 56). Germany had indeed managed to condition its loans on Russian orders from its industries, and France felt it deserved to be treated in similar fashion (Siegel 2014, 60). After 1887 the Russian influence became such that potential borrowers also had to take into account Russian will. In 1912 the French ambassador to Turkey remarked that the Russian government "abused the power of the French market as an instrument of its own political ends" (Feis 1930 [1965], 135)!

Sack (1927) details the criticisms of the Russian bond issue of 2.25 billion francs authorized by the ukase of 17 March 1906. Many observers felt that the timing of the issue—just before the convocation of the first Duma—had been planned in order to avoid having to obtain the approval of the new parliament, which would have been difficult at the time. A propaganda campaign on this issue was orchestrated in Paris. Questioned in parliament by Jean Jaurès when the Russian empire sought to raise capital once again on the Paris market, Finance Minister Joseph Caillaux declared, "The government will only admit bonds that are accompanied by all the legal guarantees we are entitled to demand from the borrowing government."[58] Accordingly, the French government was indeed responsible for admitting foreign bonds to trading in France. Several years later, Foreign Minister Pichon championed the issuance of a new Russian bond, asserting that "French savers run no risk" (Jolly 1960, 2691). Caillaux's statement implied that the quality of the borrowing country's credit was scrutinized before its debt was admitted to the market. However, in light of the sovereign defaults that occurred on the Paris market, this assumption needs to be qualified. Either no credit analysis was performed or it was performed on highly accommodative terms. In practice, economic and geostrategic considerations often played an important role in the granting of admission to the market or not (Feis 1930). The opacity with which the government admitted or denied admission to the market had already been strongly criticized at the turn of the century, particularly by left-wing circles (Lysis 1910, 5–7). For a number of years after the repudiation was declared the French government was accused of adopting a far too lenient attitude toward Russia.[59] That leniency can clearly be attributed to strategic reasons related to strengthening the Franco–Russian Alliance.

The liability of the French government was also invoked because, although it did not promote Russian bonds directly, it nevertheless encouraged its citizens to buy them in the name of Franco–Russian friendship. Several sources dating from before the repudiation stress the role played by the French government in placing Russian bonds with the general public.[60] For example, the government had not just authorized but also advised the miners' fund to invest in Russian bonds.[61] The involvement of the French government in the dissemination of Russian bonds was probably the most frequently cited ground for invoking its liability and therefore was the factor that raised the greatest hope France would repay some or all of the Russian debt. In fact, the French Foreign Affairs archives show that in many instances the French government was worried about the safety of the Russian loans and its responsibility in their diffusion (Renouvin 1959). As for Great Britain, the Secretary of State for Foreign Affairs Sir Edward Grey had stressed in 1914 that British financiers would naturally consider that the government was under some obligation if it attempted to interfere in the flotation of securities. This explained why the Foreign Office left the financiers to deal with the loans (Feis 1930 [1965], 85).

In addition to its visible actions, the French government was undoubtedly morally liable because of its covert activities. Even if it only encouraged the Russian government to subsidize the French press, the French government's involvement is not in doubt. In 1904 the French finance minister, Maurice Rouvier, and de Verneuil, the honorary chairman of the stockbrokers' syndicate, advised Russia's finance minister, Vladimir Kokovtsov, to bribe the French press in order to offset speculative attacks on Russian bonds (Long 1972). Subsequently, so as not to expose the Russian government directly, Rouvier recommended that an employee of the French treasury, a certain Lenoir, serve as an intermediary between the Russian government and the French press (Long 1972). Eventually, Bignon and Flandreau (2011, 627) mention evidence that "senior politicians instructed the Russian to pay certain papers who then used the bribe monies to buy votes in parliament."

Figures who later played a key role in deciding whether or not to repay the bondholders had thus been personally involved in the original decision to support Russia. De Verneuil, who had been directly involved in Russia's corruption of the French press, was appointed chairman of the General Commission when it was set up in 1918. Klotz, the French finance minister from 12 September 1917 to 20 January 1920, was certainly not neutral either, since in 1888 he had founded an illustrated newspaper, La Vie Franco-Russe, to promote stronger ties with Russia.

No quantitative study to date has demonstrated the efficiency of the corruption of the French press in terms of financial results.[62] To be sure, computing the return on investment from bribes is a difficult exercise. Long (1972) writes that Russian officials disagreed about its impact. Raffalovitch said that corruption reduced the number of sell orders for

Russian bonds and hence served to stabilize prices. Similarly, a letter from the Russian finance minister, Sergei Witte, indicates that, in his opinion, no Russian bond could have been issued in France without the support of the French press. Conversely, Ambassador Alexander Nelidov viewed the action taken as unsatisfactory because it had failed to counterbalance anti-Russian propaganda and the influence on the French press of negative articles in newspapers published by the empire's enemies, the Germans, British, and "Jews." Bignon and Flandreau (2011) aver that corruption was almost unavoidable, especially when the country was in a difficult situation. Long (1972) maintains that corruption yielded a profitable return on investment since the 2.5 million francs spent on bribes had not only ensured the placement of almost 2 billion francs' worth of Russian bonds over the same period but also enabled Russia to remain the gold standard despite the Russo–Japanese War and the troubles of 1905. It would be worth analyzing the efficiency of the corruption campaign in more detail. In any case, it raises a question for counterfactual history: what would the Russian empire's borrowing capacity have been without the campaigns to bribe the press?

At the time of the repudiation it is unlikely that investors knew the extent of the corruption surrounding the Russian bonds issued in the previous decades. Nonetheless, even if the public was unaware of the role played by members of the government, they could not ignore either the strong recommendations to buy Russian bonds or France's support when it admitted all the successive Russian bond issues to the official list. Last, discussion of French military intervention in Russia was interpreted as an admission of French liability.

A decree published on 15 January 1919 required French citizens to declare by 1 March 1919 their assets and interests in countries that were formerly part of the Russian empire or the kingdom of Romania.[63] Investors were also required to present their Russian and Romanian bonds and other securities to be stamped. Contrary to what one might think, the measure was initially greeted with wariness by investors, who believed it was a prelude to a tax, and with resentment by the banks because of the additional workload the inventory created.[64] Suspicion soon gave way to curiosity, then hope, as investors saw the inventory as a prelude to repayment. In 1921 the General Commission offered to resume the inventory of bonds, which it felt was worth completing.[65] The exact amounts held by French citizens remained hard to determine. Gaudin de Villaine opined that since some Russian bonds were tradable on several markets and in various currencies, investors switched between financial markets in order to benefit from the best exchange rate.[66]

In February 1919 the National League for Claims of Small Investors in Russian Securities (Ligue nationale de revendication des petits porteurs de valeurs russes) asked the General Commission to lobby the government to intervene specifically in favor of small investors, offering them the same treatment as residents of the French regions devastated by the war.[67] That proposal, submitted to the authorities, was considered with some sympathy. A law passed on 25 July 1919 authorized holders of Russian bonds living in war-ravaged regions or who had fought for France to use their bond coupons to subscribe for a new bond for national defense, for up to 50 percent of the amount subscribed (Reynaud 1924).

Over the following years there were many questions and speeches in both houses of parliament. In the senate on 31 May 1919, for example, Senator Maurice Couyba questioned Finance Minister Klotz about "what France intends to do for the Russian bondholders."[68] The minister's response was another masterpiece of ambiguity. After condemning the repudiation, Klotz reminded his audience of the French government's action in connection with the Russian bonds since 1917. The purpose of that action was to assist French savers "who subscribed for Russian bonds out of enthusiasm and a deep desire to serve the interests of their country and not to make a lucrative financial transaction." He went on to claim that "the government would be neglecting all its duties if it failed to address the matter of the Russian bondholders." Last, he asserted that "on this matter [i.e., what France intends to do for the Russian bondholders] the past must answer for the future," concluding that the Russian bondholders would not be forgotten in an upcoming consolidation operation, although he did not commit the government to this. On the basis of this speech, French investors would have reason to conclude that the French government would initiate actions to help them. Time would reveal that this was a promise—but a promise with-

out a commitment. Anatole de Monzie, supported by Gaudin de Villaine, would recall this pledge and the hopes it raised.[69]

According to de Monzie, the French position was guided by the
political situation in Russia. In his view France had agreed to advance
funds to Russia as long as there was hope of Russian repayment in the
near future. Trust was successively placed in tsarism (1915–16), in Pavel
Miliukov and Kerensky (1917), then in Kolchak and Denikin (1918). In
de Monzie's view, by 1919 the prospects of Russian reunification were so
slim that the French government had decided to decline all liability.[70]
According to the French financial press, de Monzie's speeches and his
ceaseless reminders of French liability helped buoy Russian bond prices.[71]

The Russian bondholders' defense committees also began to lobby
the French government to exchange the coupons. This, combined with
the ambiguity of Klotz's declarations, the partial admission of Russian
coupons in exchange for French bonds in 1918, and the parliamentary
debates about the Russian bonds, explains why in January 1920 Russian
bondholders were still hoping for the publication of a new decree in
their favor.[72] That hope proved to be short-lived, however, because in
February 1920 *Le Rentier* expressed its skepticism over the chances of
success of the various initiatives undertaken.[73] Those fears were confirmed when, responding to a question from the member for the Tarn
region, Joseph de Belcastel, the new finance minister, Frédéric François-
Marsal said he was opposed to any exchange of Russian coupons to pay
for the new French bond.[74] However, the rejection of that particular
proposal did not sound the death knell of French hopes. Only a few
months later *Le Rentier* asserted that, in its position as a creditor, France
would not abandon the Russian bondholders.[75]

In March 1920 a rumor of a French initiative resurfaced on the
Bourse. It was to the effect that the French government was willing to
buy back the Russian perpetual bonds at a yield based on the nominal
yield and would exchange them for French bonds. The government
would thus stand in the stead of small investors and deal with Russia in
its own name.[76] The mechanism of this rumored initiative is similar to
one that took place in Italy in 1918 (see below). Within a few months,
however, Senator Gaudin de Villaine resumed his offensive. In a written

question dated 15 June 1920 he asked the finance minister to outline the measures that would be taken to assist the Russian bondholders, particularly the miners, since the government had allowed the miners' fund to invest in Russian bonds. This request was ignored.[77]

Not all the lobbying by the General Commission went unrewarded, however. According to its members, the commission's efforts expedited the passage of a law giving companies and individuals based in Russia more time to honor their commitments.[78] Although irrelevant to most French holders of Russian bonds, that achievement, albeit modest, undoubtedly contributed to a sense that France would not leave its citizens in the lurch. Moreover, the commission could claim some credit for this small success.

The tenacity of some senators on the Russian bond case is notable. In January 1921 de Monzie reopened the debate with a written question asking what steps the government was taking to defend the rights acquired by French citizens in Russia before the war.[79] In May 1921 hopes that a French solution could be found were strong once again, and repayment of the Russian bonds was discussed as a serious domestic policy issue. A section of the press and probably of the general public also still believed the government had significant liability.[80] *Le Rentier* again urged holders of Russian securities to write to their representatives in the lower house and the senate to advance their cause.[81]

On 20 October 1922 Gaudin de Villaine submitted a draft resolution to the French senate on repayment of the bonds. In his bill Gaudin de Villaine claimed that repayment of the Russian bonds should be considered as reparation for war damage. In his view the nonpayment of the Russian coupons was a consequence of the overthrow of the tsarist regime, which itself was a direct result of the war.[82] In his argument Gaudin de Villaine pinned liability on the French state ("subscription was encouraged by the leaders of the nation"), on the issuing banks, which he accused of having misled French investors about the quality of Russian credit ("the Russian bond operation is a terrible act by men of finance"), and on the investors themselves ("a capitalist big or small must know that he runs a risk whenever he invests his money"). Given that shared liability, the senator counseled that holders of Russian bonds be repaid 50 percent of the face value. In his opinion half of the repayment should be covered by the French government and half by the banks that handled the placement of the bonds in France. Only bonds issued or guaranteed by the Russian state and previously declared by the owners would be eligible. On this basis, Gaudin de Villaine estimated the total amount France would have to pay at around 2 billion francs. He considered the payment by the state or the banks as an advance, which would be repaid as soon as Russia resumed the servicing of its debt. The proposal was reported in the French and foreign press.[83]

Barely a month after submitting his draft resolution, Gaudin de Villaine spoke again in the senate.[84] He started by recalling the liability of the French government, which, "directly or indirectly convinced these unfortunate taxpayers to raise billions, by using every method of advertising to claim that subscribing for Russian bonds was a patriotic act, and especially a blue-chip investment." He then submitted another draft resolution on payment of the coupons on Russian bonds. He had already put forward this idea in his correspondence with the finance ministers Paul Doumer and Charles de Lasteyrie.[85] In his letters Gaudin de Villaine pointed to several sources of funds that could be used to repay the bondholders: first, the French share of the Russian gold paid by the Bolsheviks under the Treaty of Brest-Litovsk and recovered by the Allies after the Treaty of Versailles; second, the 116 million in gold rubles registered in the account of the former Russian government and deposited in France; third, the funds repatriated by the Russian brigades in Salonika and deposited with the treasury. The correspondence reveals strong divergences in the interpretations of the ministers and the senator. While there was agreement that the Brest-Litovsk gold had been deposited in France, some of the other events referred to by Gaudin de Villaine were disputed. His proposals were referred to the finance commission and were never followed through on, so far as is known.

At the end of 1922 Georges Bonnefous and André Tardieu submitted a bill on the Russian bonds to the lower house.[86] Unlike earlier proffers, this one did not involve repayment of the holders of Russian bonds by the French state. Rather, it sought to facilitate the creation of mutual funds that could be used to repay the bonds. The idea defended by its authors was to encourage the holders of Russian bonds to form a mutual fund. They would pay a membership fee that would raise capital, the income from which would be used to repay the principal via a random draw. That proposition, both unrealistic and likely to lead to large-scale fraud, was referred to the finance commission, which seems not to have followed it up. In practice, it appears that similar attempts were made, notably by Foncier National Bordelais (Foncier National Bordelais 1922).

In November 1923 another draft resolution on the Russian debt was submitted to the lower house.[87] Its scope was modest, referring to repayment of only some of the Russian bondholders. Considering that many people on low wages had been relying on the income from their Russian bonds to cover their needs, the authors of the bill advised that the government seek a solution whereby it paid the arrears on Russian bonds owned by people over the age of sixty with an annual income of less than 10,000 francs. The proposal was also referred to the finance commission and seems not to have been followed up. But political intervention on the Russian debt did not end in 1923. In April 1924, when the Brest-Litovsk gold was being apportioned, Prime Minister Poincaré noted that the gold returned to France paid back some of its credit with Russia (Freymond 1996, 158). That statement revived the Russian bondholders' hopes.

The debate about recognition of the Russian government and repayment of the debt was reopened in the late 1920s by various politicians, such as Edouard Herriot and Alexandre Millerand, who saw an electoral advantage in it (Carley 2000). Thus at the start of the elections in 1928, according to contemporary observers, the settlement of the Russian problem would have favored the left, whereas failure to resolve the issue would have strengthened the right (Carley and Debo 1997). Nearly ten years after the repudiation, repayment of the Russian debt was still an important political issue in France. The far-right press used the repudiation as a pretext to incriminate "Jewish finance," in particular the Rothschilds, who allegedly formed a Judeo-Bolshevik conspiracy to exploit French investors (Bonzon 1924, 1924a), an accusation already present in some of Gaudin de Villaine's speeches.[88]

As can be seen, the ideas, proposals, suggestions, and occasional initiatives were enormously varied. Despite claiming nonliability, the French government did intervene, albeit on a very modest scale. It is legitimate to wonder whether the government's desire to intervene was influenced by developments outside France. On the one hand, the wish to intervene may have waned whenever another credible payer seemed potentially about to repay the debts. Why would France repay the bonds if the Bolshevik government were about to fall? On the other hand, financial intervention could be justified by the successes of the White armies since, in the event of a White victory, France could expect its advances to be repaid. The decisions to intervene therefore were probably influenced by the victories of the White armies and by announcements of a resumption of negotiations by the Bolsheviks.

BAILOUTS AND NONBAILOUTS IN OTHER COUNTRIES

By far the largest quantity of Russian bonds was held in France, but the issue of whether the national government should repay the bonds was also raised in other countries. French investors and politicians therefore watched the attitudes of Belgium, the United States, Italy, Japan, and Britain with interest.

The governments in those countries took decisions that varied widely. The broad range of attitudes stemmed from such factors as a tradition of nonintervention, the amounts at stake, and the government's expectations.

Although engaged alongside France in the First World War, Belgium adopted a very different position from its ally. The Belgian government, which had never advanced funds to Russia, refused to intervene in favor of Belgian citizens who owned Russian bonds.[89] That decision dealt a severe blow to those holders, especially as payment of the coupons had been suspended since the German occupation of Belgium, long before the 1917 revolution. Given the late entry of the United States into the First World War and the limited involvement of the government in the issuance of Russian bonds in the United States, neither the holders of Russian bonds nor the issuing syndicates seem to have ever expected the American government to intervene.[90] Only a small quantity of the bonds had been purchased there, and the United States had always been loath to intervene.

The announcement in May 1918 that Italy's finance minister would accept Russian bonds in exchange for subscription to a new Italian government bond attracted much commentary on the Paris Bourse.[91] Unlike France, which accepted Russian coupons only as 50 percent payment for a national subscription, Italy appears to have authorized the exchange of the Russian 5 percent perpetual bond at 50 percent of their nominal value (and the other Russian perpetual bonds at proportional values). On the day this news was announced on the Paris Bourse—21 May 1918—the 5 percent Russian bond of 1906 was trading at 47 percent of par. Italy's action was therefore very generous in that the bonds were exchanged for more than their market value. French financiers called for a similar intervention in France, which they described as being ingenious.[92]

In Japan the government considered itself responsible and intervened directly by buying back the Russian bonds from their holders. According to Freymond (1996, 46), the transaction entailed no losses for the bondholders. Last, as mentioned above, the British government paid the coupons on Russian treasury bonds due 28 January 1918, although it refused to recognize any liability whatsoever.[93] An inventory of British claims against Russia was initiated in June 1918. The Corporation of Foreign Bondholders encouraged holders of Russian state and municipal bonds to lodge complaints with the Foreign Office.[94]

Seeking Other Potential Payers

L ong before the Russian bonds were repudiated, the redrawing
of territorial boundaries as a result of wars, annexations, and
inheritances had raised the issue of the debt of territories that
had either become independent or been incorporated into new
nations. This issue was central in the case of the Russian bonds because
the Russian revolution led to a division of the empire and the creation of
new independent nations. Some of these sooner or later returned to the
Russian fold, usually as new Socialist republics, whereas others enjoyed
genuine independence during the interwar period. What was the liability of these new nations toward French creditors? did they have any obligation to repay the former debt? and if so, on the basis of which criteria
should the debt be apportioned to each?

Debt and the Succession of States: Historical Precedents

The issue of the succession of states and the apportionment of debt after
the succession dates back at least to the Middle Ages. The treaty govern-
ing the cession of Dauphiné to the French crown in the first half of the
fourteenth century explicitly states France's liabilities with regard to existing debt (Feilchenfeld 1931, 20–21). In the seventeenth century Grotius, one of the fathers of international law, analyzed the implications of

the succession of states for sovereign debt in *De Jure Belli ac Pacis* (On the law of war and peace). That fundamental analysis was followed by an extensive body of international law literature.[1] Until the nineteenth century most authors agreed that the successor state was liable for the debt of its predecessor. Hoeflich (1982) describes the reasons put forward at the time. One was the analogy of succession in private law, whereby the successor state, occupying a place similar to that of its predecessor in the community of nations, is bound to assume its obligations. Another reason was the concept of continuity: although states are only legal constructs, the real borrower is the population, which remains the same.

Those legal positions were strongly criticized later, as the reference to private law was challenged. The idea of succession was not rejected, however, since the concept of "unjust enrichment" was invoked to justify the assumption of debt. Hoeflich (1982) showed how geopolitical factors could influence the positions adopted by states. Many states were far from consistent, claiming the succession to be legal or illegal depending on their interests at the time. It is therefore unsurprising that even at the beginning of the twenty-first century the law of the succession of states is still described as "particularly fragile and undecided" (Eisemann 2002).

Succession still applied to sovereign debt in the early nineteenth century. For example, all the former Spanish colonies agreed to assume a portion of the debt of their former colonial master, and Belgium took on some of the Dutch debt when it gained independence (Feilchenfeld 1931, 205–9, 251). Reaching an agreement was almost always a protracted process. For example, following Belgian independence it took twelve years to determine the proportion of the debt to be taken over by Belgium (Collet 2012a). Over the course of the nineteenth century the United States and Britain, out of pure self-interest (Hoeflich 1982), challenged the traditionally accepted concept of the succession of debt. After the acquisition by the United States of numerous territories and Britain's creation of a vast empire, succession would have put them in the unenviable position of having to repay the debts of the territories they had conquered. When Texas was annexed in the 1840s the U.S. government did assume the Texan debt but only because it considered repayment morally fair!

A further step was taken in 1898, when, after the Spanish–American War, the United States refused to recognize Cuba's debts, which it considered odious. According to the United States, the capital raised by the debt issue benefited not the Cuban people but the Spanish crown and therefore ought not to be charged to Cuba but assumed by Spain. The Belgian and French governments and associations of bondholders in those two countries, where the Cuban debt was held, protested against the Americans' position (Feilchenfeld 1931, 331). In fact, some bonds were from the onset considered to be odious, as their proceeds had helped crush the Cuban insurrection, whereas others were viewed as more legitimate, as their proceeds had been used for constructive purposes. Collet (2013) exploits the divergences between the various Cuban bonds to show that investors required a premium to compensate for the risk that a bond might be declared odious. Eventually the United States recognized none of the bonds. After lengthy negotiations Spain partially bailed out holders of Cuban bonds but barely.

The concept of odious debt enjoyed some success and is still regularly invoked by countries that issued debt to satisfy the wishes of a dictator. The United Kingdom also invoked odious debt after several of its territories were annexed, and when it did agree to repay debt that act was invariably presented as one of fairness or generosity rather than a legal obligation (Hoeflich 1982). The annexation of some colonies led to the assumption of debts by the conquering state. The colonization of the Congo by Belgium is an example. It seems likely, however, that Belgium assumed the debt above all because doing so was an advantageous financial arrangement for Leopold II (Harms 2005).

Another textbook case of the succession of states, that of the Ottoman empire, must certainly have interested French investors in the early twentieth century. Revolts began in Bosnia-Herzegovina in 1875 and were followed by similar movements in Bulgaria, Montenegro, and Serbia until Russia intervened. Those military events, combined with a financial situation severely weakened by extravagant discretionary spending by several successive sultans, triggered a total default on the Ottoman debts in 1876 (Wynne 1951 [2000], 413–15).

The Russo–Turkish War of 1877–78 ended with the signing of the Treaty of San Stefano on 3 March 1878. The treaty endorsed the cession of various territories from Turkey to Russia, the creation of several new nations recognized as independent (Montenegro, Romania, and Serbia) and Bulgaria's acquisition of newfound autonomy. However, given British and Austro–Hungarian opposition to the treaty, Germany proposed convening a conference in Berlin, to which all the main European powers—Germany, Austria, France, Italy, United Kingdom, Russia, and Turkey—were invited. While the Ottoman debt barely got a mention at San Stefano, it was a central issue at the Berlin Conference (Feilchenfeld 1931, 233–34).

The Berlin Conference ended with the recognition of several states' partial liability for the management of the Ottoman debt. The discussion of the debt sought to determine the respective liability of each state and the guarantees to offer bondholders. Under the Treaty of Berlin, signed on 13 July 1878, Bulgaria, Montenegro, and Serbia were required to assume part of the Ottoman public debt, the amounts to be determined later. But other countries that acquired new territories, mainly Russia, were exempted from all liability. At the time, the Ottoman debt was still in default. The conference urged the Ottoman empire to accept the establishment of a financial commission that would centralize the claims of the various creditors in order to reach an agreement acceptable to all the parties (Wynne 1951 [2000], 426–27).

Over the next few years the same dual situation, liability and exemption, recurred with cessions of territories. In 1881 Greece was held liable for a share of the debt in exchange for newly acquired territory, whereas no claims were upheld against Austria–Hungary after it finally annexed Bosnia-Herzegovina (Feilchenfeld 1931, 232–45). Although established in principle, the practical division of the Ottoman debt remained deadlocked. In 1881 the Treaty of Mouharrem resolved some of the issues, particularly by creating a Council of the Ottoman Public Debt, but it did not settle the apportionment.

Not until the Treaty of Lausanne in 1912, which ended the war between Turkey and Italy, were the practical terms of the transfer of the Ottoman debt explicitly laid down in a treaty (Feilchenfeld 1931, 356–61). After Tripoli and Cyrenaica were annexed, Italy accepted a share of the debt. The Treaty of Lausanne, signed on 18 October 1912, based the amounts to be paid annually by Italy on the revenues of the annexed territories, previously allocated to servicing the Ottoman public debt.[2]

The First Balkan War further complicated the apportionment process. Although the Treaty of London, which ended the First Balkan War, contained a provision on financial settlement, the outbreak of the First World War interrupted the negotiations. The settlement of the Ottoman debt after the First World War became more complex than ever. The signing of the Treaty of Lausanne on 24 July 1923 ended the debates over the shares to be assumed by each country. A distinction was drawn between the territories ceded before and after the First Balkan War, specifically, before and after 17 October 1912. The successor states were allocated a share of the debt proportional to the revenues of the annexed territories for the years 1910–11 or 1911–12. The only difference lay in scope, with the earlier group referring to the empire in October 1912, the latter referring to a smaller area (Feilchenfeld 1931, 466–67; Wynne 1951 [2000], 490–91). The amount actually due by each country was not decided until November 1924 and sparked numerous objections that were finally arbitrated by the League of Nations in April 1925. The division of the Ottoman debt resulted in an unusually complex apportionment of liability. Turkey was assigned 65 percent, Greece 9 percent, Syria and Lebanon 8 percent, Iraq 5 percent, Yugoslavia 4 percent, and Palestine 3 percent; the remainder was assigned to Bulgaria, Albania, Hedjaz, Yemen, Transjordania, Italy, Nejd, Maan, and Assyria.

The positions of the United States and Britain were guided by the concept of fairness, which had the advantage of being highly flexible over time. To my knowledge, neither the United States nor Britain objected to the apportionment of the Ottoman debt when the Ottoman empire disintegrated. In the nineteenth century America and Britain acquired new territories, but in the twentieth century their territorial expansion stabilized, and Britain was later faced with the independence of most of its colonies. Twentieth-century geopolitics altered American and British interests, particularly their position on the succession of debt. While they were expanding territorially, their interest was to reject succession; but when the trend reversed, they supported recognition of debts by the successor states.

In the case of the Russian repudiation, in which France and Britain were creditors, it is hardly surprising that a common position was found. In a joint communiqué dated 28 March 1918 the Inter-Allied Committee on War Purchases and Finance published a resolution adopted in early February of the same year.[3] It stipulated that "the obligations of Russia bind and will bind the new state or the group of new states that represent or will represent Russia" (Klotz 1924, 78–79).

In light of the above, what might the expectations of French investors in the early twentieth century have been in terms of the succession of states and debts? More than likely the concept of the succession of states would have seemed extremely complex. They would certainly have been aware of the conflicting examples of Cuba and the Ottoman empire, since most of the Cuban bonds were held in France and Belgium, and Ottoman debt had been present in Paris since the Crimean War (Romey 2007, 289). Those two cases probably left room for only limited optimism. Even in the best-case scenario, in which third parties would repay part of the Russian debt, the Ottoman example showed that repayment by successor states was likely to be slow and not necessarily executed by all the parties.

The peace talks that followed the First World War rekindled interest, given that the peace treaties signed at the time all contained clauses on public debt apportionment (Feilchenfeld 1931, 431). The treaties were far from consistent, however. In the case of Germany alone, three situations resulted: a cession of territory without an assumption of debt (e.g., the annexation of Alsace-Lorraine by France); a cession of territory with a partial debt assumption of debt (e.g., the annexation of Eupen and Malmedy by Belgium); and a cession with full assumption (e.g., the annexation of Memel by Lithuania).

Whatever the sentiment of French investors at the time, one can reasonably assume that even without having a clear idea of the obligations of successor states they would have been attracted by promises of repayment from third countries.

Promises, Promises

The repayment of the debt issued by the tsarist regime was not a priority for the newly established governments. In fact, some regions probably wanted a clean break in order to underscore their newly acquired independence. Therefore, it might seem surprising that some countries were willing to assume a share of the tsarist debt. Their motivations—excluding an unlikely ethical motive—are easy to sum up. For some countries the recognition of debt seems to have been limited to debt owned by its own population.[4] It was thus a domestic policy matter that may have been a way to reject the Bolshevik revolution, that is, a way of asserting attachment to a capitalist economy, or an attempt at economic recovery. When the proposal to recognize the debt extended beyond national borders, geopolitical motives are likely. Some recognition seems to have been motivated by a desire to secure military aid in order to ensure the nation's survival, while others were hoping to strengthen trade relations with Western countries.

A PRINCIPLE APPLICABLE TO RUSSIA?

The apportionment of the Russian debt was mentioned as early as January 1918.[5] At the time, it was seen as a subsidiary issue of a general peace treaty, and, apparently, a peace that did not include Russia was not envisaged at the time. Members of the National Securities Office (Office National des Valeurs Mobilières) commented that if a treaty led to the autonomy or secession of territories and if this in turn led to an apportionment of debts, then French interests would be best represented by diplomatic channels. When that comment was made, debt apportionment did not seem likely. The recognition of autonomy was presented as a necessary but not a sufficient condition for apportionment. On the stock exchange the issue was addressed indirectly: market practitioners considered it would be inadmissible for Russia not to repay its debt if it did not break up into a number of smaller states.[6] At the level of French diplomacy the possibility of a succession of states became part of the prevailing view at a very early stage. The joint declaration by France and Britain explicitly provides for this possibility by stipulating that the obligations of Russia bind and will bind the new state or *all the new states* that represent or will represent Russia.

Although Germany obliged Russia to pay an amount in gold to protect German holders of Russian bonds, none of the treaties signed by the two countries referred to an apportionment of the debt as a result of territorial changes (Feilchenfeld 1931, 535). On the contrary, the Brest-Litovsk Treaty assigned full liability for the Russian debt to Russia. Germany maintained the same position in the case of Romania (see Treaty of Bucharest of 7 May 1918) after the cession of territories that had previously belonged to that country.

The apportionment of the imperial debt between Russia and the new states was mentioned in *Gazette du Commerce et de l'Industrie* on 13 July 1918.[7] The author of the article reported that a substantial amount of formerly Russian assets now belonged to the new states. Although he did not propose a basis for apportionment, he estimated that the amount involved was worth more than 4.5 billion rubles in the form of railways as well as land mortgaged to the Imperial Land Mortgage Bank for the Nobility. The General Commission for the Protection of French Interests in Russia soon included the concept of the succession of states in its arguments.[8]

The tone adopted by the foreign minister, Stéphen Pichon, radically changed in a letter to the chairman of the National Securities Office dated October 1918.[9] Citing the case of Poland, the minister made it clear that the successor states were liable for the public debt. In his view the terms of the assumption of the Russian debt, particularly the mechanism for its division, should be settled as part of the negotiations between the Allied governments. Despite this change of tone, until 1920 French policy toward Russia would focus on an almost reunified Russia repaying the debt. Anatole de Monzie criticized the dominant influence of certain civil servants who were behind this policy toward Russia.[10] In his opinion the sole debtor approach was contrary to French interests. Despite the proposals of repayment by some states that declared their independence, France continued to back the proponents of a united Russia, thus alienating the new states.

The positions of the various Russian representatives in Paris were more radical. Recognizing the successor states' liability for the Russian debt would have been tantamount to recognizing their secession. Members of the Russian Political Conference in Paris were quick to express their views to the chairman of the Peace Conference. In their opinion only Poland had a legitimate claim as a separate state because it had been declared independent by what they considered to be the last legitimate government of Russia. Finland's share of the debt could also be discussed, given the historical separation between Russian and Finnish finances (Eliacheff 1919, 237–39). Conversely, the other secessions were not considered valid. Until August 1920 the Soviets were counting on a settlement that took the liability of the successor states into account. At his meeting with de Poulpiquet du Halgouët, Leonid Krasin cited the Ottoman example.[11]

In February 1921 the issue of repayment by the successor states was raised at the international conference on the protection of private interests in Russia.[12] It was quickly dismissed by the chairman of the General Commission, Joseph Noulens, a former French ambassador to Russia, who thought negotiations could not be opened with those states unless Russia participated. In Noulens's opinion the debt ought to be apportioned at an international conference to which Russia and all the creditor states and successor states would be invited.

France's relatively passive stance toward the successor states was undoubtedly adopted for geopolitical reasons. From late January 1918 on, some French leaders thought Russia should remain united in order to act as a counterweight to the other European powers, and they therefore sought to prevent secession (Carley 1976). Furthermore, the succession of states raised the issue of France's liability toward Germany, from which it had just taken Alsace-Lorraine; unless, as Raffalovitch claimed (1919, 100, 151), the case of Alsace-Lorraine was simply different. In any case that seems to have been the position that prevailed, since the region was assigned to France unencumbered.

REPAYMENT BY THE BALTIC STATES, FINLAND, POLAND, ROMANIA, OR UKRAINE?

The Baltic states, Finland, and Poland were established on territory that had belonged to the Russian empire before the revolution. Romania was also concerned by "Russia's legacy" in terms of debt because it received Bessarabia. All these new countries managed to secure and maintain their independence during the interwar period. Conversely, other territories, including Armenia, Azerbaijan, Dagestan, Georgia, Kuban, and Ukraine, were incorporated into Russia in the early 1920s and became an integral part of the Soviet Union in December 1922.

At one time or another, almost all these territories announced their willingness to repay or to discuss the assumption of some of the Russian debt. The cases of the Baltic countries, Finland, Poland, Romania, and Ukraine are outlined below. It also appears that the governments of Azerbaijan, Georgia, and Kuban considered partial repayment at one point and that offers to this effect reached France.[13]

The Baltic States and Finland

The financial relations between imperial Russia and the Grand Duchy of Finland were extremely complex. Since the Grand Duchy enjoyed political, economic, and financial autonomy within the Russian empire, the issue of its liability was tenuous. Finland's contribution to the various wars led by Russia ranged from heavy engagement during the Crimean War to a smaller—even tiny—commitment in later wars (Eliacheff 1919, 239–40). In peacetime, according to Eliacheff, who makes no secret of his pro-Russian sentiments, Finland enjoyed a privileged position. Its status, perceived as being unfair in Russia, was criticized when Russia entered the First World War. An interministerial commission that was convened suggested the ratifying of three principles: Finland's contribution to the extraordinary expenditure of the treasury as a result of the war (proportionate to its population); setting this contribution for a five-year period, starting at 1.8 percent for 1914–19; and Finland's payment into the imperial treasury of the amounts needed to cover its contribution to the war expenditure (Eliacheff 1919, 239–40). The proposal was not implemented, but in 1919 the lawyer Boris Eliacheff considered it an interesting basis for apportionment of liability.

The Baltic States and Finland were among the first countries to be recognized as independent by Russia. In a series of treaties signed in 1920 the Russian Soviet Federative Socialist Republic recognized Estonia, Latvia, Lithuania, and Finland as independent states. When these peace treaties were signed, they included the issue of the Russian debts. With astounding generosity, the Russian Soviet Federative Socialist Republic relieved the new states of any liability for Russian debt (Delaisi 1930, 17; Eisemann, 2002). Russia's generosity was evidently not to the taste of the creditor states, which considered the offending article illegitimate. Many contemporary lawyers criticized such a unilateral decision (Apolston and Michelson 1922).

Russia's position was undoubtedly motivated by several factors. These probably included a concern not to alienate the neighboring countries over an issue that did not cost Russia anything as long as the debt continued to be repudiated. In any case, as Feilchenfeld points out (1931, 539), Bolshevik Russia could hardly have expected a third country to repay a debt that it had itself canceled. Moreover, Russia had everything to gain by encouraging other states to reject liability for the prewar Russian debt. Russia was thus no longer isolated on the question of the debt. With the exception of Romania, all the successor states eventually supported Russia's position, although their stance was criticized.

Poland

Poland was mentioned as a potential payer as early as October 1918. Of the states that managed to remain independent during the interwar period, Poland, given its economic development, was probably the one that would have to assume the largest share of the debt after Russia. It was also in the best position to do so.[14] Raffalovitch (1919, 100) argued that Poland should assume a share of the Russian debt as well as buy back the railways financed by Russian bonds on its territory. While Poland's borders were not final, the amounts to assign to it were the subject of bitter debate. According to Eliacheff (1919, 245), the "new" Poland should occupy only the territory of the former Kingdom of Poland. Illogically, while the population was used as the basis for debt apportionment in the case of Finland, Eliacheff recommended using revenues in the case of Poland—a much more advantageous arrangement for Russia. He justified this on the grounds of Poland's rapid economic development, which did not reflect the population criterion. After demonstrating that there was insufficient data to calculate the share to be charged to Poland, Eliacheff (1919, 259–60) proposed basing it on direct and indirect taxes, stamps, and other levies. Using this methodology, which excluded contributions to state revenues and state lands and repayment of the treasury, Eliacheff found Poland liable for 13 percent of the Russian debt.[15] That figure is similar to the one proposed by Apolstol and Michelson (1922), who assigned 12.6 percent of Russia's public debt to Poland.

In a convention dated 28 June 1919 appended to the Treaty of Versailles, Poland accepted liability for part of the Russian debt. The convention stipulated that a conference would be convened between the Allied powers and Poland to determine its obligations more precisely. Despite that document, in a written question in May 1920 Edouard Daladier asked Foreign Minister Alexandre Millerand whether Poland had accepted its share of the Russian foreign debt and whether France would require all the Russian republics that had belonged to the empire to assume their share of Russia's foreign debt.[16] The end of the Russo–Polish War and the Peace of Riga signed on 18 March 1921 led to a redrawing of Polish, Russian, and Ukrainian borders. In a gesture of generosity similar to the one it extended to the Baltic States, one probably forced by the outcome of war, the Russian Soviet Federative Socialist Republic relieved Poland of any liability for the Russian debt.

The contradictions between the treaty of 28 June 1919 and that of 18 March 1921 were not lost on the French government, which reacted soon after the latter was published by protesting vigorously to the Polish government.[17] After expressing its surprise, France stressed the importance of the recognition of Russia's foreign debt and pointed out that French capital invested in Russia had "ultimately rendered inestimable services to Poland in the general war that had enabled Poland's resurgence." Between a threat and a reminder of duty, the text left little doubt as to the expectations of the French government, which deemed baseless the provisions of the Treaty of Riga on the succession of the Russian debt. The issue of Poland's liability was raised again later, particularly during the Franco–Russian negotiations of the 1920s. The far-right press and its representatives also demanded repayment by Poland (Bonzon 1924).

Ukraine

Ukraine experienced a turbulent period with a succession of governments between 1917 and 1921. France paid special attention to the country, not only for military reasons but also because France had invested heavily there before the war. According to Kosyk (1981, 56), more than half of the foreign investment in Ukraine came from France. Independence movements began to emerge there in March 1917. The Central Rada, a central council representing various Ukrainian organizations, was established that month. At the end of May a Ukrainian delegation traveled to Saint Petersburg to negotiate autonomy with the provisional government. Their application was rejected, leading to direct assumption of autonomy by the Central Rada, which proclaimed independence in June and set up a national government, the General Secretariat of Ukraine (Kosyk 1981, 78). Lacking capable leaders, an organized army, and a bureaucracy, the new country soon proved to be ungovernable (Subtelny 1994, 348). The Bolsheviks' seizure of power after the October Revolution opened up the question of relations between Russia and Ukraine. The Bolsheviks, who were thinly represented in Ukraine, took a pragmatic position. Too weak to overthrow the Central Rada and the partisans of the provisional government who had retreated to Ukraine, they made the best of a bad situation and strove to maintain cordial relations with their new neighbor, at least until they could eliminate the partisans. The respite was short-lived, as Bolshevik troops headed into Ukraine in late 1917 (Kosyk 1981, 156; Subtelny 1994, 350). Meanwhile, France had opened negotiations with the new country. It is not surprising therefore that in December 1917 Ukraine was considered a separate entity on the Paris Bourse. This decision reflected the belief that Ukraine would not follow the Bolshevik course.[18]

The first clashes took place between the forces of Simon Petliura, Ukraine's minister of war, and the Red Army troops led by Vladimir Antonov-Ovseyenko. A string of military successes for the Bolsheviks created a critical situation for the Central Rada, which hoped a foreign intervention might reverse the situation. The French government, eager to maintain an Allied front in the east, gave the Ukrainian government de facto recognition on 5 January 1918 (Carley 1976). That late recognition was not enough to ensure its continuity, however. The Treaty of Brest-Litovsk drastically changed the balance of power. Represented at the treaty talks, the members of the Central Rada eventually promised to supply food in exchange for German military support (Subtelny 1994, 353). In practice the treaty led to the division of Ukraine into German and Austro–Hungarian spheres of influence and to the introduction of a new government that replaced the Central Rada.

In late April 1918 a new provisional Ukrainian government was established under Hetman Pavlo Skoropadski.[19] His conservative regime remained under the sway of Germany. The new government neverthe-less developed a foreign policy that led to the signing of a peace treaty with Russia on 12 July 1918. Opposition to Skoropadski's regime, which receded temporarily, returned with a vengeance when it became clear that the Central Powers were going to lose the war. The Treaty of Brest-Litovsk, which confirmed German–Ukrainian rapprochement, must have left the French with a bitter taste (Kosyk 1981, 260). That develop-ment and the anticipation of Germany's defeat may explain the position adopted by the Ukrainian government on the Russian bonds. On 26 September 1918 the hetmanate apparently declared its intention to pay advances for the coupons of the tsarist and provisional government bonds deposited in Ukrainian banks before 1 November 1918.[20] Shortly afterward an insurrection led by Petliura and others attacked the govern-ment. By mid-December the rebels had seized power and restored the Ukrainian National Republic (Subtelny 1994, 359). Yet far from stabiliz-ing the country, the new government was faced with total anarchy, as no fewer than six armies—Ukrainian, Bolshevik, White, Polish, the En-tente, and anarchist—were operating on its territory.

In January 1919 the delegation of the Ukrainian republic offered to assume part of the Russian debt.[21] As a successor to Russia but also to maintain its alliance with France, Ukraine declared it was willing to assume a 30 percent share. According to the Ukrainian representatives, that figure corresponded to Ukraine's share on the basis of its population and wealth. On several occasions in 1920 Ukraine reaffirmed its will-ingness to assume some of the Russian debt. At the Conference of San Remo Ukraine again offered to repay 30 percent of the former Russian debt.[22] In return Ukraine asked to recover 30 percent of the Russian gold from the Bolsheviks and 30 percent of the domestic bills and bonds issued before the revolution. Ukraine also expressed the wish to be represented so that its citizens could be considered for compensation by Russia in the future.

The military situation in Ukraine deteriorated further in 1919. After repulsing a second Bolshevik offensive in the summer of 1919, the country faced another onslaught in December. It took the Russian troops almost another year to defeat their last White and Ukrainian opponents. But in November 1920 the country was still prey to armed groups opposed to the Bolshevik government. The last opposition movements were not eradicated until late 1921. The incorporation of the Ukrainian Soviet Socialist Republic into the Soviet Union in December 1922 definitively foreclosed any possibility of repayment by Ukraine as an independent entity.

Romania and Bessarabia

Romania was the only successor state the Soviets did not exempt from liability for the tsarist debt, a fact that can be explained by the Soviet Union's refusal to sanction the integration of Bessarabia into Romania. In a treaty signed on 28 October 1920 Romania eventually recognized its liability for the share of the Russian debt corresponding to the territory of Bessarabia. However, the Romanian agreement yielded payment for only one security, the Akkerman Railway bond (Freymond 1996, 94–95). The practical terms of this were established in 1934. These provided for the exchange of expired coupons for Romanian 4.5 percent bonds (at 50 percent of the nominal value of the coupons) and the exchange of the bonds themselves for Romanian bonds of the same nominal value.

Despite that apparently good news French investors drew only meager gains from the exchange. During the interwar period, the bonds of the Kingdom of Romania suffered a spectacular series of defaults, followed by as many restructurings (Ureche-Rangau 2008). In early 1941 the Romanian government declared a general retroactive moratorium on public foreign debt. After years of talks an agreement was finally reached in 1959. This offered only symbolic compensation to the holders of Romanian bonds but settled the fate of those held in France once and for all.

A Joint Agreement

In late 1920 France suggested settling the apportionment of the Russian debt under a broad agreement. In a memorandum to the British embassy the political affairs division noted explicitly that Russia should not be the only entity to incur the burden of the Russian debt.[23] It proposed establishing an international body to apportion the debt that would be tasked with determining the amounts to be assumed by each of the parties and with transferring the funds. According to the authors of the memorandum, the mechanism could be based on the one set up by the treaties of 1918. No such body was ever established, but in 1921 some Russian bondholders remained convinced that the Russian debt would be apportioned on the basis of criteria to be determined.[24] The Committee for the Defense of Belgian Interests in Russia (*Comité de défense des intérêts belges en Russie*) mentioned the liability of Estonia, "Livonia," Lithuania, Poland, Romania, Georgia, Armenia, Azerbaijan, and, to some extent, Ukraine. Citing the case of Austria, the committee recognized the complexity of the methods that could be used to determine the respective share of each state but proposed that it be based on each entity's capacity to contribute (based on revenues from the railways, customs, or a tax on naphtha).

When the question of the Russian debt was addressed by the de Monzie commission, the apportionment of the imperial debts between the states that emerged from the ruins of the empire resurfaced. According to Delaisi (1930, 17), a consensus was reached that the secession of the Baltic countries, a large share of Poland, and a slice of Bessarabia should be reflected in a 25 percent reduction in the Soviet Union's share of the debt. Delaisi (1930) says these states were all in agreement. However, responding to a question from a member of the audience during a lecture he gave called "The Soviets and the Russian Debt in France," Delaisi (1930, 40) acknowledged that an agreement existed in principle but that no demand for funds had been sent to the countries concerned. And, in his opinion, even if such a demand were expressed, those countries would be unable to repay their share of the debt, other than by supplying raw materials.

Although agreements were reached, no payments were actually made in the name of the succession of states. The thorny issue of the terms of apportionment had long held back the negotiations on the Ottoman debt. The Russian case was likely to be equally complex. Depending on the criteria used, the respective shares assigned to each territory would have varied considerably. An apportionment based on the size of the states or, to a lesser extent, on the size of the population would have left Russia liable for the bulk of the debt; an apportionment based on actual investments or on the revenues of each region would have been more disadvantageous for the other states.

Eisemann (2002) considers that Russia is no longer the debtor for all the bonds. He claims that some of those obligations would be the liability of the Baltic countries, Poland, and Romania. In a moment of history repeating itself, the issue of the succession of states and their debts was raised again when the Soviet Union collapsed in 1991.

The Paris Peace Conference and the Treaty of Versailles: Paving the Way for German Repayment of the Russian Debt

Even before the end of the First World War investors hoped the repayment of the Russian bonds would be addressed in the peace talks. As early as January 1918 the *New York Times* opined that the question of the Russian debt would be settled in the peace treaties.[25] In August 1918 the members of the General Commission asserted, "Settlement of the Russian debt will definitely be included in the clauses of the peace treaty." A few months later John Maynard Keynes, the British treasury's delegate at Versailles, wrote a memorandum on compensation payments (Keynes 1971, 340–41). He referred explicitly to the possibility that, as part of the reparations, Germany might assume a portion of the debt issued by Allied countries and owned by German citizens. He argued that Germany might be forced to assume the Russian, Italian, Serbian, Belgian, or Romanian debt.

In January 1919, as the Paris Peace Conference opened, there was fresh enthusiasm for Russian bonds on the Paris Bourse, based on the hope that the conference would have a positive outcome for the Russian bondholders.[26] That hope was dashed when it was announced that the Bolshevik government had been invited to the negotiating table.[27] The impact of the conference was not limited to the Paris market since Russian bondholders in London were hopeful, too.[28] The Committee for the Defense of Belgian Interests in Russia worked to ensure that the peace conference did not alter Russia's liabilities without the consent of the bondholders.[29]

In the end Russia was conspicuously absent from the peace talks in Paris and consequently did not have an opportunity to express its opinions when the Treaty of Versailles was drafted. Despite its absence Russia was mentioned several times as part of the treaty. Regarding the fate of the Russian bonds, several points are noteworthy. First, Article 15 of the Treaty of Versailles canceled the provisions of the Treaty of Brest-Litovsk, and Article 19 provided for the transfer to the Allies of the gold paid to Germany by Russia under that treaty (Thomson 1966, 23–24). Articles 25 and 29 stipulated the opening of the Black Sea and the Baltic Sea to the Allies, facilitating their access to the regions threatened by the Bolsheviks.

Two articles, 116 and 117, subsequently took on great importance for the repayment of the Russian debt and formed the basis of numerous arguments on this issue. Article 116 stipulated that Germany should recognize the independence of all the territories that had belonged to the Russian empire, that it should accept the revocation of the Treaty of Brest-Litovsk, and—a factor of vital importance to the Russian bondholders—that the Allies should uphold Russia's right to demand reparations from Germany (Thomson 1966, 310). Article 117 strengthened the provisions of Article 116 by obliging Germany to recognize all the treaties that the Allies signed in future with the successor states to the Russian empire. Although some leaders of the White armies disagreed with the wording of those articles, particularly with respect to the successor states, they attempted to take advantage of them for military purposes, specifically by asking for weapons and German logistical support (Thomson 1966, 313–14). Last, Article 259 of the treaty provided for the transfer of all the amounts Germany had received under the Treaty of Brest-Litovsk (Apolston and Michelson 1922).

In 1919 Raffalovitch (1919, 100), hardly an impartial observer, said that part of the Russian debt should be assigned to the states "more responsible than others for the war, such as Prussia." That opinion was shared by other authors of Russian origin, such as Eliacheff (1919, 130). The economic and financial commission of the Russian Political Conference also considered Russia's claim on reparations from Germany to be legitimate. The commission felt that the claim should be treated in the same way as those of other countries that had been fully or partly occupied by Germany, such as Belgium and France (Eliacheff 1919, 266).

Naturally, Germany considered Article 116 of the Treaty of Versailles unacceptable.[30] In December 1921, shortly after Chicherin issued a memorandum offering to recognize the tsarist debts, the Riga-based newspaper *Novyi Put'* described the chronology of the Russian debt. The article distinguished between prewar and war debt and claimed that the latter had served only to enrich France and Britain. The position of those two countries on their own war debt also diverged significantly from Russia's line of conduct. Whereas France and Britain assigned their debt to Germany as part of the reparations, Russia refused to follow suit. The author of the article avowed that Russia never wanted to "participate in the plunder of the German people" but that "by refusing to take part in the despoiling, it erased its obligations stemming from the war debt."[31]

In practice, repayment by Germany would soon prove illusory. On 15 December 1921 Germany notified the Inter-Allied Reparations Commission that it was unable to meet the next scheduled payment (Apolston and Michelson 1922). If Germany was already unable to repay the reparations directly attributable to the war, demanding that it pay for Russia was practically senseless. Negotiations between Russia and Germany opened in early 1922. According to rumors on the Bourse in March 1922, the outcome of those negotiations was that Russia refused to demand reparations under the Treaty of Versailles.[32] The Treaty of Rapallo, signed by Germany and Russia on 16 April 1922, confirmed the rumors (Davis 1926) and finally extinguished all hope that Germany would repay the Russian debt.

Recent Econometric and Financial Research

I have sought thus far in the book to identify all the potential reasons Russian bond prices remained resilient despite the formal announcement of their repudiation. My purpose here is to determine the relative importance of each of these factors from a quantitative perspective.

Several approaches might have been taken to determine the respective role of each of these factors. In theory it is possible to construct a model of market prices for the repudiated Russian bonds by incorporating each of the factors for hope plus a factor reflecting the market's risk-free rate of return. The advantage of this approach is that it would show the importance of each factor explicitly and directly. Unfortunately, it would be hard to perform in practice. It would require the creation of a set of variables whose quantification (how could the probability of a bailout by the French government be measured?) or at least frequency (how could daily price movements be elicited on the basis of much lower-frequency data?) would be questionable.

Event studies, a common methodology in finance, might also have been possible. An event study seeks to determine whether a particular type of event generates an abnormal return at or shortly before the time it occurs. This method involves determining a normal rate of return, which is a highly debatable undertaking in a time of war, and, even more important, the delimitation of periods during which the type of event can be isolated. In relation to companies, event studies are often used to analyze, for example, the impact of share buybacks on value. The event methodology is well suited to corporate studies because the events are known and easy to identify, and it can be assumed that no other major event will have an impact on market prices a day before or after the buyback is announced. In the case of the Russian bonds, however, this approach is clearly not realistic. War alone generates events every day, and it is therefore next to impossible to isolate individual events to ensure that other factors have no influence on prices.

Consequently, two main approaches were preferred here. The first seeks to determine the dates on which market prices for Russian bonds underwent major changes. Determining the dates corresponding to extreme returns is relatively standard in this type of analysis. The approach has several advantages. First, it forces the researcher to consider the simultaneous impact of several events on prices. Second, contemporary sources have to be examined to determine market participants' expectations at the time the events occurred. That reveals factors that the researcher might not have thought of spontaneously, and it avoids ex post bias. It is tempting, when one knows how the historical events unfolded, to focus on events that are *now* considered as major. Several studies of financial assets in wartime (such as Willard, Guinnane, and Rosen 1996; Weidenmier 2002; Frey and Waldenström 2007) have shown that the dates perceived as crucial at the time and the dates that historians consider key do not always match perfectly.

However, analyzing the dates that coincide with large market movements is not entirely foolproof. First, the method cannot capture a situation in which several factors occurring on the same day had opposite effects on prices. Second, the determination to find a single explanatory factor for a strong variation in prices can easily lead to overinterpretation. As Cutler, Poterba, and Summers (1989) point out, it is often impossible to attribute some large price changes to a specific cause. Two previous studies (Oosterlinck, 2003a; Oosterlinck and Landon-Lane 2006), presented and developed in this chapter, were based on this type of approach. The first examines the biggest variations in the return on the 4.5 percent Russian bond issued in 1906 over the period January

1918—December 1919 (Oosterlinck, 2003a). The second study, by Oosterlinck and Landon-Lane (2006), is also based on an analysis of major changes from January 1915 to December 1919 but excludes general shocks affecting the French market as a whole.

The second approach attempts to isolate the impact of a specific factor: expectations of a bailout. That analysis, drawn mostly from Bernal, Oosterlinck, and Szafarz (2010), compares the trends of two similar securities traded in both London and Paris. Since measures were introduced during the war to prevent arbitrage, any price differences that appeared after the repudiation can be attributed to differing expectations of a bailout by French and British investors.

Last, the reactions of market prices of Russian bonds reflect changes in traders' expectations. These usually result either from a change in assessment or from a revision of expectations based on new information. Depending on the origin of the information, the amount of time elapsed between the time an event occurred and the time it was reported on markets must have varied enormously. It seems obvious that news from French sources would have reached the markets faster than news from Russia. But it would be a mistake to assume that the speed at which news traveled from Russia to France remained constant over the period under review. Until November 1918 the flow of information from Moscow or Petrograd remained steady because it transited through Scandinavia. The subsequent severing of diplomatic ties between Russia and Sweden considerably extended that timeframe.[1] The subsequent vagaries of the civil war made communications between different parts of Russia—and therefore between Russia and other countries—even more complex.

Major Shocks Affecting Returns on Russian Bonds

To identify the events that caused the biggest changes in Russian bond prices, I analyzed the daily returns of the 4.5 percent bond of 1906 between 1 January 1918 and 31 December 1920. I left 1921 out of the analysis for several reasons. First, the number of quotes in 1921 was much lower than in the previous years (187 observations for 1921 compared with 209 for 1920, 277 for 1919, and 260 for 1918). Second, and most important, 1921 was characterized by long periods in which prices remained constant. From late May to early August 1921, for example, prices changed only five times and remained within a range of 27 percent and 27.75 percent of par. Prices indicated renewed trading (and also increased) between early March and early May 1921, in August 1921, and at the very end of December 1921. Those movements can reasonably be attributed to the short-lived Kronstadt rebellion, to the negotiations and the signing of the Anglo–Soviet Trade Agreement, to Krasin's announcement that Russia would recognize the debt, and to the preparations for the Cannes conference.

The price trend between January 1918 and December 1920 shows far more movement than in 1921. Returns are therefore analyzed over that period. The standard formula for the realized return on a bond is

$$r_t = (P_{t+1} - P_t + D_t)/P_t$$

where r_t is the realized return, P_t the bond price in time t, and D_t any coupon paid in t. The returns are calculated on a daily basis. In order to avoid having to integrate returns calculated over longer periods, which would introduce a strong bias for periods when trading was only intermittent, the analysis uses only the returns observed between two consecutive trading days.

Table 6.1 shows the daily returns and their characteristics over the period under review. As mentioned above, the average market price remained relatively high over the entire period. Although the average return is close to zero, there are spikes.

Table 6.1. Descriptive statistics of prices and returns on the 4.5 percent Russian bond of 1906

	Price	Realized return (%)
Mean	52.88	−0.02
Median	54	0.00
High	66.5	6.53
Low	26.5	−6.27
Standard deviation	7.86	1.69

To identify extreme events, the analysis focuses on the days on which the return is more than 2.5 standard deviations from the mean. In other words, I focus on the days for which the return is above 4.20 percent or below 4.25 percent.

Table 6.2 shows the dates corresponding to extreme returns and the suggested explanations for these spikes. The rightmost column groups the explanations into five types: a French bailout (B), the First World War in France and other factors specific to the Paris Bourse (F), recognition of the debt by newly created or third countries (N), military events in Russia (R), and announcements about the debt by the Soviets or other revolutionary movements (S).

Extreme returns were recorded on a total of eighteen dates. No explanation could be suggested for six of the dates, but there are several for three of them.[2] Most of the spikes—fifteen of the eighteen—are associated with positive news. More surprisingly, most of the shocks, thirteen, occurred in 1920, compared with just two in 1918 and three in

Table 6.2. Dates of extreme shocks and suggested explanations

Date	Return (%)	Suggested explanation	Type
1–2 February 1918	4.55	French government announces it will pay the February coupon (31 January 1918)	B
6–7 November 1918	−6.27		
25–26 April 1919	6.53	Denikin's and Kolchak's victories	R
		Expectations of the imminent demise of Bolshevism	R
		Rumors of Bolshevik proposals to negotiate the debt	S
16–17 October 1919	4.27	14 October 1919: Denikin's troops reach Orel	R
		16 October 1919: Yudenich's offensive against Petrograd	R
24–25 November 1919	4.98		

Table **6.2.** *continued*

Date	Return (%)	Suggested explanation	Type
8–9 January 1920	4.38	U.S. Secretary of State Robert Lansing suggests continuing the blockade of Russia	R
10–11 February 1920	5.88		
16–17 February 1920	5.05		
25–26 March 1920	5.88	Senator Anatole de Monzie's speech to the Senate (26 March)	B
16–17 June 1920	5.75	Gaudin de Villaine submits a written question	B
24–25 June 1920	4.44	Announcement by Millerand making French recognition of the Soviets conditional on debt recognition	B
		Creation of the Commission on the Liquidation of the Russian Debt	B
8–9 July 1920	5.95	Conference in Spa	F
28–29 July 1920	−4.44		
10–11 August 1920	4.88	France recognizes Wrangel's government	R
		Politburo mentions debt recognition (*Le Matin* on 12 August 1920)	S
19–20 August 1920	4.88	Polish victories in the Russo–Polish War	R
23–24 August 1920	4.60	Polish victories in the Russo–Polish War	R
25–26 August 1920	−5.49		
29–30 September 1920	6.03	Copenhagen talks on the assumption of the debt and declarations by Krasin (mentioned on 27 September 1920)	S

1919. Consequently, it seems that few of them can be attributed directly to the First World War. However, this timing may reflect a microstructure problem. Since the market was less liquid in 1920, the shocks may be linked to trades involving only a small number of securities. Unfortunately, a lack of data on trade volumes makes it impossible to test that hypothesis.

Most of the spikes seem to have been responses to military news. Armed action—particularly the offensives led by Kolchak, Denikin, and Yudenich—seem to have played a key role in 1919. Most of the spikes in 1920 were linked to the unexpected Polish victory in August. After military news, the second factor that caused major price changes was expectations of a French bailout and the related lobbying. Recognition of the debt was the third factor by order of importance. Only a minor role was played by factors specific to the French market and expectations that a third country would assume the debt.

The military factors identified by the analysis concur with the literature on the Russian civil war. The major shifts in market prices indeed reflect the main episodes of the war. One exception, the announcement by U.S. Secretary of State Robert Lansing that the blockade of Russia would not be lifted, seems to have had more of an impact on market prices than historians would ordinarily consider justified. The impact of expectations of a bailout was felt on prices when the decision to pay the coupons was taken and when negotiations on this issue began. The literature on sovereign default rarely considers "domestic bailouts." Yet the Russian example shows that expectations of a bailout by one's own government are one of the factors most likely to trigger sharp changes in prices. Indeed, somewhat surprisingly, the declarations on the debt by various Russian factions seem to have had less impact. The repudiation itself does not show up in bond prices. This may be because rumors had already impacted prices before the repudiation announcement or because a positive event occurred on the same date. The shocks related to debt recognition are mainly visible at the end of 1920. Counterintuitively, investors apparently continued to hope for a Russian repayment despite previous unkept promises. Last, one shock is attributable to a factor that affected the market in general, namely, information about the conference in Spa. At the conference most of the Allied powers signed an agreement on the disarmament of Germany, which seems to have been perceived as positive on the Paris Bourse.

The above results overlap with some of the results in Oosterlinck (2003a). The earlier study analyzed the returns on Russian bonds in greater detail, but only for the years 1918 and 1919. By omitting 1920—which, as already shown, concentrated most of the shocks in the period 1918–20—I was able to investigate more deeply the role of each of the grounds for hope. According to those findings, all of the grounds for hope influenced market prices. In the period studied, news from the Russian front was the main factor to which Russian bond prices reacted. In this analysis, news from the French front explains some of the extreme returns. Intuitively, Russian bond prices were also affected by negative news that had a marketwide impact. Announcements by the Soviets had the smallest impact, although the repudiation is visible in this analysis. The possibility of a French bailout shows up on one date only. Last, the Treaty of Versailles and Ukraine's announcement that it would recognize a share of the debt had a positive influence on Russian bond returns. The latter two observations suggest that market participants did give some credence to the probability of repayment by Germany or another country.

In summary, both studies highlight the predominant influence of events, whether actual or rumored, connected to the Russian civil war. Expectations of repayment by France had a strong influence in 1920 but less so in the previous years. Announcements of a Soviet or White repayment played only a secondary role. Repayment by a third country is visible in just one of the two analyses. The impact of the events affecting the French market as a whole should not be underestimated. To identify their exact role, a different methodology, detailed below, was applied to the data.

Main Shocks Specific to Russian Bonds

The analysis of the shocks impacting the returns on Russian bonds can indicate the bonds' sensitivity to the release of information of various types. The methodology used cannot isolate the factors specific to Russian bonds, however. Some events influenced the market as a whole. An extreme return could thus be the result of an event extraneous to the Russian bonds. One could assume, for example, that the bombing of the Bourse during the war would have affected Russian bonds as much as French ones. Therefore, to separate market effects from effects specific to Russia, Oosterlinck and Landon-Lane (2006) analyzed the prices for Russian bonds on the basis of the identification and estimation of a structural VAR model.

To separate the factors affecting the French bond market in general from those affecting Russian bonds specifically, two weekly data series were collected from the *Bulletin de la Cote de la Compagnie des Agents de Change de Paris* for the period 1 January 1915 to 31 December 1919. The securities selected for analysis are the 4.5 percent Russian bond of 1906 and the 3 percent French perpetual bond. The descriptive statistics for the two bonds are shown in table 6.3.

The methodology used to determine the shocks specific to the Russian bonds relies on a structural VAR under the assumption that the shocks impacting the Russian bond do not have a simultaneous impact on the French bond.[3] All the empirical results are presented in Oosterlinck and Landon-Lane (2006) and summarized in table 6.4. This shows the date of occurrence of the major shocks (defined in this case as being

Table 6.3. Descriptive statistics for the Russian bond of 1906 and the 3 percent French perpetual bond (1915–19)

| | 1906 Russian bond | | 3% French perpetual bond | |
	Price	Weekly return (%)	Price	Weekly return (%)
Mean	72.09	−0.18	63.03	0.02
Median	74.75	0.00	62.75	0.00
High	94.75	13.04	73.5	3.49
Low	45	−9.80	56.75	−3.50
Standard deviation	15.16	3.05	3.76	0.85

Source: Oosterlinck and Landon-Lane (2006).

Table 6.4. Dates of the extreme shocks specific to the Russian bonds and suggested explanations

Date	Shock	Suggested explanation	Type
16–23 May 1917	+	20 May 1917: the Russian Provisional Government recognizes the debt and renounces a separate peace	S
29 August– 5 September 1917	–		
16–23 January 1918	–	17 January 1918: Soviet-German peace talks	R
		21 January 1918: Soviet Central Committee repudiates the debt	S
30 January– 6 February 1918	+	31 January 1918: French government announces it will pay the February coupon	B
24–31 July 1918	+	25 July 1918: Ekaterinburg is taken	R
		26 July 1918: French troops land in Murmansk; rumors of a Japanese intervention	R
		25 and 26 July 1918: Expectations of a French government intervention on the debt	B
2–9 October 1918	+		
15–22 January 1919	+	14–16 January 1919: British–Soviet meeting in Stockholm; Soviets apparently willing to make concessions on the debt (announcement made public by Wilson on 20 January 1919)	S S
		21 January 1919: Soviet government announces its willingness to repay part of the debt	B
		16 January 1919: Announcement of the inventory of Russian bonds in France	

continued

Table 6.4. *continued*

Date	Shock	Suggested explanation	Type
23–30 April 1919	+	23–25 April 1919: Denikin's and	R
		Kolchak's victories	R
		25 April 1919: Expectations of the	R
		imminent demise of Bolshevism	R
		28 April 1919: Rumors that Lenin	
		had fled to Budapest	S
		26 April 1919: Rumors about	
		Bolshevik proposals for debt	
		negotiations	
30 April–7 May 1919	+	2 May: News that the Bolsheviks	R
		had evacuated Petrograd	
		3 May: News confirming the	R
		weakened position of the	
		Bolsheviks	N
		3 May: Treaty of Versailles	
7–12 May 1919	–		
12–17 May 1919	+	13 May 1919: Denikin's victories in	R
		southern Russia; Estonian troops	
		move on Petrograd	
		15 May 1919: Rumors that the	
		Bolsheviks had evacuated	R
		Petrograd	
15–22 October 1919	+	14 October 1919: Denikin's troops	R
		reach Orel	
		16 October 1919: Yudenich's	R
		offensive against Petrograd	
24–31 December 1919	–	24 December 1919: Revolt against	R
		Kolchak in Irkutsk	

Source: Oosterlinck and Landon-Lane (2006).

more than two standard deviations from the mean) as well as their sign, the suggested explanation, and the type of explanation.

No shocks specific to Russia are observed prior to 1917 (see table 6.4). This might seem surprising at first glance because it implies that the Russian bonds were influenced only by marketwide shocks that also affected French bonds. This unexpected fact can be attributed to the First World War. For an investor at the time, bad news from the Russian front probably meant bad news for France since Russia was an ally. Similarly, any French military defeat was likely to affect the market as a whole and was therefore already priced into the bond. That there was no shock reaction to the February and October Revolutions seems to indicate either that French investors did not consider them major events or that they did not yet perceive their future importance.

The analysis reveals a total of thirteen major shocks: two in 1917, four in 1918, and seven in 1919. An interpretation is suggested for ten of the shocks, and even several for five of them. Unfortunately, it is impossible to determine which of several potential causes was decisive; it is also likely that each of these causes contributed to the shock in question. In general, every reason for hope—a change in the Soviet position, a French bailout, military intervention, or repayment by a third country— triggered a shock in Russian bond prices at least once. Causes of a military nature predominate (seven occurrences), followed by announcements of debt recognition or repudiation by the revolutionary governments (four occurrences), expectations of a bailout by France (three occurrences), and repayment by a third country (one occurrence). The limited impact of debt recognition by third countries can undoubtedly be attributed to the period analyzed since most of the recognitions by third countries occurred after 1919. Last, it seems that from April 1919 on, prices reacted mainly to military news from the Russian front.

These results partly corroborate the studies presented earlier, with some dates even matching perfectly. The military factors correspond to events usually perceived as major by historians. There were also rumors of military events on the Paris Bourse, for example, that Lenin had fled. The signing of the Treaty of Versailles again emerges as a key date. In this particular case, the methodology reveals that it is not the marketwide impact of the treaty which is reflected in prices but elements specific to

Russia. This tends to confirm that what is actually measured here is the hope of repayment by Germany.

The analysis of the extreme shocks affecting Russian bond prices can therefore be used to determine the types of event likely to dramatically change investors' expectations. The method does not show the size of the impact of the various factors on valuation. Indeed, market prices for Russian bonds may incorporate factors valued by the market but for which there are only a few observable changes. Expectations of a bailout by the French government are a typical example. In the absence of new information confirming or denying a bailout, the method described above cannot be used to measure the impact of these expectations on the formation of Russian bond prices. An approach based on the no-arbitrage principle, presented below, shows that expectations of a French bailout were far from negligible; they actually accounted for a relatively large portion of the value of Russian bonds.

The Impact of Expectations of a Bailout

Bernal, Oosterlinck, and Szafarz (2010) analyze expectations of bailout based on the no-arbitrage concept. According to the law of one price (LOP), two equivalent securities must be worth the same, aside from transaction costs, on all the markets where they are traded. If LOP is not respected, financial market participants engage in arbitrage, which eventually reestablishes the single price.[4]

The particular situation that arose from the First World War made any arbitrage between France and Britain impossible for several years. From the beginning of the war, various measures were introduced on the French and British financial markets to prevent the enemy from selling securities there. The global nature of the war and its vicissitudes convinced the leaders of those two countries of the importance of limiting the resources available to the enemy as much as possible. Stock exchanges were initially closed down. In London all international arbitrage was eventually prohibited. Similarly, in Paris the purchase and sale of securities owned by foreign citizens or persons living abroad were declared illegal. The ban on arbitrage did not disappear when the armistice was signed; arbitrage did not resume until September 1919 (Michie 1999, 194). From 6 January 1916 to 30 August 1919, arbitrage between Paris and London was therefore impossible.

Bernal, Oosterlinck, and Szafarz (2010) took advantage of this particular international no-arbitrage situation to determine the expectations of French and British market participants of a bailout.[5] To do so, they analyzed the trend in market prices for the same security, the 4.5 percent bond of 1909 listed in both Paris and London.[6] Market prices were taken from the *Bulletin de la Cote de la Compagnie des Agents de Change de Paris* for France and from the *Financial Times* for London; the data cover the period from 8 January 1916 to 31 August 1919, a time when arbitrage between London and Paris was materially impossible.[7]

Since the same security is used for this price comparison, in theory it ought to be worth the same in Paris and London. There is indeed no reason to suppose that either of these markets had access to privileged information or had superior valuation techniques at the time. In other words, even with a no-arbitrage condition, the value of the bonds should be very similar on both markets. Figure 6.1 takes up the trend in prices for the 4.5 percent Russian bond of 1909 on the Paris and London markets.

In general, the prices on the two stock exchanges follow a similar trend. Until early 1918 the difference between the two series is only minor. After the repudiation, however, a widening gap emerges between the two series. That impression is verified statistically. As shown in the analysis in table 6.5, there is indeed a nonsignificant difference between prices on the two markets before the repudiation. Conversely, after the repudiation the difference is strongly significant, with the same Russian bond trading at almost 3 percent higher in Paris than in London. The difference is even more pronounced in relative terms: considering the average level of Russian bond prices at the time, the difference was equivalent to 6.5 percent.

Bernal, Oosterlinck, and Szafarz (2010) attribute the difference in prices observed after the repudiation to different expectations of a bailout in France and Britain. This is indeed the only element that could potentially explain that differential if one makes the reasonable assumption

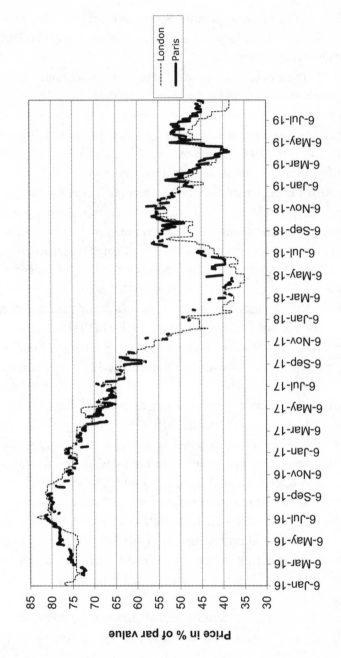

Figure 6.1. Comparison of prices for the 4.5 percent Russian bond of 1909 in London and Paris. Prices in percent of par value from January 1916 to end of August 1919. *Source:* Bernal, Oosterlinck, and Szafarz (2010).

Table 6.5. Descriptive statistics of the prices for the 4.5 percent bond of 1909 on the London and Paris stock exchanges and their differences (two subperiods: 6 January 1916–8 February 1918 and 9 February 1918–31 August 1919)

	Price before repudiation			Price after repudiation		
	London	Paris	Difference	London	Paris	Difference
Mean	72.56	72.45	0.12	44.80	47.73	−2.93***
	Difference not statistically significant			*** Difference significant at 1% confidence level		
Standard deviation	7.66	7.29	1.98	5.32	5.47	2.51
Median	74.00	74.15	0.50	46	48.5	−3.00
Low	40.00	46.00	−7.00	35	37.7	−10.75
High	83.50	81.50	5.00	54.5	57.75	3.70

Source: Bernal, Oosterlinck, and Szafarz (2010).

that investors on both sides of the Channel had access to similar information. A microstructure effect can also be ruled out because this would also have been present before the repudiation.

The impact of expectations of a bailout is therefore far from negligible. The measurement that indicates the difference in expectations between London and Paris gives a minimum value for its impact on the valuation of the bonds. It is unlikely that British investors set much store by a domestic bailout, since the British government had mostly adopted a noninterventionist policy in the past. However, if British investors were also expecting a bailout, even a minimal one, then the total impact of such expectations in France should be revised up and would therefore exceed the mean of 3 percent shown above. Eventually, the analysis also shows that bailout expectations influenced the dynamic of the bond price series.

Conclusion

The primary aim of this book is to understand something that, at first glance, might seem strange: the robust performance of Russian bonds after their repudiation. (As a reminder, the 5 percent bond of 1906 was trading above 45 percent of par more than two years after it was repudiated and was still valued at around 20 percent of par at the end of 1921.) I have also tried to set a specific but extreme case of repudiation in the broader context of theories about sovereign debt.

In hindsight, market prices seem at first to have reflected either unusual naivety or irrational behavior. In fact, this supposed anomaly can be interpreted on the basis of the so-called peso problem. This theory shows that ex post analysis often overlooks events that might have had an extreme impact on prices at the time but that, in the end, did not occur. Jorion and Goetzmann (1999) attributed the equity premium puzzle to a peso problem. According to them, investors were expecting an extreme crash further down the line and demanded a premium in exchange for taking on that risk. Since most studies in finance are based on uninterrupted markets, such as the U.S. market, the premium seems excessive ex post.

This book shows that French investors were actually far from irrational and that many had legitimate reasons to hope for repayment.

Historical precedents seemed to indicate that countries eventually re-negotiated their debts in the medium or long term in order to be able to borrow on capital markets again. The shifting position of the Bolsheviks, alternating between promises of repayment and rejection of liability, might have pointed to the possibility of a negotiated outcome. Threats of trade sanctions against Russia, already devastated by years of war (world war, then civil war), might also reasonably have seemed credible and effective. If threats were not sufficient, the possibility that the Bolshevik government would be overthrown by Allied troops or White armies could not be ruled out. At times the Whites' victory seemed only a mat-ter of days away. Last, even if the Bolsheviks remained in power, French investors could hope to be repaid by France, which is what happened when the Mexican debt was repudiated in 1867. Finally, if all those possibilities of repayment failed, investors could still expect partial re-payment by the countries created or enlarged as a result of the dismem-berment of the Russian empire.

Quantitative research confirms the importance of these expecta-tions, which ultimately enabled Russian bonds to continue being quoted at extremely high prices. It is not possible to determine the respective importance of each reason for hope in the overall valuation of the secu-rities. However, it seems reasonable to assume that each cause that re-sulted in a spike in market prices contributed to the overall robust per-formance of Russian bonds. On the basis of extreme changes in returns, the overthrow of the Bolsheviks was undoubtedly a major source of hope. Soviet proposals of repayment and expectations of a bailout by the French government were also considered important by investors. The hope of repayment by countries founded on the ruins of the Russian empire or by Germany seems to have had less influence. The differences can perhaps be explained by the amounts the investors could hope for in each scenario. If the White armies took power, they would probably rec-ognize all the debt. If repayment followed an about-face by the Soviets, it would be the result of lengthy negotiations that would sharply reduce the amounts repaid to investors. Similarly, a French intervention would probably never have exceeded 50 percent of par. As for repayment by a third country, this would have covered at most 30 percent of the out-standing debt.

Having so many grounds for hope, French investors seem to have been victims of enormous bad luck. This must be qualified by the fact that the probabilities of repayment by each source were most likely not independent. For example, if the Bolsheviks decided to recognize the debt, the French government no longer had any reason to intervene. Similarly, the French government probably lost some of the incentive to bail out its citizens whenever a newly created state recognized part of the former Russian debt. Oosterlinck and Ureche-Rangau (2008) suggest analyzing Russian sovereign debt as a portfolio of negatively correlated securities, with each security representing one of the potential payers. That approach can be debated. The changes in probability are not always mutually exclusive (when one appears, another disappears). If the newly created countries had agreed to repay almost 25 percent of the amounts due, is it irrational to think that the probability of the Soviet Union re-paying its share would have strongly increased? In any case, the ap-proach presented by Oosterlinck and Ureche-Rangau (2008) explains, through a diversification effect, why prices for the repudiated Russian bonds remained so high.

The repudiation of the Russian bonds deviates somewhat from the reasons usually offered to explain the repayment of sovereign debt. First, an additional factor—the debtor country's desire for political recognition—seems to have played a key role in the negotiations on debt repayment. This factor is not usually presented as a reason in the literature on sovereign debt. Second, the Soviet repudiation is one of those rare cases in which, even though the creditor countries deployed the full range of sanctions (reputation, military, trade, etc.) against the debtor state, a solution was not found in due course. Should the Russian case therefore be seen as a counterexample that could challenge tradi-tional theories? Probably not.

The inefficiency of the sanctions against Russia can be attributed to several factors. Debt repudiation was a strong symbolic gesture. Its supporters intended to signal a clean break with capitalism. It could therefore be seen as spearheading the ideology of the Bolshevik govern-ment. For the Bolsheviks, loss of reputation, seen by some as the main incentive for repayment, might in fact have been synonymous with suc-cess or at least with loyalty to an ideal. Repaying the loans to gain a good reputation would have been a direct betrayal of Lenin, who had criticized the plundering of the world by coupon-cutting capitalists. It is symptomatic that a negotiated solution was not reached until after the fall of the Iron Curtain. The ideological aspect thus undoubtedly limited the scope of the negotiations and the threat of reputational loss.

With respect to military sanctions, two factors are illustrative. First, such interventions had only lukewarm support from the Allied governments. There was no massive deployment of troops to force Russia to repay. Second, the purpose of both Allied military action and the civil war was to overthrow the Bolsheviks, not to force them to repay the debt. Consequently, it is easy to understand that the Bolsheviks had little incentive to engage in repayment negotiations.

The failure of trade sanctions can be ascribed to the lack of coordination between the creditor countries. Far from forming a homogeneous group, the creditors were worried about diverse issues. In France, where bondholders were extremely numerous, repayment of the bonds generated a great deal of political lobbying since every bondholder was a voter. In Britain, trade concerns prevailed, and pressure groups lobbied the government to reopen trade with Russia. In their opinion the potential economic benefits of trade were worth sacrificing the Russian debt for. The Anglo–Soviet Trade Agreement, signed in March 1921, made any further threats of trade sanctions ineffectual. Another factor also naturally played in Soviet Russia's favor. Given the size of its market and wealth of natural resources, excluding Russia from international trade might well have done more damage in the long term to the countries excluding it than to Russia itself. The Russian case therefore shows that the effectiveness of trade sanctions is dependent on the coordination of the creditor countries and that sanctions can be realistically considered only against small or, at most, medium-sized countries.

Last, the Russian case shows how the duration of the negotiations can alter their chances of succeeding. A multilateral conference to settle the Russian debt question was not convened until more than four years after the repudiation. The failure of the conferences at Genoa and The Hague sent the protagonists back to square one. The subsequent bilateral negotiations between France and the Soviet Union also took almost four years to reach a conclusion. They did lead to a repayment proposal, but the French government rejected it as insufficient. The length of the negotiations certainly affected the parties' willingness to find common ground. As relations between the two countries gradually returned to normal, the fate of the Russian bondholders became a problem whose solution became less and less of a priority. As a result, of all the defaults listed by Reinhart and Rogoff (2009), the Russian one is the one for which bondholders had to wait the longest before a settlement was agreed upon.

Epilogue

These days the pricing of a bond seems unrelated to the nationality of its holder. In other words, the financial markets do not seem to put a different value on a bond according to the nationality of the person holding it.[1] However, the Russian repudiation offers a historical counterexample. In the 1920s the British Union of Russian Bondholders indicated that, although it was not customary to mention the bondholders' nationality, the negotiations between Britain and the Soviet Union would not take the claims of non-British nationals into account (British Union of Russian Bondholders, 8). In 1921 the Committee for the Defense of Belgian Interests in Russia came to the sad conclusion that "Belgians own more unpaid coupons per bond held than nationals of other countries, particularly France, Britain, the Netherlands and Switzerland."[2] The difference in the valuation of Russian bonds highlighted by Bernal, Oosterlinck, and Szafarz (2010) can indeed be related to the disparate treatment afforded Russian bondholders. Having failed to secure a collective settlement, each country negotiated with Russia unilaterally. The result was that two holders of the same bond were not treated identically if they were not of the same nationality.

In July 1986 Britain and the Soviet Union signed an economic agreement that provided explicitly for the repayment of the Russian bonds held by British nationals. The practicalities of repayment were outsourced to Price Waterhouse (Freymond 1995, 110), which asked the bondholders to make themselves known.[3] In total, slightly fewer than 950,000 securities were presented by roughly 3,700 bondholders. On average the bonds were redeemed for 476 francs. Following the British precedent, negotiations were reopened between France and Russia. The first informal meetings were held at the end of 1989 (Freymond 1995, 113). A Treaty of Friendship and Cooperation, signed in Rambouillet in October 1990, stipulated that France and the Soviet Union agreed, inter alia, to promptly settle the financial disputes outstanding between the two parties (Freymond 1995, 114; Bayle 1997, 126). The breakup of the Soviet Union, which triggered the creation of another array of new countries, delayed the repayment process, chiefly because agreements needed to be signed by each of the successor states. The Treaty of Paris, signed on 7 February 1992 and implemented on 1 April 1993, reiterated the wording of the Rambouillet pact with respect to outstanding financial disputes. Through a series of bilateral agreements Russia eventually became the sole debtor for the outstanding debt held by Western countries (Bayle 1997, 127).

After more than three years of negotiations, the parties signed a memorandum of understanding (MoU) on 26 November 1996. Russia's wish to issue a new bond in Luxembourg probably accelerated the negotiation process. On 25 November 1996 France's finance minister, Jean Arthuis, and its foreign minister, Hervé de Charrette, announced the imminent signing of an agreement providing for the payment of a lump sum of $300 million for all of Russia's French creditors (Bayle 1997, 131). The amount was raised to $400 million the next day. On 27 May 1997 France and the Russian Federation signed an agreement on the final settlement of debt issued between the two countries prior to 9 May 1945 (Szurek 2002). The agreement was approved by the Act of 19 December 1997, passed by the French parliament. In practice the terms of the compensation payout were entrusted to a monitoring committee, analyzed by Muxart (2002) and discussed by Paye (2002). Deschamps (2002) and Baillet (2002) have described the rights of the Russian bondholders as a result of the Franco–Russian agreements.

The adventure of the Russian bonds issued in France before 1917 ended with a decree published in the *Journal Officiel* on 23 August 2000.[4] The decree defines the securities eligible for compensation:

1. Debt securities issued or guaranteed before 7 November 1917 by the government of the Russian Empire or by local authorities located on its territory;
2. Debt securities issued after 7 November 1917 but before 9 May 1945 by governments who administered a territory that was an integral part of the Union of Soviet Socialist Republics before the latter date or by local authorities located on territories that formed part of that country before that date;
3. Debt securities and shares issued before 7 November 1917 by companies headquartered on the territory of the Russian Empire;
4. Debt securities and shares issued after 7 November 1917 and before 9 May 1945 by companies that had their headquarters on a territory that was an integral part of the Union of Soviet Socialist Republics before the latter date;
5. Certificates representing the securities defined under points 1, 2, 3, and 4;
6. Bills issued by the Imperial Bank of Russia before 7 November 1917.

French legislators had not forgotten the inventory of bonds conducted shortly after the repudiation, and they ruled that only bonds that had been stamped at that time would be eligible for repayment. Furthermore, of the abovementioned securities, the legislators considered that only those with a nominal value should be taken into account. While that decision undoubtedly facilitated repayment, it created de facto inequality between bondholders given that the repudiation had also affected bonds with no nominal value.

Numerous estimates of the value of Russian bonds had been published in the press long before the decree of 23 August 2000. For example, an article published in 1996 valued a 500-franc Russian bond at almost 37,000 francs.[5] The monitoring committee of the Franco–Russian MoU

of 26 November 1996 compiled a report setting forth the system it used
to apportion the lump sum of $400 million for final settlement.[6] The
diversity of eligible securities made it extremely difficult to assess the
claims of each creditor. Two questions had to be addressed: (1) how
could values of the various securities be converted into a single unit of
account? and, once that was done, (2) how could the compensation
payment be apportioned among the creditors? These apparently simple
questions conceal a variety of subquestions. Should a distinction be
made between shares and bonds? of the sovereign debt securities, should
a distinction be made between those explicitly guaranteed by the state
and the others? what of the securities for which the debt agreement stipulated the allocation of a specific revenue to repayment? which currency
should be used for securities issued in more than one currency? And so
on, and so forth.

The decree of 23 August 2000 set out the complex mechanism used
to value the claims.[7] Each security or liquid asset was assigned a value in
1914 gold francs in accordance with the following rules:

1. The nominal value of the debt securities issued or guaranteed before 7 November 1917 by the government of the
   Russian Empire or by local authorities located on its territory is retained as the value of the security if it is expressed
   in 1914 gold francs. If the nominal value of the security is
   expressed in another currency, it is converted at the average exchange rate for that currency against the gold franc
   during the first seven months of 1914 in order to determine the value of the security;[8]

2. The date on which the other securities, with the exception
   of certificates, are valued is set at 1917 if the loss of entitle-
   ment to the debt resulted from dispossessions occurring
   on a territory that formed part of the Union of Soviet Socialist Republics on 28 September 1939. The date is set at
   1939 if the loss resulted from annexations that occurred
   between 28 September 1939 and 9 May 1945. If the nominal value is expressed in francs, the value attributed in
   1914 gold francs is obtained by applying the rate of change

in the purchasing power of the French franc in 1917 or 1939, depending on the case. If the nominal value is expressed in certain foreign currencies, the value assigned in 1914 gold francs is obtained by applying, first, the average exchange rate of that currency against the French franc prevailing in 1917 or 1939, depending on the case; and, second, the rate of change in the purchasing power of the French franc in 1917 or 1939;[9]

3. The eligible certificates are treated as the bearer securities they represent.

This method allows the various debt securities to be valued directly. For listed securities, an alternative approach would have been to use their market value at the time of the repudiation. This would have been a more accurate assessment of the impact of repudiation on the portfolios of the various holders of securities at the time it occurred. However, that approach would have left open the question of the repayment of unlisted securities.

Regarding the apportionment of the compensation, the report by the committee responsible for monitoring the 26 November 1996 MoU discusses the various approaches. These are as follows: pro rata compensation, which would calculate the total debt and then divide the amounts received from Russia proportionally; a higher rate of compensation for bonds; a higher rate of compensation for securities guaranteed by the state; a diminishing rate of compensation; compensation reserved for the original holders; or a lump-sum indemnity for each beneficiary.[10] Each of these methods had advantages and disadvantages. Some valuation methods favored large investors more than small. The first approach would probably be the most favorable to large investors and would pay small investors only a minimal indemnity.

Given these factors, the committee suggested a combination of two methods: the lump-sum method and the pro rata method but with a cap. In practice, the repayment process would consist of three stages:

1. The apportionment of the Russian compensation payout between two groups: securities holders, and those dispos-

sessed of their assets, according to the total debt owing to
each category;

2. The amounts allocated to securities holders would be divided in two, one half divided equally between the securities holders; the other divided proportionally to the debt
but with a cap per investor;

3. The amounts allocated to the dispossessed would be divided on the basis of the same principle as for the securities
holders but with different caps.

The amended French budget for 1999 set out the calculation
method to be used for the compensation payment.[11] The approach the
legislators adopted is very similar to the one recommended by the monitoring committee. It provides a lump sum equal to 250 million francs,
divided evenly among the investors eligible for compensation. That
lump sum was also augmented by an amount:

- proportional to the total value of the portfolio of securities
  and liquid assets if that value is less than 150,000 1914 gold
  francs;
- equal to the indemnity that a portfolio of securities and
  liquid assets of a value equal to 150,000 1914 gold francs
  would receive if the total portfolio value is more than
  150,000 1914 gold francs.

The choice of method can be and certainly was criticized. Nevertheless, it addresses several of the concerns expressed by the monitoring
committee. It does not lead to a major difference between the smallest
and largest indemnities, and it acknowledges to some extent the losses
actually incurred by investors, since part of the compensation payment
is calculated on a proportional basis. Obviously, this method did not
satisfy the largest holders of Russian bonds. Already disappointed by the
amounts finally conceded by Russia, some of them saw these terms as an
additional grievance. Consequently the Franco–Russian agreement came
under harsh criticism from several associations of Russian bondholders,
which considered the amounts paid out by Russia inadequate.[12] Some

investor groups are still lobbying for additional compensation. Bayle (1997) considers that only 10 per cent of Russian bondholders (and their descendants) at most were persistent enough for their securities to still be eligible for repayment eighty years after they were repudiated. Freymond (2002) considers that, as well as being too low, the compensation payment was based on political criteria. Given the storm of criticism that the Franco–Russian agreement has attracted, it is hardly surprising that a number of lawsuits have followed. The Russian bond affair therefore seems set to continue in France, despite the Franco–Russian agreement.

Despite being strongly criticized, the Franco–Russian agreement nevertheless enabled holders of Russian bonds to obtain compensation. That situation can be seen as privileged in comparison with that of Belgian holders of Russian bonds, who have to settle for the faint hope of future payment. The substantial amounts lent by Belgium and its limited clout on the international scene explain Russia's lack of enthusiasm to reach a settlement. Yet regular appeals continue to be made in both houses of the Belgian parliament. An organization to defend the interests of Belgian holders of Russian bonds, called Scripta Russia Manent, claims four hundred members and continues to wage a relentless campaign to have its rights recognized.[13]

Appendix A: Russian Bonds Listed out of Russia (1903)

Sovereign Bonds	Maturity	Currency	Listed in
5% 1822	Perpetuity	£	Paris, Amsterdam, Berlin, London
5% Gold 1884	Right to call in 1904	Fixed parity between rubles, Reichsmark, FF, Dutch guilder, and £	Amsterdam, Berlin
4% Gold 1889	81 years	Fixed parity between rubles, Reichsmark, FF, Dutch guilder, USD, and £	Paris, Amsterdam, Berlin
4% Gold 1890 (2nd emission)	80 years	Fixed parity between rubles, Reichsmark, FF, Dutch guilder, USD, and £	Paris, Amsterdam, Berlin

continued

Sovereign Bonds	Maturity	Currency	Listed in
4% Gold 1890 (3rd emission)	81 years starting in 1891	Fixed parity between rubles, Reichsmark, FF, Dutch guilder, USD, and £	Paris, Amsterdam, Berlin
4% Gold 1890 (4th emission)	60 years starting in 1891	Fixed parity between rubles, Reichsmark, FF, Dutch guilder, USD, and £	Paris, Amsterdam, Berlin
4% Gold 1893 (5th emission)	81 years starting in 1894. Not callable before 1904	Fixed parity between rubles, Reichsmark, FF, Dutch guilder, USD, and £	Paris, Amsterdam
4% Gold 1894 (6th emission)	81 years starting in 1894. Not callable before 1904	Fixed parity between rubles, Reichsmark, FF, Dutch guilder, USD, and £	Paris, Amsterdam, Berlin
Russian 4% Conversion Railroad Bds Ser. I 1889	81 years	Fixed parity between rubles, Reichsmark, FF, Dutch guilder, USD, and £	Paris, Amsterdam, Berlin, London
Russian 4% Conversion Railroad Bds Ser. II 1889	81 years	Fixed parity between rubles, Reichsmark, FF, Dutch guilder, USD, and £	Paris, Amsterdam, Berlin, London
Russian 4% Conversion Railroad Bds Ser. III 1891	80 years	Fixed parity between rubles, Reichsmark, FF, Dutch guilder, USD, and £	Paris, Amsterdam, Berlin, London

Sovereign Bonds	Maturity	Currency	Listed in
Conversion 4% 1880	81 years starting in 1881	Fixed parity between rubles, Reichsmark, and FF	Paris, Amsterdam, Berlin
Conversion 4% 1901	Not callable before 1916, callable at will afterward	Fixed parity between rubles, Reichsmark, FF, Dutch guilder, USD, and £	Paris
Russian state loan 4% 1902	39 years. Not callable before January 1915	Fixed parity between rubles, Reichsmark, Dutch guilder, and £	Amsterdam, Berlin
Conversion 4% Kingdom of Poland 1844	61 years	Rubles	Amsterdam, Berlin
Russian State Bank Obligations 4% 1866	37 years	Rubles	Paris
Conversion 3$^{8/10}$% 1898	81 years. Not callable before 1906	Fixed parity between rubles, Reichsmark, FF, Dutch guilder, and £	Amsterdam, Berlin
Gold loan 3.5% 1894	81 years starting in 1895. Not callable before 1905	Fixed parity between rubles, Reichsmark, FF, kronor, Dutch guilder, USD, and £	Paris, Amsterdam, Berlin, London
Loan 3% 1859	Buybacks on the stock exchange	£	Amsterdam, Berlin, London

continued

Sovereign Bonds	Maturity	Currency	Listed in
Gold loan 3% 1891	81 years starting in 1892	Fixed parity between rubles, Reichsmark, FF, kronor, Dutch guilder, USD, and £	Paris, Amsterdam
Gold loan 3%, 2nd emission 1894	79 years starting in 1894	Fixed parity between rubles, Reichsmark, FF, kronor, Dutch guilder, USD, and £	Paris, Amsterdam
Loan 3% 1896	Not callable before 1911. Afterward amortization or buybacks	Fixed parity between rubles, Reichsmark, FF, kronor, Dutch guilder, USD, and £	Paris, Amsterdam, Berlin
4% loan Grand Russian Railway, 1st issue (1858), declared public debt in 1893	75 years starting in 1867. Not callable before 1916	Fixed parity between rubles, Prussian Thaler, FF, Dutch guilder, and £	Amsterdam, Paris
4% loan Grand Russian Railway, 2nd issue (1861), declared public debt in 1893	75 years starting in 1867	Fixed parity between rubles, FF, Dutch guilder, and £	Amsterdam

Sovereign Bonds	Maturity	Currency	Listed in
3% loan Grand Russian Railway, 3rd issue (1881), declared public debt in 1893	70 years starting in 1881	Fixed parity between rubles, Reichsmark, FF, Dutch guilder, and £	Amsterdam, Berlin
4% loan Grand Russian Railway, (1888), Nicolai Bonds declared public debt in 1893	64 years starting in 1888	Fixed parity between rubles, Dutch guilder, and £	Amsterdam, London
4% loan Grand Russian Railway, 4th issue (1890), declared public debt in 1893	61 years starting in 1891	Fixed parity between rubles and Dutch guilder	Amsterdam
Russian (Nicholas Railroad), 1867 4%	84 years starting in 1868	Fixed parity between rubles, FF, Dutch guilder, and £	Paris, Amsterdam, Berlin, London
Russian (Nicholas Railroad), 1869 4%	82 years starting in 1870	Fixed parity between rubles, FF, Dutch guilder, and £	Paris, Amsterdam, Berlin, London
Moscow-Jaroslaw Railroad Co. declared public debt in 1900 5%	75 years starting in 1869	Fixed parity between rubles, thalers, Dutch guilder, and £	Amsterdam, London

continued

Sovereign Bonds	Maturity	Currency	Listed in
Ivangorod-Dombrovo Railroad 4.5%	50 years	Fixed parity between rubles, Reichsmark, FF, Dutch guilder, and £	Amsterdam, Berlin
Donetz Railroad 4% 1893	65 years starting in 1894	Fixed parity between rubles, Reichsmark, FF, Dutch guilder, and £	Paris, Amsterdam
Dvinsk-Vitebsk Railroad 4%	57 years starting in 1894	Fixed parity between rubles, Reichsmark, FF, Dutch guilder, and £	Paris, London
Koursk-Kharkof-Azof Railroad 4% Serie A declared public debt in 1894	67 years starting in 1888	Fixed parity between £, Reichsmark, and Dutch guilder	Amsterdam, Berlin
Koursk-Kharkof-Azof Railroad 4% Serie B declared public debt in 1894	65.5 years starting in 1889	Fixed parity between Reichsmark, FF, and Dutch guilder	Paris, Amsterdam, Berlin
Koursk-Kharkof-Azof Railroad 4% 1894 issue	61 years starting in 1894	Fixed parity between rubles, Reichsmark, FF, £, and Dutch guilder	Paris, Amsterdam

Sovereign Bonds	Maturity	Currency	Listed in
Moscow-Koursk Railroad 4% declared public debt in 1892	66 years starting in 1887	Reichsmark	Amsterdam, Berlin
Moscow-Smolensk Railroad 4% declared public debt in 1896	81 years. Not callable before 1906	Thalers and Dutch guilders	Amsterdam, Berlin
Moscow-Yaroslavl-Arkhangel Railroad, 1897, 4% declared public debt in 1900	45.5 years starting in 1897. Not callable before 1908	Fixed parity between rubles, Reichsmark, and Dutch guilder	Amsterdam, Berlin
Orel-Griazi Railroad, serie A 4% declared public debt in 1891	63 years starting in 1888	Reichsmark	Amsterdam, Berlin
Orel-Griazi Railroad, serie B 4% declared public debt in 1891	61 years starting in 1889	Reichsmark	Paris, Amsterdam, Berlin
Orel-Griazi Railroad, 1894 4% declared public debt in 1891	60 years starting in 1894	Fixed parity between rubles, Reichsmark, FF, Dutch guilder, and £	Amsterdam

continued

Sovereign Bonds	Maturity	Currency	Listed in
Riga-Dvinsk Railroad 4%	42 years starting in 1894	Fixed parity between rubles, Reichsmark, FF, Dutch guilder, and £	Paris
South-West Railroad 4%	68 years starting in 1885	Fixed parity between rubles, Reichsmark, FF, Dutch guilder, and £	Amsterdam, Berlin
Tambof-Saratof Railroad 4%	73 years starting in 1882	Fixed parity between rubles, Reichsmark, FF, Dutch guilder, and £	Amsterdam
Transcaucasian Railroad 4%	63 years starting in 1891	FF	Paris, Amsterdam
Morchansk-Syzrane Railroad 3%	66 years starting in 1890	Rubles	Amsterdam
Riajsk-Viazma Railroad 3%	66 years starting in 1890	Rubles	Amsterdam
Transcaucasian Railroad 3%	70 years starting in 1883	Fixed parity between rubles, Reichsmark, FF, Dutch guilder, and £	Paris, Amsterdam, Berlin, London
Loans from the former Crédit Foncier Mutuel, 5% declared public debt in 1895	Non-callable	Fixed parity between rubles, Prussian Thaler, FF, Dutch guilder, and £	Amsterdam, Berlin

Sovereign Bonds	Maturity	Currency	Listed in
6% loan from 1817 to 1818	Buybacks	Rubles	Amsterdam
5% loan from 1820	Buybacks	Rubles	Amsterdam
5% loan from 1854	Callable at par	Rubles	Amsterdam, Berlin
1864 Lottery Loan	60 years starting in 1865 Lottery	Rubles	Amsterdam, Berlin
1866 Lottery Loan	60 years starting in 1866 Lottery	Rubles	Amsterdam, Berlin
Kingdom of Poland, 4% liquidation loan		Rubles	Berlin
Russian 4% rentes, 1894		Fixed parity between rubles, Reichsmark, FF, Dutch guilder, and £	Paris, Amsterdam, Berlin, London, New York
Railroad Guaranteed Bonds			
4% Lodz 1901	38.5 years starting in 1902. Not callable before 1915	Fixed parity between rubles, Reichsmark, Dutch guilder, and £	Amsterdam, Berlin
4% Moscow-Riazan 1885	60 years starting in 1885	Reichsmark	Berlin

continued

Sovereign Bonds	Maturity	Currency	Listed in
4% Moscow-Riazan 1901	43.5 years starting in 1902. Not callable before 1915	Fixed parity between rubles, Reichsmark, Dutch guilder, and £	Amsterdam, Berlin
4% Koursk-Kiev 1887	68 years starting in 1888	Reichsmark	Amsterdam, Berlin
4% Moscow-Kiev-Woronej 1895	59 years starting in 1896. Not callable before 1906	Fixed parity between rubles, Reichsmark, Dutch guilder, and £	Amsterdam, Berlin
4% Rybinsk 1895	59 years starting in 1896. Not callable before 1906	Fixed parity between rubles, Reichsmark, Dutch guilder, and £	Amsterdam, Berlin
4% Moscow-Windau-Rybinsk 1897	57.5 years starting in 1897. Not callable before 1908	Fixed parity between rubles, Reichsmark, Dutch guilder, and £	Amsterdam, Berlin
4% Moscow-Windau-Rybinsk 1898	56.5 years starting in 1898. Not callable before 1909	Fixed parity between rubles, Reichsmark, Dutch guilder, and £	Amsterdam, Berlin
4% Moscow-Windau-Rybinsk 1898	55 years starting in 1900. Not callable before 1910	Fixed parity between rubles, Reichsmark, Dutch guilder, and £	Amsterdam, London
4% Riazan-Kozlof 1886	62 years starting in 1886	Reichsmark	Berlin

Sovereign Bonds	Maturity	Currency	Listed in
4% Riazan-Ouralsk 1894	52.5 years starting in 1895. Not callable before 1905	Fixed parity between rubles, FF, Reichsmark, Dutch guilder, and £	Amsterdam, Berlin
4% Riazan-Ouralsk 1897	49.5 years starting in 1898. Not callable before 1908	Fixed parity between rubles, Reichsmark, Dutch guilder, and £	Amsterdam, Berlin
4% Riazan-Ouralsk 1898	48.5 years starting in 1899. Not callable before 1909	Fixed parity between rubles, Reichsmark, Dutch guilder, and £	Amsterdam, Berlin
4% Kozlof-Woronej-Rostof, 1887	65 years starting in 1888	Reichsmark	Berlin
4% Kozlof-Woronej-Rostof, 1889	63 years starting in 1889	Fixed parity between Reichsmark, FF, and Dutch guilder	Amsterdam, Berlin
4% South-East 1897	55 years starting in 1898. Not callable before 1908	Fixed parity between rubles, Reichsmark, Dutch guilder, and £	Amsterdam, Berlin
4% South-East 1898	54 years starting in 1899. Not callable before 1909	Fixed parity between rubles, Reichsmark, Dutch guilder, and £	Amsterdam, Berlin

continued

Sovereign Bonds	Maturity	Currency	Listed in
4% South-East 1901	51 years starting in 1902. Not callable before 1915	Fixed parity between rubles, Reichsmark, Dutch guilder, and £	Amsterdam, Berlin
4% Warsaw-Vienna 1890, serie VII	41.5 years starting in 1902	Rubles	Amsterdam
4% Vladicaucas 1885	68 years starting in 1889	Fixed parity between rubles, Reichsmark, Dutch guilder, and £	Amsterdam, Berlin
4% Vladicaucas 1894	62 years starting in 1894. Not callable before 1905	Fixed parity between rubles, Reichsmark, FF, Dutch guilder, and £	Amsterdam
4% Vladicaucas 1895	60 years starting in 1896. Not callable before 1906	Fixed parity between rubles, Reichsmark, Dutch guilder, and £	Amsterdam, Berlin
4% Vladicaucas 1897	58 years starting in 1896. Not callable before 1908	Fixed parity between rubles, Reichsmark, Dutch guilder, and £	Amsterdam, Berlin
4% Vladicaucas 1898	57 years starting in 1899. Not callable before 1909	Fixed parity between rubles, Reichsmark, Dutch guilder, and £	Amsterdam, Berlin

Sovereign Bonds	Maturity	Currency	Listed in
Securities issued by governmental institutions and guaranteed by the states			
Imperial Land Mortgage Bank for the Nobility, 5% Mortgage Lottery Bonds		Rubles	Amsterdam
Imperial Land Mortgage Bank for the Nobility, 3.5% Mortgage Lottery Bonds, 1st issue		Fixed parity between rubles, Reichsmark, FF, Dutch guilder, and £	Paris, London
Imperial Land Mortgage Bank for the Nobility, 3.5% Mortgage Lottery Bonds, 2nd issue		Fixed parity between rubles, Reichsmark, FF, Dutch guilder, and £	Paris
Imperial Land Mortgage Bank for the Nobility, 3.5% Mortgage Lottery Bonds, 3rd issue		Fixed parity between rubles, Reichsmark, FF, Dutch guilder, and £	Paris

Source: Manuel du Porteur de Fonds Russes. Emprunts émis ou garantis par l'état et côtés à l'étranger. Published in St. Petersburg by the Russian Ministry of Finance.

Appendix B: Russian Bonds Listed on Paris Stock Exchange (2 January 1917)*

---

1. Russian 4% 1863 and 1869 to be reimbursed at par
2. Russian 4% 1880 to be reimbursed at par
3. Russian 4% Gold 1889
4. Russian 4% Gold 1890 (2nd and 3rd issues)
5. Russian 4% Gold 1890 (4th issue)
6. Russian 4% Gold 1893 (5th issue)
7. Russian 4% Gold 1894 (6th issue)
8. Russian consolidated 4%, 1st and 2nd series
9. Russian consolidated 4%, 3rd series
10. Russian consolidated 4% 1901
11. Russian 3% Gold 1891–94
12. Russian 3% Gold 1896
13. Russian 3% Gold 1894
14. Russian 5% 1906 (Series 1–273)
15. Russian 4.5% 1909 (Series 37–230)
16. Russian Interior bond 4% 1894 (Series 1–112)
17. Russian 4% Donetz Railroad bond, 1893
18. Russian 4% Dwinsk-Vitebsk Railroad bond
19. Russian 4% Koursk-Kharkof-Azov Railroad bond, 1889 Serie B
20. Russian 4% Koursk-Kharkof-Azov Railroad bond, 1894
21. Russian 4% Orel-Griasi Railroad bond, 1889, serie B

22.   Russian 4% Riga-Dwinsk Railroad bond, 1894

23.   Russian 3% Transcaucasian Railroad bond, to be reimbursed at par

24.   Russian 4% Transcaucasian Railroad bond, to be reimbursed at par

25.   Russian 3.5% Imperial Land Mortgage Bank for the Nobility, (1st, 2nd, and 3rd issue)

26.   Russian 4%, Russian Peasants' Mortgage Bank, to be reimbursed at par

27.   Russian 4%, Grand Russian Railway bond, to be reimbursed at par

---

* In the section *Fonds d'Etat Etrangers* (Foreign Sovereign Bonds)

Source: Cours Authentique des Agents de Change.

Notes

Abbreviations Used in the Notes

ACAC   (1914–21), archives of the Compagnie des Agents de Change de Paris, Procès verbaux, SBF, Paris

ANPFVM   (1917–24), archives of the Association Nationale des Porteurs Français de Valeurs Mobilières

APPP   (1917–19), archives of the Préfecture de Police de Paris

JORF   *Journal Officiel de la République Française*

Preface

1. See, for example, the arguments expressed in Patrick Juillard and Brigitte Stern, eds., *Les emprunts russes aspects juridiques,* Paris: CEDIN Paris 1, Cahiers Internationaux, 2002, p. 16. See also Freymond (1995) and Bayle (1997).

2. An article published in the Belgian newspaper *Le Soir* dated 21 January 1919 gives an idea of the information available in Europe about the situation in Russia and the Bolsheviks' intentions. Entitled "The Bolsheviks nationalise women," the piece announces a decree on the nationalization of women and claims, "Commissars of Free Love have been appointed in several cities, and respectable women have been flogged for refusing to comply."

3. According to Darmon (2002), the inspectors were ordered to "take the pulse of public opinion." Copies of their reports were forwarded to the Ministry of the Interior and the Ministry of War.

4. This name dates from October 1919, when the institution was recognized as a public interest organisation. Prior to that date, it was the Office National des Valeurs Mobilières.

5. Quoted in Trotsky, *My Life:* http://www.marxists.org/archive/trotsky/1930/mylife/ch45.htm

Introduction

1. According to the figures from the Coordinated Portfolio Investment Survey (CPIS) conducted by the IMF): http://cpis.imf.org/. If one considers the eurozone as a whole the figure rises to 64.3 percent (see Lane 2006).

2. According to the same authors, in proportion war debts represented 48.33 percent of the total; prewar state debts, guaranteed loans, and municipal bonds 37.20 percent; and industrial securities 14.47 percent.

3. Feis (1930). Only one security was listed on the Lyon stock exchange, but many Russian securities were traded on the curb market (*Le Rentier,* 17 October 1921). Appendix 1 provides a list of the government and government-guaranteed securities traded outside Russia. The first list was established on the basis of the *Manuel du Porteur de Fonds Russes,* published by the Russian Ministry of Finance in 1903. Since it was published by the Russian ministry it is likely to be complete. The second list is concentrated on the Paris market. It details the securities listed on the official market (Parquet) in January 1917 on basis of the Cote Officielle de la Compagnie des Agents de Change.

4. *Le Rentier,* 27 February 1918, for the figures provided by E. Brousse. Speech to the Senate by Senator Anatole de Monzie (Senate, session of 26 March 1920, p. 390).

5. Office National des Valeurs Mobilières, "Note sur la création d'un comité de protection des intérêts français engagés en Russie," 22 January 1918, ANPFVM 440-A-17.

6. *Le Rentier,* 27 February 1918. This amount is corroborated by a subsequent study by the Commission générale pour la protection des intérêts français en Russie, *Le Rentier,* 17 October 1921.

7. The overestimation is likely to be relatively small, however, as many domestic Russian bonds were held abroad (Bovykin 1990; Bayle 1997). Bayle (1997) mentions, for example, the presence of internal loans issued in 1908 and 1914 in French portfolios.

8. Comparing the relative size of defaults across time is not an easy task. Depending on the assumption made regarding the reinvestment of the coupons and the use of the currency option embedded in most bonds, the present value of a given bond may differ dramatically. For example, Augros and Leboisne (1997) show that, depending on the assumptions made, the value in 1997 francs of the 4 percent Russian gold loan could range from 109 to 143,475 francs! Siegel (2014) estimates the total amount of imperial Russian sovereign debt as well in excess of $100 billion in early twenty-first-century terms.

9. Quoted in *Le Rentier,* 17 June 1919.

10. British Union of Russian Bondholders, 24.

11. Ibid., 24–25.

12. If one takes 1914 as the reference year, £100 would be worth between £6,350 and £49,950 (in 2005 pounds sterling) depending on the method used; either way, this is not an amount within reach for small savers. See the methods described by Law-

rence H. Officer and Samuel H. Williamson: http://measuringworth.com/calculators/ukcompare/

13. Association belge pour la défense des détenteurs de fonds publics, *Rapport annuel pour l'exercice 1920–1921*, 149–54.

14. Aulagnon, "La question russe à la veille de la conférence de Gênes," March 1922, ANPFVM 440-A-56.

15. Readers interested in the trends in investments in Russian bonds can refer to Girault (1973), who is still the leading authority on the issue. See also Siegel (2014).

16. According to Sergei Witte, who held senior posts in the imperial government, the memory of the Crimean War and Russian neutrality during the Franco–Prussian War was still fresh at the time (Ukhov 2003).

17. They estimate their number at 250.

18. "Les emprunts russes et la vénalité de la presse," *Le Crapouillot*, May 1932, 33–39.

19. Speech by Senator Anatole de Monzie to the Senate (Senate, Séance du 26 mars 1920, p. 393).

20. *L'Economiste français*, whose editor in chief was Leroy-Beaulieu, also received a stipend from the Russian government. Raffalovitch nevertheless claimed that Leroy-Beaulieu was expressing his personal opinion when he praised Russian credit (Raffalovitch 1931, 28, 128).

21. The former finance minister Kokovtsov was at this time secretary to the tsar and represented Russia in the negotiations surrounding a new bond issue in France. Kokovtsov was subsequently named finance minister again (Wieczynski 1976).

22. See in particular the article by Anatole France in *L'Humanité* on 2 February 1905, 3.

23. Speech of 18 March 1905, quoted in *Le Crapouillot*, May 1932, 35–36.

24. Marius Moutet, during the parliamentary discussion of a bill on advances to Allied governments (Chambre des députés, Séance du 31 janvier 1918, p. 250).

25. Speech of 18 March 1905, quoted in *Le Crapouillot*, May 1932, 36.

26. Letter from Maxim Gorky on the Russian bonds and reply from Anatole France, Publications périodiques, Société des amis du peuple russe et des peuples annexés, Paris, April 1906.

27. Anatole France, in *L'Européen* of 25 March 1905, quoted in Long (1972, 350).

28. Speech of 18 March 1905, quoted in *Le Crapouillot*, May 1932, 37.

29. Quoted in *Le Crapouillot*, May 1932, 37.

30. Only cash was accepted, and the futures market did not open until the beginning of 1920. See Vidal (1919) for a description of stock market activity in the first few hours of the war.

31. The months in parentheses refer to the Julian calendar. Contrary to practice in volumes about the Russian revolution, I use the Gregorian calendar here because those are the dates used in France at the time.

32. See, for example, Figes (1997), Pipes (1990), Trotsky (1995), and Werth (2004).

33. Session of 21 March 1917, quoted in the speech by Gaudin de Villaine to the Senate on 20 March 1920 (p. 396).

34. Quoted in Skidelsky (1983, 337).

35. *Le Rentier,* 27 May 1917.

36. See, for example, *Le Rentier,* 7 July 1917.

37. *Le Rentier,* 27 May 1917, and British Union of Russian Bondholders, 16.

38. *Le Rentier,* 7 July 1917.

39. *Le Rentier,* 25–27 August 1917.

40. *Le Rentier,* 27 October, 17 and 27 November 1917

41. *Le Rentier,* 17 and 27 December 1917.

42. *Le Rentier,* 17 December 1917.

43. ANPFVM, 440-A-29

44. ANPFVM, 440-A-10.

45. *Le Rentier,* 27 February 1918.

46. ANPFVM 440-A-10

47. Commission générale pour la protection des intérêts français en Russie, Bulletin no. I, 1 October 1918, p. iii, ANPFVM 440A3.

48. 2.25 billion and 1.4 billion francs.

49. More exactly, the bond traded at 45 percent of par on 15, 16, 17, 25, and 26 April 1918.

50. "Decline in Russian Bonds," *New York Times,* 26 February 1918.

51. Stephen Castle (20 February 2012), "Europe Agrees on New Bailout to Help Greece Avoid Default," *New York Times* online edition.

52. Daniel Bases (March 9, 2012), "ISDA declares Greek credit event, CDS payments triggered," Reuters.

53. Spreads were computed on a weekly basis; when there were no data on a given date, the closest value in the week was taken.

54. This date corresponds to the European Union summit proposing a 50 percent haircut for private holders of Greek debts. An alternative date could have been February 2012, when this measure was agreed upon, or March 2012, when credit default swaps were triggered. Be that as it may, choosing any of these alternatives would not change the main findings.

55. Even though Romanian bonds offered more guarantees at issuance.

56. The bonds considered were both mainly traded on the Paris Bourse, their benchmark market. In both cases the issues were heavily subscribed by small investors in a chaotic issuance environment: the end of the First World War in the case of Russia and the Great Depression for Romania. All these bonds were issued with the blessing of the French government because of their geostrategic and geopolitical benefits. They included an explicit or implicit gold clause.

57. With all the limitations that this approach implies: lackluster trading in a usually lively segment could involve a larger volume of trade than a lively session in a segment where trading is thin.

58. One stock market inspector put the matter very clearly: "The resumption of

business is adjourned until a date that no one can predict," APPP, BA 1587, 13 April 1918, see also APPP, BA 1587, 22, 24 April 1918. See also Lehmann (1997).

59. APPP, BA 1587, 3 December 1917, and APPP, BA 1587, 6 December 1917.

60. *Le Rentier,* 7 December 1917. See also APPP, BA 1587, 13 December 1917, which mentions unfulfilled *demand.*

61. *Le Rentier,* 27 December 1917.

62. APPP, BA 1587, 18 January 1918.

63. *Le Rentier,* 27 March 1918.

64. *Le Rentier,* 27 August 1918.

65. *Revue des Valeurs Russes,* no. 1, 14 September 1918.

66. *Le Rentier,* 27 August 1919.

67. APPP, BA 1572, 19 January 1920.

68. *Le Rentier,* 17 May and 7 July 1920. This wait-and-see position would crop up frequently in *Le Rentier;* see, for example, *Le Rentier,* 27 August 1920, 17 September 1920, 17 January 1921.

69. APPP, BA 1572, 25 December 1920.

70. *Le Rentier,* 17 May 1921.

71. Draft resolution in favor of Russian bondholders submitted by Senator Gaudin de Villaine, Documents Parlementaires, Senate, 22 October 1922, Annexe no. 610, p. 24.

72. One of these occasions was in late 1920 when news of Wrangel's defeat reached Paris. *Le Rentier* of 27 November 1920 mentioned that "the decline would have been steeper if trading volumes had not been so low." Similarly, *Le Rentier* of 17 January 1921, referring to the impossibility of selling large quantities of Russian bonds, said that "it would not take many buy orders to boost prices."

73. Commission générale pour la protection des intérêts français en Russie, Communication no. 1, 5 August, 1918, ANPFVM, 440-A-30.

ONE Sovereign Debt

1. There are several definitions of sovereign debt, with some authors (see, notably, Eaton and Fernandez 1995) using the term only to refer to debt issued by developing countries. The definition used here is broader and encompasses all debt issued by a sovereign state, irrespective of the creditors or type of security. For a recent study on the problem of sovereign debt, see, for example, Oosterlinck and Szafarz (2005) and Oosterlinck (2013).

2. Collateral for sovereign debt is now extremely rare (see Bulow 2002). This can be attributed notably to the difficulties of seizing collateral and to the amounts involved. In the Middle Ages a diverse array of collateral was used, including royal crowns and noble titles. See Hoeflich (1982). In some exceptional instances collateral seems to have worked. Vizcarra (2009) provides evidence of the successful use of guano as collateral for Peru's foreign debt in the nineteenth century. In this case, the success of the scheme was probably also owing to the good reputation of the British intermediaries in charge of selling the guano and collecting the revenues to service the debt.

3. It is difficult to establish a direct causal link between default and coups d'état. For an attempt to analyze this issue, see Bordo and Oosterlinck (2005).

4. Although the debt discussed here is that of American states, not the federal government, it can be considered equivalent to sovereign debt since the U.S. Constitution recognizes state sovereignty for debt.

5. These two states did repay their debts in full; the other three repaid in part.

6. Given that the law made no provisions for an individual to take a state to court, bondholders petitioned the king of Spain and then the prince of Monaco for assistance, albeit unsuccessfully.

7. See, for example, "Revolutionary finance—An example for Mr Lenin" in the *British Russian Gazette,* 30 November 1922.

8. Sack (1927) mentions mainly the Provisional Government of the Northern Region (Arkhangelsk); General Vandam's army (Pskov); the armies of General Rodzianko, General Yudenich, and Avalov-Bermont (western Russia); the Central Rada, the Hetmanate (seven months) and the Directorate (two months) in Ukraine; the volunteer armies of General Denikin and General Wrangel in the south; the Crimean Regional Government; the Don Army; the Kuban Rada; General Dutov's army (Orenburg); the Urals Regional Government (Ekaterinburg); the Provisional Siberian Government; Admiral Kolchak (Omsk); Ataman Semenov (Chita); Medvedev's government (Vladivostok), etc.

9. However, democratically elected leaders may decide to repudiate debts, as Rafael Correa did in Ecuador in 2008.

10. Ochoa (2008) traces the concept back to Aristotle.

11. A. N. Sack will be frequently mentioned in this paragraph as his name has been associated with the odious debt doctrine. As shown by Ludington et al. (2010) many myths have been created around him, and his writings should be put into perspective.

12. For a more detailed description of the characteristics and the amounts invested in these financial products, see especially Oosterlinck and Szafarz (2005).

13. For a summary that includes all potential cases, see Rieffel (2003).

TWO Reputation, Trade Retaliation, and Recognition

1. Moreover, as explained below, there seems to have been no unanimous support for the repudiation within the various Socialist movements.

2. In the United Kingdom in 1873, then in the Netherlands in 1876, in France and Belgium in 1898, in Switzerland in 1912, in Germany in 1927, and in the United States in 1933.

3. Lenin (1917 [1952, 9]) stressed the support given to Kolchak and Denikin by the Mensheviks or the Socialist-Revolutionaries against the Bolsheviks.

4. Even though some states (Greece and the Confederate States of America, for example) had in the past been able to float bonds abroad without being recognized as sovereign states, the norm was to accept only bonds of recognized sovereigns on the stock exchange.

5. British Union of Russian Bondholders, 25.

6. This point needs to be put into perspective, however, since it was actually thanks to French financial support that Russia avoided default in 1905–6.

7. See, for example, *Le Rentier,* 7 July 1917.

8. This was the position of the UK chancellor of the exchequer, Bonar Law, and the Dutch finance minister; see *Le Rentier,* 17 December 1917.

9. Louis-Lucien Klotz, in the discussion in the lower house of a bill on advances to the Allied governments (Chambre des députés, 31 January 1918, p. 249).

10. "Russian Bonds Drop on Repudiation Talk," *New York Times,* 12 January 1918. And "Russian bonds were an outstanding feature of weakness owing to the reported drastic action of the Bolsheviks against foreign creditors. . . . The Petrograd message announcing that the Superior Council of National Property have drafted a decree declaring null and void all national bonds issued by the Imperial and Bourgeois Government, . . . which is held by foreigners, naturally had a bad effect on Russian bonds."

11. APPP, BA 1587, 18 January 1918.

12. APPP, BA 1587, 21 January 1918.

13. APPP, BA 1587, 21 February 1918, and Raffalovitch (1919, 80, 112).

14. *Le Rentier,* 7 July 1917

15. Commission générale pour la protection des intérêts français en Russie, Communication no. 1, 5 August 1918, ANPFVM, 440-A-30.

16. According to Hogenhuis-Seliverstoff (1981, 52), Pierre Darcy had an important position at the time, particularly through his involvement in the Russian business syndicate, the Prodameta trust, and Banque de l'Union Parisienne. Letter to the chairman of Commission générale pour la protection des intérêts français en Russie; de l'ANPFVM, dated July 1918, ANPFVM 440A18

17. British Union of Russian Bondholders, 23.

18. British Union of Russian Bondholders, 22.

19. Commission générale pour la protection des intérêts français en Russie, Bulletin no. 1, 1 October 1918, p. 12, ANPFVM 440A3. Boris Avilov (1874–1938). This Russian revolutionary was originally a Bolshevik who joined the Mensheviks after 1905. He was last politically active in 1918 (Wieczynski 1976).

20. In other words, a matter between others, alien to the claimant. Korovin, cited in Sack referenced by Hoeflich (1982). See also Eisenamm (2002)

21. British Union of Russian Bondholders, 19.

22. Marius Moutet, in the discussion of a bill on advances to Allied governments in the lower house of parliament (Chambre des députés, 31 January 1918, p. 250).

23. This reference to an article in the *Frankfurter Handelsblatt* is mentioned in an internal document at the ANPFVM (ANPFVM 440-A-35), which is undated but was probably drafted in September 1918. This assertion should be interpreted with caution, as it might have been an attempt to boost Germany's credit rating during the war.

24. See *Le Rentier,* 17 June 1918, and APPP, BA 1587, 6 May 1918.

25. APPP, BA 1587, 6 May 1918.

26. Minutes of the Executive Committee Meeting of the Commission générale

pour la protection des intérêts français en Russie, 1 August 1918, ANPFVM, 440-A-17; see also *Le Rentier,* 7 July 1918.

27. *Messager de Paris,* 12 September 1918.

28. Office National des Valeurs Mobilières, Memo on the formation of a committee to protect French interests in Russia, 22 January 1918, ANPFVM 440-A-17.

29. Minutes of the Executive Committee Meeting of the Commission générale pour la protection des intérêts français en Russie, 1 August 1918, ANPFVM, 440-A-17.

30. *Le Rentier,* 7 September 1918. See also the speech by Senator Anatole de Monzie to the Senate (Senate, 26 March 1920, p. 391).

31. Commission générale pour la protection des intérêts français en Russie, Communication no. 1, 5 August, 1918, ANPFVM, 440-A-30.

32. Much of the information presented here comes directly or indirectly from this source, which was probably the most comprehensive database available to investors at the time.

33. Commission générale pour la protection des intérêts français en Russie, Communication no. 1, 5 August 1918, ANPFVM, 440-A-30.

34. Commission générale pour la protection des intérêts français en Russie, Communication, 24 September 1918.

35. Annuaire 1915–20, p. 128.

36. Speech by Senator Anatole de Monzie to the Senate (Senate, Séance du 26 mars 1920, p. 391). The first name is not mentioned in the text, but the person in question is likely Fernand des Closières, who was involved in the agreements reached regarding the Ottoman debt.

37. Letter to the chairman of the Commission générale pour la protection des intérêts français en Russie (ANPFVM), dated July 1918, ANPFVM 440A18

38. Presentation document of Union des Valeurs Russes, ANPFVM 440-A-13.

39. *Le Rentier,* 7 March 1925.

40. Ibid.

41. Commission générale pour la protection des intérêts français en Russie, "Note sur la protection des intérêts privés en Russie," undated but probably published after 1926, ANPFVM 440-A-43.

42. Ibid.

43. See appendix 1 for an inventory of these associations compiled in the late 1920s.

44. *Corporation of Foreign Bondholders,* 45th Annual Report, 1918, p. 31.

45. *Corporation of Foreign Bondholders,* Annual Reports, 1919, 1920, 1921.

46. Association belge pour la défense des détenteurs de fonds publics, Central Committee Annual Report for 1914–19, p. 8.

47. This observation was made by the association, which was founded in 1898 (Borchard, 1951 [2000], 213). Association belge pour la défense des détenteurs de fonds publics, Annual Report for 1920–1921, p. 147.

48. For a view of Belgian involvement in Russian industry, see Peeters and Wilson (1999).

49. Annuaire 1915–20, pp. 127.

50. Ibid., pp. 126–28.

51. Ibid.

52. Minutes of the International Conference for the Protection of Private Interests in Russia, 10–13 February 1921, ANPFVM 440-A-25.

53. Association belge pour la défense des détenteurs de fonds publics, Annual Report for 1920–1921, p. 157.

54. Commission générale pour la protection des intérêts français en Russie, Report submitted to the Annual General Meeting of 30 September 1921.

55. *Le Rentier,* 17 June 1922.

56. Commission générale pour la protection des intérêts français en Russie, "Note sur la protection des intérêts privés en Russie," undated but probably published after 1926, ANPFVM 440-A-43.

57. Letter from Foreign Minister Stéphen Pichon to the chairman of Office National des Valeurs Mobilières, 23 October 1918, ANPFVM 440-A-10.

58. APPP, BA 1588, 31 January 1919.

59. *The Economist,* 1 and 15 February 1919.

60. Commission générale pour la protection des intérêts français en Russie, Bulletin no. 15, 1 November 1919, p. 212, ANPFVM 440A29.

61. APPP, BA 1572, 17 January 1920.

62. Speech by Anatole de Monzie to the Senate (26 March 1920, p. 395).

63. "Topics in Wall Street," *New York Times,* 28 February 1920.

64. "The Russian Peace Offer," *New York Times,* 28 February 1920

65. "Les offres de Kameneff pour la reconnaissance des dettes de la Russie," *Le Matin,* 12 August 1920.

66. Letter from du Halgouët to Foreign Minister de Fleuriau, (1999), vol. 1920, tome 2.

67. APPP, BA 1572, 29 March 1920.

68. APPP, BA 1572, 18 May 1920.

69. APPP, BA 1572, 30 June and 20 July 1920.

70. *Le Rentier,* 17 May 1920.

71. *Le Rentier,* 27 September 1920.

72. *Le Rentier,* 7 December 1920 and 27 August 1921.

73. "France Wants Gold of Soviets Seized," *New York Times,* 11 June 1920.

74. Association belge pour la défense des détenteurs de fonds publics, Annual Report for 1920–21, p. 155.

75. "Can't Attach Roubles for Czarist Debts," *New York Times,* 14 July 1921.

76. APPP, BA 1572, 10 January 1921.

77. Question from Communist member René Nicod (27 January 1921), Chambre des députés, 17 February 1921, p. 667; question from Senator Lederlin (16 March 1921), Senate, 24 March 1921, p. 325).

78. British Union of Russian Bondholders, 22, Glenny (1970).

79. Glenny 1970, 68–69.

80. For a detailed analysis of the treaty negotiations, see Glenny (1970).

81. British Union of Russian Bondholders, 22.

82. See, for example, the letter from the foreign minister to the chairman of the General Commission for the Protection of French Interests in Russia, 27 April 1921, ANPFVM 440-A-10.

83. *Le Rentier,* 27 August 1921.

84. See, for example, Liesse A., "La situation en Russie: A propos de l'accord commercial avec l'Angleterre," *L'Economiste Français,* 2 April 1921.

85. Letter from the foreign minister to the chairman of the General Commission for the Protection of French Interests in Russia, 27 April 1921, ANPFVM 440-A-10.

86. APPP, BA 1572, 11 June 1921.

87. *Le Rentier,* 27 August 1921.

88. Liesse A., "La situation en Russie et les intérêts de la France," *L'Economiste Français,* 5 November 1921, and Testis, "Lettre d'Angleterre," *L'Economiste Français,* 3 December 1921.

89. Written question from Senator Anatole de Monzie (3 April 1921), Senate, 23 April 1921, p. 1030.

90. "Russian Bonds Are Active," *New York Times,* 3 August 1921.

91. Commission générale pour la protection des intérêts français en Russie, Deuxième Série, Bulletin no. 5, November–December 1921, pp. 162–163, ANPFVM 440A1.

92. Ibid.

93. Ibid., p. 164.

94. Letter from the French Foreign Ministry to the British embassy, 8 November 1921, ANPFVM 440-A-10.

95. Commission générale pour la protection des intérêts français en Russie, Deuxième Série, Bulletin no. 5, November–December 1921, pp. 165–166, ANPFVM 440A1.

96. Ibid., pp. 166–167.

97. APPP, BA 1572, 7 November 1921.

98. "Stock markets. Revival in Russian bonds expected. Foreign bondholders and the outlook,"*British Russian Gazette,* 31 March 1922.

99. Ibid.

100. Commission générale pour la protection des intérêts français en Russie, "Note sur la protection des intérêts privés en Russie" undated (but probably published after 1926), ANPFVM 440-A-43.

101. Aulagnon, "La question russe à la veille de la conférence de Gênes," March 1922, ANPFVM 440-A-56.

102. *Le Rentier,* 7 May 1922.

103. "Russian Bonds at London: Scope of Their Recovery on Lloyd George's New Policy," *New York Times,* 24 April 1922.

104. *Le Rentier,* 17 June 1922.

105. *Le Rentier,* 7 July 1922. "The Russian Stock and Share Markets in June," *British Russian Gazette,* 30 June 1922.

106. "The Russian Stock and Share Markets in July," *British Russian Gazette*, 31 July 1922.

107. *Le Rentier*, 27 September 1922.

108. "The Russian Stock and Share Markets," *British Russian Gazette*, 30 November 1922.

109. Senator Adrien Gaudin de Villaine had already spoken out in defense of bondholders over the Panama scandal. His speeches on Russian bonds mingled anti-Communist and anti-Semitic sentiment, since Gaudin de Villaine viewed Bolshevism as an "accident of the great war, of the great Jewish-German war on Catholicism and France in particular." For more details on his life, see Robert and Cougny (1889–91) and Jolly (1960, 1791). Draft resolution in favor of Russian bondholders submitted by Senator Gaudin de Villaine, Documents Parlementaires, Senate, 22 October 1922, Annexe no. 610, p. 24.

110. See the correspondence between the U.S. State Department and the Russian ambassador and Russian financial attaché (1934), *American Journal of International Law* 28, no. 1: 12, 13, 15, 16.

111. *Le Rentier*, 17 August 1924.

112. On Jean Herbette's position, see Denéchère (2003).

113. Commission générale pour la protection des intérêts français en Russie, "Note sur la protection des intérêts privés en Russie," undated but probably published after 1926, ANPFVM 440-A-43.

114. *Le Rentier*, 27 December 1924.

115. Germany was granted a favored-nation clause at the end of 1925 (Davis 1927). This may have influenced the French position, particularly by kindling a fear that the Germans would eject France from Russia.

116. JORF, 1 July 1920, p. 9269.

117. APPP, BA 1588, 16, 17, 18 January 1919.

118. The metal content of the franc germinal had been defined in 1803. As a result of the First World War, France was forced to leave the gold standard. Following unsuccessful attempts to return to prewar parity, Poincaré devalued the currency in 1928. In terms of metallic content this new franc, the Franc Poincaré, was worth one-fifth of its predecessor (Sédillot 1979, 144).

119. Commission générale pour la protection des intérêts français en Russie, Deuxième Série, Bulletin no. 5, November–December 1921, p. 168, ANPFVM 440A1.

120. *Le Rentier*, 17 August and 7 November 1924.

121. *Le Rentier*, 17 August 1924.

122. *Le Rentier*, 7 November 1924.

123. Which the negotiations had fuelled (Delaisi 1930, 19).

124. *Le Rentier*, 7 December 1924.

125. Ibid.

126. British Union of Russian Bondholders, 26.

127. See *Le Rentier*, 7 July 1917.

128. *Le Rentier,* 27 February 1918.

129. Letter from Foreign Minister Stéphen Pichon to the chairman of the National Securities Office, 23 October 1918, ANPFVM 440-A-10.

130. Ibid.

131. "Conditions in Russia," *The Economist,* 1 March 1919, and "Soviet Russia's Conditions," *The Economist,* 31 May 1919.

132. APPP, BA 1572, 18 May 1920.

133. *Le Rentier,* 27 December 1924.

134. British Union of Russian Bondholders, 12.

135. British Union of Russian Bondholders, 30–32.

THREE Military Intervention and the Impact of War Events

1. Those fears were expressed notably by the former U.S. vice-president, John Quincy Adams.

2. Oosterlinck, Ureche-Rangau, and Vaslin (2014) show that, following Waterloo, the threat not to liberate France prompted the regime of Louis XVIII to honor France's debts.

3. In this case the price evolution actually reflects financial repression (see Oosterlinck 2010).

4. See, for example, Frey and Kücher (2000, 2001), Brown and Burdekin (2002), Oosterlinck (2003), Frey and Waldenström (2004), and Waldenström and Frey (2008).

5. APPP, BA 1587, 9 and 10 December 1917.

6. APPP, BA 1587, 6 December 1917.

7. APPP, BA 1587, 14 December 1917 and 17 January 1918.

8. "Russian Bonds Drop on Repudiation Talk," *New York Times,* 12 January 1918.

9. "Russian bonds, the market for which was still weak, though from the extent of the fall in prices it was evident that the proposal of the present administration to repudiate foreign loans is not taken seriously as would be the case if the Government were considered a stable one."

10. APPP, BA 1587, 19 December 1917 and 22 January 1918.

11. *Le Rentier,* 27 February 1918.

12. APPP, BA 1587, 24 June, 1 and 3 July 1918.

13. An American detachment was subsequently sent, and two regiments landed at Vladivostok on 19 August. The position of the United States mainly manifested a wish to avoid direct conflict with the Bolsheviks.

14. APPP, BA 1587, 29 July 1918.

15. APPP, BA 1587, 24 June 1918.

16. Tsaritsyn was later renamed Stalingrad, then Volgograd.

17. Commission générale pour la protection des intérêts français en Russie, Communication no. 1, 5 August 1918, ANPFVM, 440-A-30.

18. APPP, BA 1587, 13 August 1918.

19. *Revue des Valeurs Russes,* no. 1, 14 September 1918.

20. An inventory of all the self-proclaimed governments is beyond the scope of this book. In the mid-nineteenth century Siberia was the theater of nationalist movements. After the Bolsheviks came to power, the Socialist-Revolutionaries and Kadets formed an alliance to set up a Siberian Regional Council in Tomsk with governmental powers, then declared Siberia's independence on 9 February 1918. Another government, established in Samara on 8 June 1918, based on the results of the Constituent Assembly elections in November 1917, proclaimed itself the only legitimate Russian government.

21. APPP, BA 1587, 23 and 24 December 1918.

22. APPP, BA 1588, 7 and 8 January 1919.

23. APPP, BA 1588, 25 April 1919.

24. APPP, BA 1588, 26, 28 April, 2, 15 May 1919.

25. APPP, BA 1588, 4 April 1919

26. APPP, BA 1588, 26 April 1919.

27. *The Economist,* 3, 10, and 17 May 1919.

28. *The Economist,* 31 May 1919.

29. *The Economist,* 14 June 1919, 19 July 1919.

30. *The Economist,* 27 September 1919 and 18 October 1919.

31. *The Economist,* 20 September 1919.

32. *The Economist,* 1 November 1919.

33. *The Economist,* 8 November 1919.

34. APPP, BA 1572, 8 March 1920.

35. APPP, BA 1588, *Le Rentier,* 27 May 1920.

36. Association belge pour la défense des détenteurs de fonds publics, Annual report for 1920–21, p. 154.

37. APPP, BA 1572, 13 August 1920.

38. APPP, BA 1572, 3 September 1920.

39. *Le Rentier,* 17 October 1920.

40. *Le Rentier,* 27 November 1920.

41. Jacques Bonzon, "Guerre de Pologne et de Crimée et l'Emprunt, L'activité française & étrangère," *Revue économique, financière et politique,* 38, September–October 1920.

42. JORF, 12 December 1920, p. 20482.

43. Chambre des députés, 18 December 1920, p. 6766.

44. APPP, BA 1572, 9 March 1921.

45. APPP, BA 1572, 9 and 12 March 1921. See also Association belge pour la défense des détenteurs de fonds publics, Annual report for 1920–21, p. 154.

46. Letter from Mr Struve to Alexandre Millerand, Ministère des Affaires Etrangères, (1999), 1920, vol. 2.

47. Association belge pour la défense des détenteurs de fonds publics, Annual report for 1920–21, p. 154.

48. *The Economist* estimated the amount advanced to Denikin at almost £95 million, half of which was in military hardware and thus impossible to resell. *The Economist,* 8 November 1919.

49. Commission générale pour la protection des intérêts français en Russie, Bulletin no. 15, 1 November 1919, p. 215, ANPFVM 440A29.

50. "Russia Fails to Pay $50,000,000 Bonds," *New York Times*, 18 June 1919; "Overseas Correspondence," *The Economist*, 19 July 1919.

51. "To Protect Bondholders," *New York Times*, 29 May 1919.

FOUR   A French Bailout?

1. He exchanged 60 percent of it for expired, capitalized coupons of former bonds (Sack 1927).

2. The relatively high interest rate as well as a prize associated with the bond undoubtedly also played a role in the success of this bond in France (see *Le Rentier*, 7 June 1921).

3. ACAC, minutes of the Chambre Syndicale des Agents de change de Paris, 10 May 1869.

4. *Le Rentier*, 7 June 1921.

5. Although some transactions involved high amounts, the French intervention can be seen as modest compared with the amounts invested by the French population.

6. See also Senator Anatole de Monzie's speech to the Senate (Senate, 26 March 1920, p. 390).

7. These agreements were mentioned by Albert Grodet during the discussion in the lower house of a bill on advances to Allied governments (Chambre des Députés, 31 January 1918, p. 248).

8. This advance was made not only to pay the coupons but also to cover the Russian government's general expenditure. Anatole de Monzie's speech to the Senate (Senate, 26 March 1920, p. 390).

9. "Stock markets. Revival in Russian bonds expected. Foreign bondholders and the outlook," in *British Russian Gazette*, 31 March 1922.

10. British Union of Russian Bondholders, 15.

11. Quoted in *Le Rentier*, 27 May 1917.

12. Albert Grodet during the discussion in the lower house of a bill on advances to Allied governments (Chambre des Députés, 31 January 1918, p. 248).

13. *Le Rentier*, 17 December 1917, APPP, BA 1587, 30 January 1918.

14. *Le Rentier*, 27 December 1917.

15. Office National des Valeurs Mobilières, Note sur la création d'un comité de protection des intérêts français engagés en Russie, 22 January 1918, ANPFVM 440-A-17.

16. The Socialist Party, represented by Marius Moutet, also raised this point during the discussion in the lower house of a bill on advances to Allied governments (Chambre des Députés, 31 January 1918, p. 250).

17. *Le Rentier*, 27 January 1918.

18. Ibid.

19. APPP, BA 1587, 21 January 1918.

20. *Le Rentier,* 27 February 1918. Rumors that the January coupons would be paid began circulating on 28 January 1918, APPP, BA 1587, 28 January 1918.

21. APPP, BA 1587, 1 February 1918.

22. 360 votes in favor and 112 against (Chambre des Députés, 31 January 1918, p. 251).

23. Albert Grodet during the discussion in the lower house of a bill on advances to Allied governments (Chambre des Députés, 31 January, p. 249).

24. Marius Moutet during the discussion in the lower house of a bill on advances to Allied governments (Chambre des Députés, 31 January, p. 250).

25. Marius Moutet during the discussion in the lower house of a bill on advances to Allied governments (Chambre des Députés, 31 January, p. 250).

26. Statement by Emmanuel Brousse during the discussion in the lower house of a bill on advances to Allied governments (Chambre des Députés, 31 January, p. 250), reported in *Le Rentier,* 27 February 1918.

27. *Le Rentier,* 27 August 1918.

28. Statement by Raoul Péret, chairman of the Budget Commission, to the *Petit Journal* on 31 August 1918 (quoted in *Revue des Valeurs Russes,* no. 1, 14 September 1918).

29. *Revue des Valeurs Russes,* no. 1, 14 September 1918.

30. APPP, BA 1587, 8 April 1918.

31. *Le Rentier,* 17 April 1918.

32. "In the current upheaval, the suspension of the payment of Russian coupons is going unnoticed," APPP, BA 1587, 13 April 1918.

33. APPP, BA 1587, 1 May 1918.

34. APPP, BA 1587, 3 and 21 May 1918.

35. *Le Rentier,* 27 May 1918. This proposal was reiterated in August of the same year.

36. "We are expecting the French government to resume payment of the coupons in some form," APPP BA 1587, 25 July 1918

37. APPP BA 1587, 26 July 1918. APPP BA 1587, 9 September 1918.

38. Commission générale pour la protection des intérêts français en Russie, Communication no. 1, 5 August, 1918, ANPFVM, 440-A-30.

39. *Revue des Valeurs Russes,* no. 1, 14 September 1918.

40. *Le Rentier,* 27 May 1918.

41. Statement by Raoul Péret, chairman of the Budget Commission, to the *Petit Journal* on 31 August 1918 (quoted in *Revue des Valeurs Russes,* no. 1, 14 September 1918). Which, as the only holder of Russian bonds, would then turn against Russia. That idea would be taken up by the National League for Claims of Small Investors in Russian Securities, which cited the Swiss example (Minutes of the general council meeting of the National Securities Office of 26 March 1919).

42. This recalled the action taken by the United States when Texas was annexed. The Texan debts were partly assumed even though the U.S. government did not recog-

nize any liability for them (see Hoeflich [1982] for the legal aspects and Burdekin [2006] for the impact of the annexation on market prices).

43. *Le Rentier,* 27 February 1918.

44. *Revue des Valeurs Russes,* no. 1, 14 September 1918.

45. APPP BA 1587, 17, 18, and 20 September 1918.

46. *Le Rentier,* 17 June 1919.

47. Letter by Stéphen Pichon, foreign minister, to the chairman of the National Securities Office, 23 October 1918, ANPFVM 440-A-10.

48. Commission générale pour la protection des intérêts français en Russie, Communication, dated 24 September 1918.

49. Letter by Stéphen Pichon, foreign minister, to the chairman of the National Securities Office, 23 October 1918, ANPFVM 440-A-10.

50. ANPFVM 440A18

51. Letter by Mr Thiébaut to Mr Pichon of 10 May 1918, ANPFVM 440-A-10.

52. The main assets were Briansk, assets in the Donbas and Banque Russo-Asiatique (which controlled the Yusovka, Parviainen and Putilov factories).

53. Letter from Mr Thiébaut to Mr Pichon of 10 May 1918, ANPFVM 440-A-10.

54. Letter sent to the chairman of the Commission générale pour la protection des intérêts français en Russie or the ANFVM, dated July 1918, ANPFVM 440A18.

55. Minutes of the general council meeting of the National Securities Office of 20 January 1919.

56. Draft resolution in favor of holder of Russian bonds, presented by Senator Gaudin de Villaine, parliamentary records, Senate, 22 October 1922, Annex no. 610.

57. From the description of the bonds published in the *Manuel des porteurs de fonds russes* (1903) and Bayle (1997), it seems that Russia didn't have to pledge a specific stream of revenues as guarantee for its bonds. By contrast, loans issued by cities (St. Petersburg, Kiev, Moscow, etc.) were usually guaranteed by all the revenues, real estate, and resources of the cities (Bayle 1997).

58. Quoted in Sack (1927), http://www.odiousdebts.org/odiousdebts/publications/dettes_publiques.html

59. *Le Rentier,* 7 June 1921.

60. *Le Rentier,* 27 May 1917.

61. Association belge pour la défense des détenteurs de fonds publics, Annual report 1920–21, p. 148.

62. Bignon and Flandreau (2011) estimate, however, the amounts paid by Russia during the Russo–Japanese War and exploit a leak to the press from BNP/Paribas to estimate the costs of bribes. For new issues they represented on average 0.5 percent of the amounts raised.

63. JORF, 15 January 1919, pp. 538–39.

64. APPP BA 1588, 16 January 1919. APPP BA 1588, 17 January 1919.

65. Commission générale pour la protection des intérêts français en Russie, Report presented to the Ordinary General Meeting on 30 September 1921.

66. Draft resolution in favor of holder of Russian bonds, presented by Senator

Gaudin de Villaine, parliamentary records, Senate, 22 October 1922, Annex no. 610, p. 25.

67. Minutes of the general council meeting of the National Securities Office of 26 February and 26 March 1919.

68. Quoted in *Le Rentier,* 17 June 1919.

69. Speeches by Anatole de Monzie and Adrien Gaudin de Villaine to the Senate (Senate, 26 March 1920, p. 390). Adrien Gaudin de Villaine's speech to the Senate (Senate, 27 February, in response to a question on 5 February) and session of 26 March 1920, p. 398).

70. Anatole de Monzie's speech to the Senate (Senate, 26 March 1920, p. 390).

71. *Le Rentier,* 7 May 1921.

72. *Le Rentier,* 27 January 1920.

73. *Le Rentier,* 7 February 1920.

74. *Le Rentier,* 17 February 1920.

75. *Le Rentier,* 27 May 1920.

76. APPP, BA 1572, 8 March 1920.

77. Senate, session of 29 June 1920, p. 1057.

78. Commission générale pour la protection des intérêts français en Russie, Report presented to the Ordinary General Meeting of 30 September 1921.

79. Senate, question of 18 January 1921 and response in the session of 3 February 1921, p. 89.

80. *Le Rentier,* 17 May and 7 June 1921

81. *Le Rentier,* 17 May 1921.

82. Bill to support Russian bondholders submitted by Senator Gaudin de Villaine, parliamentary records, Senate, 22 October 1922, Annex no. 610, pp. 24–27.

83. "Bill to Aid Holders of Russian Bonds," *New York Times,* 29 October 1922, and *Le Rentier,* 27 November 1922.

84. Speech by Adrien Gaudin de Villaine to the Senate (Senate, 23 November 1922, p. 1399).

85. Bill to support Russian bondholders submitted by Senator Gaudin de Villaine, parliamentary records, Senate, 23 November 1922, Annex no. 691, pp. 117–119.

86. Bill to facilitate the creation of mutual funds for the full reimbursement of Russian sovereign bonds owned by French citizens submitted by Georges Bonnefous and André Tardieu, members of parliament, parliamentary records, Chamber of Deputies, 22 December 1922, Annex no. 5325, p. 624.

87. Bill inviting the government to find a way to assist small investors in Russian bonds submitted by Messrs. Ouvré, Gaborit, and Prévet, members of parliament, parliamentary records, Chamber of Deputies, 30 November 1923, Annex no. 6674, pp. 447–48.

88. Bill to support Russian bondholders submitted by Senator Gaudin de Villaine, parliamentary records, Senate, 23 November 1922, Annex no. 691, pp. 117–19.

89. Association belge pour la défense des détenteurs de fonds publics, Annual report for 1920–21, p. 148.

90. "To Protect Bondholders," *New York Times,* 29 May 1919.

91. APPP, BA 1587, 21 May 1918.

92. Ibid.

93. *Le Rentier,* 27 January 1918.

94. Corporation of Foreign Bondholders, 45th Annual Report, 1918, p. 31.

FIVE   Seeking Other Potential Payers

1. For a literature review, see Feilchenfeld (1931) and Hoeflich (1982).

2. The amount was to correspond "to the average of the sums which in each of the three years preceding that of the declaration of war have been assigned to the service of the public debt under the revenues of the two provinces."

3. The Inter-Allied Commission on War Purchases and Finance meet for the first time in Paris on 2 January 1918 to determine the terms and coordinate the financial actions of the Allied countries. The first meeting was attended by representatives of the United States, Belgium, Britain, France, Japan, Italy, Romania, and Serbia (Klotz 1924, 77–78). After the war the issue of the Inter-Allied debt would give rise to numerous controversies (see Homberg 1926 for a contemporary account of the events, and Artaud 1978, for a more recent analysis).

4. Determining the citizenships of many individuals remained an arduous task following the partition of the Russian Empire (see, for example, Lohr 2012 for an in-depth analysis of this problem).

5. Office National des Valeurs Mobilières, Note sur la création d'un comité de protection des intérêts français engagés en Russie, 22 June 1918, ANPFVM 440-A-17.

6. APPP, BA 1587, 23 January 1918.

7. *Torgovo-Promyshlennaia Gazeta,* Commission générale pour la protection des intérêts français en Russie, Bulletin no. 1, 1 October 1918, p. 12, ANPFVM 440A3.

8. Commission générale pour la protection des intérêts français en Russie, Communication 1, 5 August, 1918, ANPFVM, 440-A-30.

9. Letter from Stéphen Pichon, the foreign minister, to the chairman of the National Securities Office, 23 October 1918, ANPFVM 440-A-10.

10. Speech by Senator Anatole de Monzie to the Senate (session of 26 March 1920, p. 393).

11. Letter from du Halgouët to de Fleuriau, Ministère des Affaires Etrangères (1999), vol. 1920, tome 2.

12. Minutes of the International Conference for the Protection of Private Interests in Russia, 10–13 February 1921, ANPFVM 440-A-25.

13. Speech by Senator Anatole de Monzie to the Senate (session of 26 March 1920, p. 394). I have not found any other record of those offers. In any case, given the relative size and economic importance of the three countries, their offer probably concerned only a small portion of the debt. For Azerbaijan, see also Feilchenfeld 1931, 543–44.

14. Association belge pour la défense des détenteurs de fonds publics, Annual report for 1920–21, p. 156.

15. The inclusion of all the contributions reduced Poland's share from 12.98 percent to 8.07 percent. That factor shows how sensitive the determination of the amounts due was to the definition of *revenues*.

16. Les nouvelles économiques et financières, 27 May 1920, ANPFVM 440-A-18.

17. Letter from the foreign minister to the Polish Legation, 30 April 1921, ANPFVM 440-A-10. See also Ministère des Affaires Etrangères (2004), vol. 1921, tome 1.

18. APPP, BA 1587, 22 December 1917.

19. The honorific title *Hetman* reflects Skoropadski's Cossack origins.

20. Document dated 26 September 1918, translated by the Danish delegation and sent on 29 September 1918 to ANPFVM. The enthusiastic title of the original document, apparently published in *Finances et économie populaire*, was "On reconnaît les emprunts du Tsar" (The tsar's bonds have been recognized), ANPFVM A40.

21. Speech by Senator Anatole de Monzie to the Senate (session of 26 March 1920, p. 394).

22. Letter dated 16 June 1920 from the chairman of the delegation of the Ukrainian National Republic to Paris to Joseph Noulens, chairman of the international conference of Russian creditors, ANPFVM 440-A-13.

23. Memorandum from the political affairs division to the British embassy regarding the settlement of the Russian debt and the damages suffered by foreigners in Russia, Ministère des Affaires Etrangères (1999), vol. 1920, tome 3.

24. Association belge pour la défense des détenteurs de fonds publics, Annual report for 1920–21, p. 156.

25. "Russian Bonds Drop on Repudiation Ralk," *New York Times,* 12 January 1918.

26. APPP BA 1588, 20, 21, 22 January 1919.

27. APPP, BA 1588, 31 January 1919.

28. *The Economist,* 1 March 1919.

29. Letter from the foreign minister published in *Courrier de la bourse et de la banque* on 27 February 1919, ANPFVM 440-A-52.

30. As the German delegates said at the Genoa Conference after the Treaty of Rapallo was signed, *Le Rentier,* 27 April 1922.

31. Commission générale pour la protection des intérêts français en Russie, second series, Bulletin no. 5, November–December 1921, p. 168, ANPFVM 440A1.

32. "Stock markets. Revival in Russian bonds expected. Foreign bondholders and the outlook," *British Russian Gazette,* 31 March 1922.

six Recent Econometric and Financial Research

1. "Conditions in Russia," *The Economist,* 4 January 1919.

2. The positive shocks of February 1920 could be attributed to the "Bankers' Memorandum," or the plan to convene a major international conference to resolve the exchange rate crisis (see, for example, Mouton 1995). The shock of 28 July 1920 might have followed Lloyd George's and Millerand's meeting at Boulogne-sur-Mer on the re-

sumption of economic ties with Russia, see Ministère des Affaires Etrangères (2005), 1921, Annexes 1920–21, 423–33.

3. For the more technical aspects, readers can refer to Oosterlinck and Landon-Lane (2006).

4. In the present case, they would buy bonds where they were cheapest and immediately resell them where they were worth the most. After deducting transaction costs, the difference between the two prices would be a net gain for the arbitrageurs.

5. From November 1923 to January 1924 *Le Rentier* published a series of articles referring to advantageous arbitrages on Russian bonds, aimed at benefiting from price differences in the spot and forward markets. This type of arbitrage is different from that described here, which compares the prices for the same security in different countries. See *Le Rentier*, 27 November, 7 and 17 December 1923, and 7 January 1924.

6. The 4.5 percent bond of 1909 was also listed in Amsterdam. At the time, serial numbers were associated with a specific stock exchange, which meant that bonds could not be traded elsewhere (see *Le Rentier*, 7 December 1923 for a description of this system in relation to the 5 percent Russian bond of 1906).

7. Since the quotation system was different in London, I have used the average of buy and sell prices for the London data.

Epilogue

1. Obviously, a distinction is made between domestic and foreign debt, but that distinction does not apply to the nationality of the bondholders, only to the currency in which the bond was issued.

2. Association belge pour la défense des détenteurs de fonds publics, Annual report for 1920–21, p. 149.

3. There seems to have been arbitrages in listed bonds that had been issued on several markets, but this had only a small impact according to Freymond (1995, 110).

4. JORF, no. 195, 24 August 2000.

5. "Emprunts russes: un remboursement sans intérêt," *Libération*, 27 November 1996

6. Available on: http://www.finances.gouv.fr/fonds_documentaire/pole_ecofin/international/paye.htm

7. JORF, no. 195 24 August 2000.

8. The valuation method varied depending on the currency and on whether or not a value in francs is shown on the security.

9. The decree sets forth how each will be treated.

10. According to the committee, the rate of compensation would be around 2 percent.

11. JORF, 31 December 1999, pp. 19981–82.

12. Such as Union des Porteurs d'Emprunts Russes, http://empruntsrusses.win nerbb.com/, Association Française des Porteurs d'Emprunts Russes, and Association Fédérative Internationale des Porteurs d'Emprunts Russes. Newspaper articles that ap-

peared during the negotiations show that this disagreement dates back to the very first hours of the talks. See, for example, "Dette. Les porteurs d'emprunts ruses crient à la manipulation," *La Tribune,* 28 March 1997, and "Les porteurs d'emprunts russes contre l'Etat français," *Le Figaro,* 29 March 1997.

    13. See especially the article "Titres russes: la Belgique en justice?," *Le Soir,* 7 April 2007.

References

Anderson, Chandler P. 1934. "Recognition of Russia." *American Journal of International Law* 28, no 1: 90–98.

Apostol, Paul, and Alexandre Michelson. 1922. "Les questions d'ordre international soulevées par le problème de la Dette russe." In *Le problème financier Russe: La Dette publique de la Russie,* ed. Arthur Raffalovich, Paul Apostol, Alexandre Michelson, M. Bernatzky, and W. Novitsky, 55–161. Paris: Payot.

Association Belge Pour la Défense des Détenteurs de Fonds Publics. 1919–22. *Rapports annuels du comité central.* Anvers: Neptune.

Association financière, industrielle, commerciale russe et Comité des représentants des banques russes à Paris. 1922. *La débâcle des Soviets et la restauration économique de la Russie, Aperçu des mémoires présentés à la Conférence de Gênes.* Paris: Société anonyme de l'imprimerie I. Rirachovsky.

Association Nationale des Porteurs Français de Valeurs Mobilières. 1920. *Annuaire 1915–1920.* Paris: Association nationale des porteurs français de valeurs mobilières.

Artaud, Denise. 1978. *La question des dettes interalliées et la reconstruction de l'Europe (1917–1929).* Lille: Atelier de reproduction des thèses de Lille III.

Augros, Jean-Claude, and Nicolas Leboisne 1997. "Risque Souverain et Indemnisation: le Cas des Empruntes Russes (1919–1997)." *Bulletin Français d'Actuariat* 1, no 1: 1–20.

Baillet, Francis. 2002. "Les droits des porteurs en dehors du système de répartition de l'indemnité conventionnelle." In *Les emprunts russes: aspects juridiques,* ed. Patrick Juillard and Brigitte Stern, 279–95. Paris: CEDIN Paris 1, Cahiers Internationaux.

Bainville, Jacques. 1919. *Après la guerre: Comment placer sa fortune?* Paris: Nouvelle Librairie Nationale.

Barnett, Vincent. 2001. "Calling up the Reserves: Keynes, Tugan-Baranovsky and Russian War Finance." *Europe–Asia Studies* 53, no 1: 151–169.

Baudhuin, Fernand. 1945. *Précis de finances publiques,* Bruxelles: Editions Bruylant.

Bayle, François. 1997. *Emprunt russe: indemnisation mode d'emploi.* Paris: Balland.

Bernal, Oscar, Kim Oosterlinck, and Ariane Szafarz. 2010. "Observing bailout expectations during a total eclipse of the sun." *Journal of International Money and Finance* 29, no. 7: 1193–1205.

Bignon, Vincent, and Marc Flandreau. 2011. "The Economics of Badmouthing: Libel Law and the Underworld of the Financial Press in France before World War I." *Journal of Economic History* 71, no. 3: 616–53.

Boissière, Gustave. 1925. *La compagnie des agents de change et le marché officiel à la bourse de Paris.* Paris: Arthur Rousseau.

Bonzon, Jacques. 1924. *Les emprunts russes et les "révélations" du journal "L'humanité," Conférence prononcée le 2 février 1924.* Conflans-Sainte-Honorine: Publication de l'idée libre.

———. 1924a. *Les emprunts russes et les Rothschild, Conférence prononcée le 29 mars 1924.* Conflans-Sainte-Honorine: Publication de l'idée libre.

Borchard, Edwin M. 1913. "International contractual claims and their settlement." *Judicial Settlement of International Disputes* 13: 1–60.

———. 1951. *State Insolvency and Foreign Bondholders.* Vol. 1. New Haven: Yale University Press. Reprint, Washington: Beard Books, 2000.

Bordo, Michael D., and Christopher M. Meissner. 2006. "The role of foreign currency debt in financial crises: 1880–1913 versus 1972–1997." *Journal of Banking & Finance* 30, no. 12: 3299–3329.

Bordo, Michael David, and Kim Oosterlinck. 2005. "Do political changes trigger debt defaults? And do defaults trigger political changes?" Paper presented at the Conference on the Political Economy of International Finance, Ann Arbor, Michigan, October 28–29.

Bovykin, V. I. 1990. "Les emprunts extérieurs russes." *Revue d'économie financière* 14, no. 2: 81–92.

British Union of Russian Bondholders and Edouard Luboff. No date. *Russia's Debts. The case of British holders of Russian Bonds.* London: British Union of Russian Bondholders.

Brown, William O., Jr., and Richard C. K. Burdekin. 2002. "German debt traded in London during the Second World War: A British perspective on Hitler." *Economica* 69, no. 276: 655–69.

Bulow, Jeremy. 2002. "First world governments and third world debt." *Brookings Papers on Economic Activity* 2002, no. 1: 229–55.

Bulow, Jeremy, and Kenneth Rogoff. 1989. "A Constant Recontracting Model of Sovereign Debt." *Journal of Political Economy* 97: 155–78.

———. 1989a. "Sovereign Debt: Is to Forgive to Forget?" *American Economic Review* 79, no. 1: 43–50.

Burdeau, Geneviève. 2002. "L'or russe dans le règlement du contentieux financier franco-russe." In *Les emprunts russes: aspects juridiques,* ed. Patrick Juillard and Brigitte Stern, 151–69. Paris: CEDIN Paris 1, Cahiers Internationaux.

Burdekin, Richard C. K. 2006. "Bondholder gains from the annexation of Texas and implications of the US bailout." *Explorations in Economic History* 43, no. 4: 646–66.

Carley, Michael Jabara. 1976. "The origins of the French intervention in the Russian Civil War, January-May 1918: a reappraisal." *Journal of Modern History* 48, no. 3: 413–439.

———. 2000. "Episodes from the Early Cold War: Franco-Soviet Relations, 1917–1927." *Europe-Asia Studies* 52, no. 7: 1275–1305.

———. 2006. "A Soviet Eye on France from the rue de Grenelle in Paris, 1924–1940." *Diplomacy and Statecraft* 17, no. 2: 295–346.

Carley, Michael Jabara, and Richard Kent Debo. 1997. "Always in need of credit: The USSR and Franco–German economic cooperation, 1926–1929." *French Historical Studies* 20, no. 3: 315–56.

Collet, Stéphanie. 2012a. "Sovereign Bonds: Odious Debts and State Succession." PhD diss., Université Libre de Bruxelles.

———. 2012b. "A Unified Italy? Sovereign Debt and Investor Scepticism." Paper presented at the American Economic Association Annual Meeting, Chicago, January 6–8.

———. 2013. "The financial penalty for 'unfair' debt: The case of Cuban bonds at the time of independence." *European Review of Economic History* 17, no. 3: 364–87.

Collet, Stephanie, and Kim Oosterlinck. 2012. "Lending Money to the 'Executioners': The Case of the 1906 Russian Loan." Paper presented at the Workshop in Money, History and Finance, Rutgers University, New Brunswick, N.J., September 24.

Comité des Représentants des Banques Russes à Paris. 1921. *Banque et monnaie. Dette de l'état: Questions économiques soulevées par les événements de Russie, Rapports et documents, octobre 1919–juillet 1921.* Paris: Imprimerie Rirachovsky.

Commission Générale pour la Protection des Intérêts en Russie. 1919–22. *Bulletins.* Paris: Association Nationale des Porteurs de Valeurs Mobilières

Corporation of Foreign Bondholders. 1918–22. *Annual General Report of the Council of the Corporation of Foreign Bondholders.* London: Corporation of Foreign Bondholders.

Cosnard, Michel. 2002. "Les créances au titre de l'intervention occidentale de 1918–1922." In *Les emprunts russes: aspects juridiques,* ed. Patrick Juillard and Brigitte Stern, 121–49. Paris: CEDIN Paris 1, Cahiers Internationaux.

Cruces, Juan J., and Christoph Trebesch. 2011. *Sovereign Defaults: The Price of Haircuts.* No. 3604. CESifo Group Munich.

Cutler, David M., James M. Poterba, and Lawrence H. Summers. 1989. "What moves stock prices?" *Journal of Portfolio Management* 15, no. 3: 4–12.

Darmon, Pierre. 2002. *Vivre à Paris pendant la grande guerre.* Paris: Fayard.

Davies, Norman. 1972. *White Eagle, Red Star: The Polish–Soviet War, 1919-20.* London: Macdonal.

Davis, Malcolm W. 1927. "Soviet Recognition and Trade." *Foreign Affairs* 5: 650–62.

de Monzie, Anatole. 1931. *Petit manuel de la Russie nouvelle*. Paris: Firmin Didot.

Delaisi, Francis. 1928. *Comment les Soviets régleront la dette russe (d'après les travaux de la Commission officielle franco-soviétique)*. Paris: Librairie A. Delpeuch.

———. 1930. "Les Soviets et la dette russe en France." In *Les Soviets et la dette russe en France: les Soviets et les Organisations de la Paix. France et Russie*, ed. Dotation Carnegie pour la Paix Internationale, 7–40. Paris: Publications de la Conciliation Internationale.

Denéchère, Yves. 2003. *Jean Herbette (1878–1960), Journaliste et ambassadeur*. Brussels: Peter Lang.

Deschamps, Thomas. 2002. "Les droits des porteurs français après les accords franco-russes." In *Les emprunts russes: aspects juridiques*, ed. Patrick Juillard and Brigitte Stern, 253–77. Paris: CEDIN Paris 1, Cahiers Internationaux.

Eaton, Jonathan, and Mark Gersovitz. 1981. "Debt with potential repudiation: Theoretical and empirical analysis." *Review of Economic Studies* 48: 289–309.

Eaton, Jonathan, and Raquel Fernandez. 1995. "Sovereign debt," NBER Working Paper 5131.

Eichengreen, Barry, and Richard Portes. 1986. "Debt and Default in the 1930s: Causes and Consequences." *European Economic Review* 30, no. 3: 599–640.

———. 1989. "After the deluge: Default, negotiation, and the readjustment during the interwar years." In *The International Debt Crises in Historical Perspective*, ed. Barry Eichengreen and Peter Lindert, 12–47. Cambridge: MIT Press.

Eichengreen, Barry, Ricardo Haussmann, and Ugo Panizza. 2005. "The pain of original sin." In *Other People's Money: Debt Denomination and Financial Instability in Emerging Market Economies*, ed. Barry Eichengreen and Ricardo Hausmann, 13–47. Chicago: University of Chicago Press.

Eisemann, Pierre Michel. 2002. "Emprunts russes et problèmes de succession d'états." In *Les emprunts russes: aspects juridiques*, ed. Patrick Juillard and Brigitte Stern, 53–78. Paris: CEDIN Paris 1, Cahiers Internationaux.

Eliacheff, Boris. 1919. *Les finances de guerre de la Russie*. Paris: Giard et Brière.

English, William B. 1996. "Understanding the costs of sovereign default: American state debts in the 1840's." *American Economic Review* 86, no. 1: 259–75.

Erce, Aitor, and Javier Diaz-Cassou. 2011. "Selective sovereign defaults." Globalization and Monetary Policy Institute Working Paper 127.

Esteves, Rui Pedro. 2013. "The bondholder, the sovereign, and the banker: Sovereign debt and bondholders' protection before 1914." *European Review of Economic History* 17, no. 4: 389–407.

Faure, Fernand. 1920. "Les créances françaises et le gouvernement bolcheviste." *Revue Politique et Parlementaire* 3: 155–61.

Feilchenfeld, Ernst Hermann. 1931. *Public Debts and State Succession*. New York: Macmillan.

Feis, Herbert. 1930. *Europe, The World's Banker, 1870–1914: An Account of European Foreign Investment and the Connection of World Finance with Diplomacy Before World War I*. New Haven: Yale University Press. Reprint, New York: Norton, 1965.

Ferguson, Niall. 2001. *The Cash Nexus*. New York: Basic Books.

Fiddick, Thomas. 1973. "The 'Miracle of the Vistula': Soviet Policy versus Red Army Strategy." *Journal of Modern History* 45, no. 4: 626–43.

Figes, Orlando. 1997. *A People's Tragedy: The Russian Revolution, 1891–1924,* London: Penguin Books.

Fink, Carole. 1993. *The Genoa Conference: European Diplomacy, 1921–1922.* Syracuse: Syracuse University Press.

Fishlow, Albert. 1985. "Lessons from the past: Capital markets during the 19th century and the interwar period." *International Organization* 39, no. 3: 383–439.

Flandreau, Marc. 2003. "Caveat emptor: Coping with sovereign risk under the international gold standard, 1871–1913." In *International Financial History in the Twentieth Century, System and Anarchy,* ed. Marc Flandreau, Carl-Ludwig Holtfreich, and Harold James, 17–50. Cambridge: Cambridge University Press.

———. 2013. "Sovereign states, bondholders committees, and the London Stock Exchange in the nineteenth century (1827–68): New facts and old fictions." *Oxford Review of Economic Policy* 29, no. 4: 668–96.

Flandreau, Marc, and Frédéric Zumer. 2004. *The Making of Global Finance.* Paris: OECD Publishing.

Flandreau, Marc, and Juan H. Flores. 2009. "Bonds and brands: Foundations of sovereign debt markets, 1820–1830." *Journal of Economic History* 69, no. 3: 646–84.

Flandreau, Marc, Juan H. Flores, Norbert Gaillard, and Sebastián Nieto-Parra. 2009. "The End of Gatekeeping: Underwriters and the Quality of Sovereign Bond Markets, 1815–2007." National Bureau of Economic Research Working Paper w15128.

Foncier National Bordelais. No date. *Remboursement des Emprunts Russe.* Bordeaux: Imprimerie Delmas.

Frey, Bruno S., and Daniel Waldenström. 2004. "Markets work in war: World War II reflected in the Zurich and Stockholm bond markets." *Financial History Review* 11, no. 1: 51–67.

———. 2007. "Using Financial Markets to Analyze History: The Case of the Second World War." *Historical Social Research/Historische Sozialforschung* 32, no. 4: 330–50.

Frey, Bruno S., and Marcel Kucher. 2000. "History as reflected in capital markets: The case of World War II." *Journal of Economic History* 60, no. 2: 468–96.

———. 2001. "Wars and markets: How bond values reflect the Second World War." *Economica* 68, no. 271: 317–33.

Freymond, Joël. 1995. *Les emprunts russes de la ruine au remboursement: histoire de la plus grande spoliation du siècle.* Paris: Edition du Journal des Finances.

———. 2002. "Historique de la revendication des porteurs." In *Les emprunts russes: aspects juridiques,* ed. Patrick Juillard and Brigitte Stern, 187–96. Paris: CEDIN Paris 1, Cahiers Internationaux.

Fuentes, Miguel, and Diego Saravia. 2010. "Sovereign defaulters: Do international capital markets punish them?" *Journal of Development Economics* 91, no. 2: 336–47.

Gans, H. 1909. "L'intervention gouvernementale et l'accès du marché financier." *Revue Politique et Parlementaire* 59: 249–64.

Gibson, Heather D., Stephen G. Hall, and George S. Tavlas. 2012. "The Greek financial crisis: Growing imbalances and sovereign spreads." *Journal of International Money and Finance* 31, no. 3: 498–516.

Girault, René. 1961. "Sur quelques aspects financiers de l'alliance franco-russe." *Revue d'histoire moderne et contemporaine* 8, no. 1: 67–76.

———. 1973. *Emprunts russes et investissements français en Russie, 1887–1914.* Paris: Armand Colin. Reprint, Paris: Comité pour l'Histoire Economique et Financière de la France, 1993.

Gleichen, Lord Edward. 1988. *Chronology of the Great War.* London: Greenhill.

Glenny, Michael V. 1970. "The Anglo–Soviet Trade Agreement, March 1921." *Journal of Contemporary History* 5, no. 2: 63–82.

Harms Robert. 2005. "King Leopold's Bonds." In *The Origins of Value: The Financial Innovations That Created Modern Capital Markets,* ed. William N. Goetzmann and K. Geert Rouwenhorst, 343–57. New York, Oxford University Press.

Harrison, Mark, and Andreai Markevich. 2012. "Russia's Home Front, 1914–1922: The Economy." Working Paper Cage Online Working Paper Series 74.

Heathcote, Jonathan, and Fabrizio Perri. 2013. "The international diversification puzzle is not as bad as you think." *Journal of Political Economy* 121, no. 6: 1108–59.

Hoeflich, Michael H. 1982. "Through a glass darkly: Reflections upon the history of the international law of public debt in connection with state succession." *University of Illinois Law Review* 54: 39.

Hogenhuis-Seliverstoff, Anne. 1981. *Les relations franco-soviétiques, 1917–1924.* Paris: Publications de la Sorbonne.

Homberg, Octave. 1926. *La grande injustice: La question des dettes interalliées.* Paris: Bernard Grasset.

Hornbeck, J. F. 2013. "Argentina's Defaulted Sovereign Debt: Dealing with the 'Holdouts.'" *Congressional Research Service Report for Congress.* Accessed December 16, 2014. http://fas.org/sgp/crs/row/R41029.pdf.

International Monetary Fund (IMF). 2004. *Evaluation Report: The IMF and Argentina 1991–2001,* Washington, D.C.: IMF.

Jolly, Jean, and Adolphe Robert. 1960. *Dictionnaire des parlementaires français: notices biographiques sur les ministres, sénateurs et députés français de 1889 à 1940.* Paris: Presses Universitaires de France.

Jorgensen, Erika, and Jeffrey Sachs. 1989. "Default and renegotiation of Latin American foreign bonds in the interwar period." In *The International Debt Crises in Historical Perspective,* ed. Barry Eichengreen and Peter Lindert, 49–85. Cambridge: MIT Press.

Jorion, Philippe, and William N. Goetzmann. 1999. "Global stock markets in the twentieth century." *Journal of Finance* 54, no. 3: 953–80.

Keynes, John Maynard. 1971. *Collected Writings of John Maynard Keynes.* Vol. 16: *Activities 1914–1919: The Treasury and Versailles,* ed. Elizabeth Johnson. London: Macmillan.

Khalfan, Ashfaq, Jeff King, and Bryan Thomas. 2003. "Advancing the odious debt doctrine." Center for International Sustainable Development Law. Working Paper COM/RES/ESJ 11.

Klotz, Louis Lucien. 1924. *De la guerre à la paix: Souvenirs et documents.* Paris: Payot.

Kohlscheen, Emanuel. 2006. "Why Are There Serial Defaulters?: Quasi Experimental Evidence from Constitutions." *ESRC World Economy and Finance Research Programme,* Birkbeck, University of London, no. 0003.

Kosyk, Volodymyr. 1981. *La politique de la France à l'égard de l'Ukraine: mars 1917–février 1918.* Paris: Université de Paris-I, Panthéon-Sorbonne, Institut d'histoire des relations internationales contemporaines.

Lane, Philip R. 2006. "The real effects of European monetary union." *Journal of Economic Perspectives* 20, no. 4: 47–66.

———. 2012. "The European sovereign debt crisis." *Journal of Economic Perspectives* 26, no. 3: 49–67.

Lehmann, Paul-Jacques. 1997. *Histoire de la Bourse de Paris.* Paris: Presses Universitaires de France.

Lenin, Vladimir Ilyich. 1917. *Imperialism: The Highest Stage of Capitalism.* Translated by Foreign Language Publishing House. Reprint, Moscow: Foreign Language Publishing House, 1952.

Leroy-Beaulieu, Paul. 1906. *Traité de la science des finances. Vol. 2: Le Budget et le Crédit public.* Paris: Guillaumin.

Lienau, Odette. 2014. *Rethinking Sovereign Debt: Politics, Reputation and Legitimacy in Modern Finance.* Cambridge: Harvard University Press.

Lohr, Eric. 2012. *Russian Citizenship: From Empire to Soviet Union.* Cambridge: Harvard University Press.

Long, James William. 1972. "Russian manipulation of the French Press, 1904–1906." *Slavic Review* 31, no. 2: 343–54.

Ludington, Sarah, Mitu Gulati, and Alfred L. Brophy. 2010. "Applied Legal History: Demystifying the Doctrine of Odious Debts." *Theoretical Inquiries in Law* 11, no. 1: 247–81.

Lysis. 1910. *Contre l'oligarchie financière en France.* Paris: Albin Michel.

Manasse, Paolo, Nouriel Roubini, and Axel Schimmelpfennig. 2003. "Predicting Sovereign Debt Crises." IMF Working Paper WP03/221.

Manuel du Porteur de Fonds Russes. 1903. *Emprunts émis ou garantis par l'état et côtés à l'étranger.* Published in St. Petersburg by the Russian Ministry of Finance.

Martin, Léon. 1921. "La protection des intérêts privés français en Russie." *Revue Politique et Parlementaire* 106: 212–36.

Mauro, Paolo, Nathan Sussman, and Yishay Yafeh. 2006. *Emerging Market and Financial Globalization: Sovereign Bond Spreads in 1870–1913 and Today.* Oxford: Oxford University Press.

McGillivray, Fiona, and Alastair Smith. 2003. "Who can be trusted? Sovereign debt and the impact of leadership change." Working Paper, Department of Politics, New York University.

Michie, Ranald C. 1999. *The London Stock Exchange: A History.* Oxford: Oxford University Press.

Ministère des Affaires Etrangères. 1999–2005. *Documents diplomatiques français.* Paris: Imprimerie Nationale.

Ministère des Finances de Russie. 1903. *Manuel du Porteur de Fonds Russes: Emprunts émis ou garantis par l'état et côtés à l'étranger.* St. Petersburg: Trenké et Fusnot.

Mitchener, Kris James, and Marc Weidenmier. 2005. "Empire, public goods, and the Roosevelt corollary." *Journal of Economic History* 65, no. 3: 658–92.

———. 2010. "Supersanctions and sovereign debt repayment." *Journal of International Money and Finance* 29, no. 1: 19–36.

Mitchener, Kris James, Kim Oosterlinck, Marc Weidenmier, and Steve Haber. 2015. "Victory or Repudiation? Predicting Winners in Civil Wars Using International Financial Markets," *Journal of Banking and Finance* 60 (November 2015): 310–19.

Mourin, Maxime. 1967. *Les Relations franco-soviétiques, 1917–1967.* Paris: Payot.

Mouton, Marie-Renée. 1995. *La société des nations et les intérêts de la France, 1920–1924.* Bern: P. Lang.

Muxart, Anne. 2002. "Le système de mise en œuvre législative et réglementaire du mémorandum d'accord franco-russe du 26 novembre 1996 relatif à l'indemnisation de français spoliés ou dépossédés par l'URSS." In *Les emprunts russes: aspects juridiques,* ed. Patrick Juillard and Brigitte Stern, 197–242. Paris: CEDIN Paris 1, Cahiers Internationaux.

Neymarck, Alfred. 1872. *Aperçus financiers, 1868–1872.* Paris: E. Dentu.

Noulens, Joseph. 1933. *Mon ambassade en Russie soviétique, 1917–1919.* Paris: Plon.

Ochoa, Christiana. 2008. "From Odious Debt to Odious Finance: Avoiding the Externalities of a Functional Odious Debt Doctrine." *Harvard International Law Journal* 49, no. 1: 109–59.

Oosterlinck, Kim. 2003. "The bond market and the legitimacy of Vichy France." *Explorations in Economic History* 40, no. 3: 326–44.

———. 2003a. "Why do investors still hope? The Soviet repudiation puzzle 1918–1919." Working Paper, Centre Emile Bernheim, Solvay Business School, ULB WP-CEB: No. 03–010.

———. 2006. "Sovereign bonds during troubled times: A historical perspective." In *Contemporaneous Issues in International Finance,* ed. Robert S. Uh, 33–49. New York: Nova Science Publishers.

———. 2010. "French Stock Exchanges and Regulation during World War II." *Financial History Review* 17, no. 2: 211–37.

———. 2013. "Sovereign debt defaults: Insights from history." *Oxford Review of Economic Policy* 29, no. 4: 697–714.

Oosterlinck, Kim, and Ariane Szafarz. 2005. *Les obligations souveraines.* Brussels: Editions Larcier, Collection Cahiers Financiers.

Oosterlinck, Kim, and John S. Landon-Lane. 2006. "Hope Springs Eternal—French Bondholders and the Soviet Repudiation (1915–1919)." *Review of Finance* 10, no. 4: 507–35.

Oosterlinck, Kim, and Loredana Ureche-Rangau. 2005. "Entre la peste et le choléra: le détenteur d'obligations peut préférer la répudiation au défaut. . . ." *Revue d'économie financière* 79, no. 2: 309–31.

———. 2008. "Multiple potential payers and sovereign bond prices." *Finance* 29, no. 1: 31–52.

———. 2012. "Interwar Romanian sovereign bonds: The impact of diplomacy, politics and the economy." *Financial History Review* 19, no. 2: 219–44.

Oosterlinck, Kim, Loredana Ureche-Rangau, and Jacques-Marie Vaslin. 2014. "Baring, Wellington and the Resurrection of French Public Finances Following Waterloo." *Journal of Economic History* 74, no. 4: 1072–1102.

Özler, Şule 1989. "On the relation between reschedulings and bank value." *American Economic Review* 74, no. 5: 1117–31.

Pasvolsky, Leo, and Harold Glenn Moulton. 1924. *Russian Debts and Russian Reconstruction: A Study of the Relation of Russia's Foreign Debts to Her Economic Recovery*. London: McGraw-Hill.

Paye, Jean-Claude. 2002. "Quelques réflexions sur les travaux de la commission du suivi." In *Les emprunts russes: aspects juridiques*, ed. Patrick Juillard and Brigitte Stern, 242–52. Paris: CEDIN Paris 1, Cahiers Internationaux.

Peeters, Wim, and Jérôme Wilson. 1999. *L'industrie belge dans la Russie des tsars*. Alleur-Liège: Éditions du Perron.

Pipes, Richard. 1990. *La révolution russe*. Paris: Presses Universitaires de France.

———. 1995. *Russia Under the Bolshevik Regime, 1919–1924*. London: Fortuna Press.

———. 1998. *The Unknown Lenin: From the Secret Archives*. New Haven: Yale University Press.

Poincaré, Raymond. 1921. "Chronique de la quinzaine." *Revue des Deux Mondes*, 15 juillet.

Raffalovich, Arthur. 1919. *Le marché financier: les dettes publiques et l'inflation pendant la guerre*. Paris: Librairie Felix Alcan.

———. 1922. "La dette publique de la Russie: dette d'avant-guerre et opérations de crédit pendant la guerre." In *Le problème financier Russe: La Dette publique de la Russie*, ed. Arthur Raffalovich, Paul Apostol, Alexandre Michelson, M. Bernatzky, and W. Novitsky, 7–54. Paris: Payot.

———. 1931. *L'abominable vénalité de la presse . . . d'après les documents des archives russes (1897–1917)*. Paris: Librairie du Travail.

Reinhart, Carmen M., and Kenneth Rogoff. 2009. *This Time Is Different: Eight Centuries of Financial Folly*. Princeton: Princeton University Press.

———. 2011. "The Forgotten History of Domestic Debt." *Economic Journal* 121, no. 552: 319–50.

Reinhart, Carmen M., Kenneth Rogoff, and Miguel A. Savastano. 2003. "Debt Intolerance." *Brookings Papers on Economic Activity* 1: 1–74.

Renouvin, Pierre. 1959. "Les relations franco-russes à la fin du XIXe siècle et au début du XXe siècle [Bilan des recherches]." *Cahiers du monde russe et soviétique* 1, no. 1: 128–47.

Reynaud, Pierre. 1924. *Etude sur les modalités de paiement des coupons de valeurs mobilières depuis 1914*. Paris: Editions de la vie universitaire.

Rieffel, Lex. 2003. *Restructuring Sovereign Debt: The Case for Ad Hoc Machinery*. Washington: Brookings Institution Press.

Robert, Adolphe, Edgar Bourloton, and Gaston Cougny, eds. 1889–91. *Dictionnaire des parlementaires français (1789–1889)*. Paris: Bourloton.

Romey, Carine. 2007. "Les transformations de l'activité boursière." In *Le marché financier français au XIXème siècle*. Vol. 1: *Récit,* ed. Pierre-Cyrille Hautcoeur, 273–310. Paris: Publications de la Sorbonne.

Rose, Andrew K. 2005. "One reason countries pay their debts: Renegotiation and international trade." *Journal of Development Economics* 77, no. 1: 189–206.

Roubini, Nouriel, and Brad Setser. 2004. *Bailouts or Bail-ins?: Responding to Financial Crises in Emerging Economies*. Washington: Peterson Institute Press.

Rouwenhorst, K. Geert. "The origins of mutual funds." Yale International Center for Finance Working Paper no. 4–48.

Sack, Alexander Nahum. 1927. *Les effets des transformations des états sur leurs dettes publiques et autres obligations financières: traité juridique et financier*. Paris: Recueil Sirey.

———. 1938. "Diplomatic Claims Against the Soviets (1918–1938)." *New York University Law Quarterly Review* 15: 507–35.

Sédillot, René. 1979. *Histoire du franc*. Paris: Sirey.

Shleifer, Andrei. 2003. "Will the sovereign debt market survive?" National Bureau of Economic Research Working Paper w9493.

Siegel, Jennifer. 2014. *For Peace and Money: French and British Finance in the Service of Tsars and Commissars*. Oxford: Oxford University Press.

Siegel, Katherine A. S. 1996. *Loans and Legitimacy: The Evolution of Soviet–American Relations 1919–1933*. Lexington: University Press of Kentucky.

Sinyagina-Woodruff, Yulia 2003. "Russia, sovereign default, reputation and access to capital markets." *Europe–Asia Studies* 55, no. 4: 521–51.

Skidelsky, Robert Jacob Alexander. 1983. *John Maynard Keynes: A Biography*. Vol. 1, *Hopes Betrayed, 1883–1920*. London: Macmillan.

Sontag, John P. 1968. "Tsarist debts and Tsarist foreign policy." *Slavic Review* 27, no. 4: 529–41.

Sturzenegger, Federico, and Jeromin Zettelmeyer. 2008. "Haircuts: Estimating investor losses in sovereign debt restructurings, 1998–2005." *Journal of International Money and Finance* 27, no. 5: 780–805.

Subtelny, Orest. 1994. *Ukraine: A History*. Toronto: University of Toronto Press.

Szurek, Sandra. 2002. "Mise en perspective de l'accord franco-russe." In *Les emprunts russes: aspects juridiques,* ed. Patrick Juillard and Brigitte Stern, 7–51. Paris: CEDIN Paris 1, Cahiers Internationaux.

Thompson, John M. 1966. *Russia, Bolshevism, and the Versailles Peace*. Princeton: Princeton University Press.

Tomz, Michael. 2007. *Reputation and International Cooperation: Sovereign Debt Across Three Centuries.* Princeton: Princeton University Press.

Tooze, Adam, and Martin Ivanov. 2011. "Disciplining the 'black sheep of the Balkans': Financial supervision and sovereignty in Bulgaria, 1902–38." *Economic History Review* 64, no. 1: 30–51.

Trotsky, Léon. 1930. *Ma vie.* Translated by Maurice Parijanine. Paris: Editions Gallimard, 1953.

———. 1930–32. *Histoire de la révolution russe.* Translated by Maurice Parijanine. Paris: Seuil Essais Edition, 1995.

Ukhov, Andrey D. 2003. "Financial innovation and Russian government debt before 1918." Yale Working Paper 03-20.

Ureche-Rangau, Loredana. 2008. *Dette souveraine en crise: l'expérience des emprunts roumains à la bourse de Paris durant l'entre-deux-guerres.* Paris: Publications de la Sorbonne.

Van Rijckhegem, Caroline, and Beatrice Weder. 2009. "Political Institutions and Debt Crises." *Public Choice* 138: 387–408.

Vidal, Emmanuel. 1919. *Les "jours noirs" à la Bourse de Paris (du 24 juillet au 4 décembre 1914).* Paris: Auguste Picard.

Vizcarra, Catalina. 2009. "Guano, Credible Commitments, and Sovereign Debt Repayment in Nineteenth-Century Peru." *Journal of Economic History* 69, no. 2: 358–87.

Waldenström, Daniel, and Bruno S. Frey. 2008. "Did Nordic countries recognize the gathering storm of World War II? Evidence from the bond markets." *Explorations in Economic History* 45, no. 2: 107–26.

Wallis, John Joseph, Richard E. Sylla, and Arthur Grinath III. 2004. "Sovereign Debt and Repudiation: The Emerging-Market Debt Crisis in the US States, 1839–1843." National Bureau of Economic Research Working Paper w10753.

Weidenmier, Marc D. 2002. "Turning points in the US Civil War: Views from the Grayback market." *Southern Economic Journal* 68, no. 4: 875–90.

Werth, Nicolas. 2004. *Histoire de l'Union Soviétique.* Paris: Presses Universitaires de France.

White, Stephen. 2002. *The Origins of Detente: The Genoa Conference and Soviet-Western Relations, 1921–1922.* Cambridge: Cambridge University Press.

Wieczynski, Joseph L., ed. 1976–96. *The Modern Encyclopedia of Russian and Soviet History.* Gulf Breeze, Fla.: Academic International Press.

Willard, Kristen L., Timothy W. Guinnane, and Harvey S. Rosen. 1996. "Turning Points in the Civil War: Views from the Greenback Market." *American Economic Review* 86, no. 4: 1001–18.

Wrangel, Petr Nikolaevich. 1930. *Mémoires du Général Wrangel.* Paris: Editions J. Tallandier.

Wynne, William H. 1951. *State Insolvency and Foreign Bondholders.* Vol. 2. New Haven: Yale University Press. Reprint, Washington: Beard Books, 2000.

Index